D1615523

Tomboys and bachelor girls

MANCHESTER
1824

Manchester University Press

Tomboys and bachelor girls

A lesbian history of post-war Britain 1945–71

Rebecca Jennings

Manchester University Press
Manchester and New York
distributed exclusively in the USA by Palgrave

The right of Rebecca Jennings to be identified as the author of this work has been asserted
by her in accordance with the Copyright, Designs and Patents Act 1988.

Published by Manchester University Press
Oxford Road, Manchester M13 9NR, UK
and Room 400, 175 Fifth Avenue, New York, NY 10010, USA
www.manchesteruniversitypress.co.uk

Distributed exclusively in the USA by
Palgrave, 175 Fifth Avenue, New York,
NY 10010, USA

Distributed exclusively in Canada by
UBC Press, University of British Columbia, 2029 West Mall,
Vancouver, BC, Canada V6T 1Z2

British Library Cataloguing-in-Publication Data
A catalogue record for this book is available from the British Library

Library of Congress Cataloging-in-Publication Data applied for

ISBN   978 0 7190 7544 5   hardback

First published 2007

16 15 14 13 12 11 10 09 08 07   10 9 8 7 6 5 4 3 2 1

Typeset
by Helen Skelton, Brighton, UK
Printed in Great Britain
by Biddles Ltd, King's Lynn

For Vicky

Contents

Acknowledgements

I would like to thank James Vernon and Harry Cocks, without whose support and guidance over many years, this book could not have been written. I am also very grateful to Laura Doan and Alison Oram, Penny Summerfield and Penny Tinkler for their invaluable comments.

I am indebted to the staff at Manchester University Press; Rob Perks at the National Sound Archive; Oliver Merrington, curator of the Hall Carpenter Newsmedia Archive, Middlesex University; the staff at The National Archive and the British Library, and all those at the Northern Listening Post, British Library, Boston Spa. I am grateful to Tessa Stone, Harold L. Smith and Gerard de Groot for advising me on related aspects of their own research.

Finally I would like to thank my family, Robert, Denise and John Jennings for their support and Andree Bellamy, who has been an inspiration to me in this research.

Some of the material in Chapter 4 was previously published in my article 'The Gateways club and the emergence of a post-war lesbian subculture', *Social History* 31/2 (May 2006) and is reproduced with the kind permission of the publisher: www.tandf.co.uk.

Introduction

In the late 1950s, Margaret Cranch, a young woman from Plymouth, completed her training as a nurse and began to consider the career options open to her. She had no interest in pursuing her nursing and was eager to leave home, so she decided to join the Women's Royal Army Corps (WRAC). She had already had a few relationships with women on her nursing course and now a friend had told her that 'there were lots of lesbians in the army'. However, she had not realised that 'there weren't meant to be lesbians in the army' and soon discovered that her 'masculine' look might threaten her army career. One evening, during the training, she was caught driving a corporal's motorbike around the camp and summoned before the Commanding Officer. The CO accused her of being a 'tomboy', which Margaret interpreted as a code word for lesbian, and informed her that the WRAC was trying to cultivate a 'more feminine' image; if Margaret did not alter her behaviour and appearance, there would be no place for her in the WRAC. Margaret sought the help of two lesbian friends, cutting her hair in a more feminine style, and learning to apply make-up before going on parade. The change of image worked: at Margaret's next interview with the CO, the officer expressed her pleasure at the change and admitted Margaret permanently into the WRAC. While Margaret Cranch was struggling with the label of 'tomboy', another woman, Diana Chapman, was walking the streets of Chelsea in search of masculine women. Born in Bristol before the war, Diana had moved to London at the age of twenty-three to embark on her training in dentistry and was therefore the archetypal 'bachelor girl' of the period. Diana had read Radclyffe Hall's lesbian novel, *The Well of Loneliness*, a few years before and formed the impression that all lesbians were 'very masculine' so, aware that the legendary lesbian club, the Gateways, was hidden some-where off the Kings Road, but having no means of discovering its exact address, Diana hoped to follow a 'tall, handsome woman with cropped hair' into the entrance of the club.[1]

In a period when lesbianism remained largely unnamed and unspoken, women drew upon a diverse range of gendered and sexual identities to express same-sex desire. Such fluid and ambiguous concepts as 'tomboy' and 'bachelor girl' were sufficiently flexible to be deployed as indicators of sexual dissidence. These terms were situational and contingent, enabling individual women to alternate between a number of sexual identity models in distinct locations and at different times. While lesbian historians have focused on the inter-war period as crucial in the emergence of new models of lesbian identity, it was in the subsequent decades, after the Second World War, that women began to take up these new definitions and deploy them to make sense of their own experiences.[2] It is this relatively uncharted territory which Tomboys and Bachelor Girls will explore, examining the different attempts to explain and articulate female same-sex desire in the 1940s, 50s and 60s and tracing the emergence of a collective lesbian identity and sense of community.

Since Michel Foucault argued, in his History of Sexuality, that notions of identity in the modern era have been predicated on a belief that sex defines the self, historians of sexuality and post-structuralist historians more broadly have devoted considerable energies to questions of identity.[3] Developing insights which have informed the cultural or 'linguistic turn' in history, post-structuralist and cultural historians, such as Joan Scott, have questioned the validity of the social historical project of reclaiming past experience, arguing that any attempt to uncover an objective 'truth' in the past must be fundamentally flawed.[4] Influenced by Foucault's work on the genealogy of the modern subject, post-structuralist historians have challenged the liberal democratic notion of the human as a centred subject, understanding the subject instead as a cultural construction which is specific to a given historical period. Recent cultural histories have therefore abandoned as impossible the attempt to uncover accurate accounts of individual experiences in the past, in favour of an examination of how individuals and societies have been presented in culture or 'discourse'. It is in this spirit that Tomboys and Bachelor Girls will explore the cultural representations of lesbianism in post-war Britain and the possibilities for presenting new identities which they suggested.

Post-structuralist approaches have proved particularly influential amongst feminist historians, enabling the monolithic and transhistorical concept of 'woman' to be replaced with a more historically specific understanding of how various cultural concepts of gender have constituted the subject category 'woman' in different ways across historical periods.

Judith Butler has taken this debate further, arguing that gender and sexual identities are cultural constructs which have to be continually reiterated or 'performed' in order to bring the subject into being. Butler's theory thus opens up the possibility that multiple versions or discourses of gender can co-exist in a given historical moment, enabling historical actors to draw on and perform different identities in different locations and times.[5] Employing this model of gender – and sexuality – as performative, this book will trace a range of gender and sexual identity models current in Britain in the post-war period, and explore the opportunities offered by specific discourses and spaces for individual women to perform distinct gendered and sexual identities.

A range of definitions of same-sex desire between women emerged from various cultural media in the post-war decades. The science of medicine and psychiatry, which had assumed an authority in the late nineteenth century to classify and explain sexual behaviour, continued to dominate the field in the mid-twentieth century. In the 1950s and 60s, an increasing number of popular psychiatry books and self-help guides sought to explain lesbianism as the result of arrested development, and characterised the lesbian as immature and emotionally stilted, unable to develop equal relationships and prone to angry outbursts and alcoholism. These representations of lesbians as isolated and potentially destructive figures were reinforced by a trend towards media coverage of divorce cases and violent crime involving lesbians. In the decades following the publication of The Well of Loneliness, literary portrayals of lesbianism prolifer-ated, aimed at an increasingly knowing readership. Lesbian characters appeared as isolated figures in the crime novels of Agatha Christie and, in the 1950s and 60s, the explosion of mass-produced pulp fiction imported largely from the US, brought with it a flood of lesbian-themed novels. Series, such as Ann Bannon's Beebo Brinker Chronicles, established lesbian char-acters within a sophisticated urban social scene, far removed from the conventional domestic femininity of the era.

Tomboys and Bachelor Girls will explore how individual women made sense of their same-sex desire in the context of these representations of lesbian-ism. Examining different aspects of daily life, such as childhood and education, work and the home, this book will analyse the opportunities open to women in the expression of their sexuality and the identities they forged. By the mid-twentieth century, increasing awareness of the poten-tial of lesbianism in same-sex environments was having an impact on girls' schools and educational institutions and there is evidence that girls growing up in the 1950s and 60s were conscious of sexual desire for women as a taboo. However, longstanding assumptions that crushes on older girls and teachers were a 'normal' aspect of girls' development, meant that intense emotional relationships between girls were largely downplayed, only gaining significance with age, in the context of a post-war cultural emphasis on marriage and motherhood as the ultimate goals for women. The figure of the 'bachelor girl' or 'career woman', which took on greater resonance with the expansion of female participation in the workplace, offered one possible alternative to domestic models of femininity and a number of careers did offer women the potential to express a non-heterosexual identity through their work. The recently established women's services and police provided an environment in which women could legitimately express many of the cultural indicators of lesbianism, such as the wearing of 'masculine' attire and uniforms, the assumption of authority and engagement in physically active, outdoor pursuits. Although contemporary concerns about lesbianism in the ranks could potentially render these occupations problematic, as Margaret Cranch's experience shows, such environments nevertheless enabled women to give new meanings to their own sexual identities and to develop social networks with other lesbians.

Tomboys and Bachelor Girls will examine the ways in which women were able to deploy ambiguous concepts such as the 'career woman' and the 'bachelor girl' to simultaneously indicate and mask a lesbian identity. Contemporary anxieties about female same-sex desire which attached to these figures offered the opportunity to deploy them as an indication of potential sexual deviance, but their very ambiguity simultaneously afforded a protection from censure which more explicit terms such as 'lesbian' did not. These cultural connections between 'deviant' and 'normative' models of sexual identity have become the focus of consider-able attention by queer theorists and historians in recent years. Queer historians have sought to analyse the institutional practices and discourses which produce sexual knowledge, and the ways in which these organise social life, and have thus concentrated their research on the binary oppo-sition of homosexuality and heterosexuality as the dominant epistemolog-ical framework of knowledge about sexuality. Teresa de Lauretis has claimed that 'queer' represents a way of rethinking lesbian and gay iden-tities and cultures

> based on the speculative premise that homosexuality is no longer to be seen
> simply as marginal with regard to a dominant, stable form of sexuality
> (heterosexuality) against which it would be defined either by opposition or
> by homology ... Thus, rather than marking the limits of the social space by
> designating a place at the edge of culture, gay sexuality in its specific female
> and male cultural (or subcultural) forms acts as an agency of social process

whose mode of functioning is both interactive and yet resistant, both participatory and yet distinct, claiming at once equality and difference.[6]

Queer theory therefore constitutes an attempt to consider the dividing line between normative and deviant sexuality through a focus on 'regimes of the normal'. Thus, while the previous affirmative model of gay and lesbian studies was associated with the attempt to 'shift' the line so as to include 'normal' homosexuals in the category of normative sexuality, queer theory claims to adopt an approach which would destabilise and hopefully dissolve the line.

However, this focus on the production of knowledge in histories of sexuality has resulted in a tendency to prioritise questions of identity at the expense of considerations of materiality. Identities are invested with meaning and deployed in the material world and recent scholarship has therefore drawn attention to the impact of space and the material environment on the construction and performance of cultural practices. In the field of the history of sexuality, gay male subcultures have thus emerged as the focus of considerable scholarly attention. Building on earlier histories, which linked the emergence of a male homosexual subculture with the development of commercial leisure venues in a capitalist society, recent work has attempted to map sites of homosexual expression as well as geographies of surveillance and regulation within the urban environment.[7] Drawing on nineteenth-century preoccupations with the modern city as a place of physical and moral degeneracy, historians have traced attempts to control deviant behaviour through legislation and policing, inevitably focusing on the figures of the male homosexual and the prostitute.[8] However, no comparable research has examined the significance of the material environment in histories of female homosexuality in the UK. Such research as has been undertaken into lesbians' spatial practices and the ways in which lesbians experience space, largely within the fields of social geography and cultural studies, has focused on abstract or contemporary analyses.[9] Theorists have emphasised the importance of gender in shaping lesbians' experience of space as distinctly different from that of male homosexuals, constructing lesbians' social interaction in terms of private friendship networks rather than the public spaces of bars and the street, which have been associated with gay men. Longstanding narratives opposing public and private space, which have historically linked the female gender with the private sphere, have shaped much of this debate.[10] Thus Manuel Castells, in his analysis of the interaction between space and society in San Francisco's urban social movements, was able to characterise lesbians as primarily oriented toward 'private space', and so dismiss them as irrelevant to his discussion.[11] In a more sociological take on this notion, Gill Valentine and others have argued that lesbians, like all women, tend to occupy a low-income bracket and are at a higher risk from violence in public places and that these factors explain lesbians' lower visibility in urban areas.[12] Such an approach owes much to feminist analyses within human geography and urban studies, which have emphasised the importance of gender in shaping an individual's experience of, and practices within, space. This research has documented the constraints placed on women's spatial behaviour and their unequal access to services in the urban environment; it has demonstrated the ways in which women have been excluded from participation in urban design to the extent that their needs have not been met in the built environment; and it has explored the historical construction of the public/private opposition and the origins of women's oppression within this mode of social organisation.[13] Recent work on contemporary lesbian spatial practices has reflected these pre-occupations, focusing on the impact of lesbians' gender identity in constructing their spatial practices and experiences as marginal.[14]

Tomboys and Bachelor Girls seeks to explore the connections between space and cultural practices in lesbian history and is therefore concerned with the material world of post-war Britain. Identities such as 'tomboy' were invested with specific meanings in particular spatial contexts, so that as a child in rural Essex in the early 1950s, Nina Jenkins could use the term to explain and excuse her desire to climb trees and be part of a boys' street gang but, when Margaret Cranch's Commanding Officer employed it in a WRAC training camp in the same period to describe the young cadet's image, it was transformed into an accusation of sexual deviance. It is only by paying attention to these material considerations that we can truly understand the meanings of women's behaviour and self-expression in a given historical context.[15]

Despite the proliferation of terms which could be deployed to indicate lesbianism in this period, same-sex desire between women in post-war Britain was shaped and defined by silence. Responding to an interviewer's question regarding the terms she used to describe her lesbian identity in the early 1960s, oral history interviewee Nina Jenkins explained:

> Do you know I can't – it's terrible, I mean I should be much more conscious of these sort of social things – but I don't ever recall words being used, in fact I'm not sure they were. I don't think they were because gay hadn't been invented; homosexual was a thing in books; lesbian was like a derogatory term that you hardly ever heard; and other people used things like poofs and queers. I loathed those words, they made my skin crawl, they still do.

So I don't think any words were ever used. I think there was just an expectation that there were people like us and there were other people.[16]

Fluid terms such as 'tomboy' and 'bachelor girl' were invested with sexual meaning in the immediate post-war decades precisely because of this absence of explicit discussion about lesbianism. Unlike male homosexuality, lesbianism was not subject to legal penalties and was therefore not an object of legislative or juridical concern. The impetus to discover a 'cure' for homosexuality was consequently not present for lesbians as for male homosexuals and the medical literature on female homosexuality was proportionately limited. This relative silence on the subject of lesbianism in post-war Britain has been replicated and reinforced by historians, who, with the exception of a number of popular studies, such as Emily Hamer's *Britannia's Glory* and, more recently, Jill Gardiner's oral history of the Gateways nightclub, have paid the period scant attention.[17] Drawn by the proliferation of official discourses on lesbianism, modern historians, as well as literary and cultural theorists, have focused instead on the inter-war period as a central moment in the development of modern notions of lesbian identity. The publicity surrounding the 1928 obscenity trial of *The Well of Loneliness* has been regarded as crucial in generating a new public awareness of lesbianism and Laura Doan's highly nuanced examination of the period, *Fashioning Sapphism*, has demonstrated the ways in which the trial and other inter-war debates about lesbianism drew upon a range of contemporary legal, sexological, literary and sartorial discourses.[18] The more recent history of lesbian politics in the 1970s and 1980s has also been the subject of a range of historical and anthropological studies, such as Lisa Power's account of the British Gay Liberation movement, *No Bath But Plenty of Bubbles*, and Sarah Green's analysis of lesbian feminist collectives in London in the 1980s.[19] Developments in gay politics in the late 1960s and early 1970s – centring around the Stonewall Riots of 1969 in the US, and the subsequent formation of the Gay Liberation Front – produced a new brand of lesbian and gay politics dependent on the principle of gay visibility as both a tool and a gauge of the success of its cause. Eve Kosofsky Sedgwick has discussed the importance of the 'closet' and its opposite 'coming out' as a paradigm for gay identity in the twentieth century, highlighting the significance of visibility to an identity with no obvious essential characteristics.[20] These definitions of gay identity have inevitably influenced the ideas of lesbian and gay historians and Elizabeth Kennedy has claimed that the Stonewall riot of 1969 has become a key moment in lesbian and gay history, marking a turning point in the grand narrative of lesbian and gay oppression: 'In the mythology of gay and lesbian history, before Stonewall gays lived furtive, closeted, miserable lives, while after Stonewall gays could be free and open. Stonewall is quintessentially about being out of the closet, fighting back, about refusing to be mistreated anymore.'[21] In the US, a number of recent studies of the post-war period have begun to complicate this picture. Madeline Davis and Elizabeth Kennedy, in their groundbreaking oral history of the post-war lesbian bar community in Buffalo, New York, have argued that the stereotyping of 'members of this community as low-life societal discards and pathetic imitators of heterosexuality, and therefore as hardly self-conscious actors in history', by '[p]opular culture, the medical establishment, affluent lesbians and gays, and recently, many lesbian feminists' has been a gross misrepresentation.[22] In contrast, they characterise butch and femme lesbians as self-conscious political actors, locating the lesbian bar communities of the mid-twentieth century within a trajectory of resistance to oppression which was to culminate in the Gay Liberation Movement of the early 1970s.

> By finding ways to socialize together, individuals ended the crushing isolation of lesbian oppression and created the possibility for group consciousness and activity. In addition, by forming community in a public setting outside of the protected and restricted boundaries of their own living rooms, lesbians also began the struggle for public recognition and acceptance.[23]

Leila J. Rupp, who has explored the post-war period in her history of same-sex love in America, has similarly emphasised the important connections between communities and activism in the immediate post-war decades and the lesbian and gay politics which emerged in the 1970s.[24] However, in the UK, the historiographical focus on the inter-war period and 1970s has encouraged the continuing interpretation of the 1940s and 1950s as decades of repression in gay history and has reinforced the mainstream historical account of the post-war decades as a period of austerity and cultural conservatism, preceding a permissive moment in the 1960s.

In addressing this neglected period in British lesbian history, this book draws on a rich variety of source material, from medical and literary constructions of the single woman and the lesbian to press reports of divorce cases and murder trials. Lesbians' own experiences of same-sex desire in the post-war decades emerge from two distinct archives. The 1960s saw the establishment of the first lesbian magazine, *Arena Three*, which provided an alternative forum for women to explore different understandings of lesbian identity, to contest many of the definitions of lesbianism current in society in the writings of psychiatrists and the media, and to build a discursive community. As the editors of *Arena Three* claimed, the desire to make contact with other women and alleviate the isolation experienced by many lesbians in Britain was the central aim of this emerging community and the magazine's impact as a historical source reflects this. In the discussions which took place in the readers' letters pages and editorial responses, a record exists of women's conceptions of their own sexual desires and identities in the period 1964–71. However, these debates also helped to construct new understandings of lesbianism, so that the magazine also documents the process by which a collective model of lesbian identity emerged. While *Arena Three* provides an invaluable insight into women's contemporary attitudes toward their own lesbian identity, *Tomboys and Bachelor Girls* also draws extensively on lesbian personal narratives contained within the Hall Carpenter Oral History Archive at the British Library. Created during the 1980s and 1990s, this archive represents a collection of life-history interviews recounting women's experiences as lesbians throughout much of the twentieth century and is therefore a product of the sense of community forged by *Arena Three* and its successors. The tensions between these two archives, and the contemporary and retrospective stories they offer of lesbian experience, provide an insight into the changing meanings of female same-sex desire in post-war Britain and are a central focus of this book.

Elizabeth Kennedy has argued that storytelling occupies a particularly significant role in lesbian culture. She suggests that the testimonies she and Madeline Davis recorded in their research into the post-war Buffalo lesbian community were not being told for the first time, but had been repeatedly narrated to other lesbians in bars and at parties as part of a process of shaping and building lesbian identity and community. Following Audre Lorde, she suggests that:

> Because the majority of lesbians grow up in a heterosexual culture, they have no guidelines and no patterns for creating a homosexual life. They, therefore, are constantly creating their lives, developing a biomythography, so to speak. Lesbians who are completely private are no exceptions; they cannot passively accept the traditional structure of a woman's life; they must create their own guidelines for living and therefore actively engage the process of storytelling.[25]

In the absence of prescribed patterns or narratives for living and describing their lives, she suggests, lesbians create their own stories, based on personal experience and shared myths, as a means of interpreting their experiences. Bonnie Zimmerman points to a political dimension to this interest in storytelling in her review of lesbian personal narratives

published in the late 1970s and early 1980s. She argues that collections of
personal narratives compiled in this period reflect a feminist commitment
to speech and self-expression as a powerful tool in resisting oppression:

> In a sense, then, contemporary lesbian feminists postulate lesbian oppres-
> sion as a mutilation of consciousness curable by language. Lesbians do share
> the institutional oppression of all women and the denial of civil rights with
> gay men. But what lesbian feminists identify as the particular, unique
> oppression of lesbians – rightly or wrongly – is speechlessness, invisibility,
> and inauthenticity. Lesbian resistance lies in correct naming; thus our power
> flows from language, vision and culture.[26]

Motivated by an ideological commitment to the notion that the personal
is political, published personal accounts, such as those contained within
the Hall Carpenter Oral History Archive, were political statements of the
existence and visibility of lesbians. As such, they served a further purpose
of reaching out to a wider community of women.

The collective nature of this narrative process facilitated the development of common themes in lesbian narratives. Biddy Martin has argued
that lesbian autobiography as a genre constructs a monolithic account of
lesbian identity in which 'lesbianism becomes the central moment around
which women's lives are reconstructed'.[27] Women who recount their life
stories as part of a collection of lesbian personal narratives are encouraged
to construct an account which emphasises and makes sense of their lives
in terms of their lesbian identity, and which minimises those experiences
which do not fit this metanarrative. The type of lesbian identity projected
by such accounts is therefore profoundly shaped by the political and
cultural meanings attributed to lesbianism at any specific historical
moment. Graham Dawson has considered this relationship between
personal narratives and wider culture in formulating his concept of
'composure'. He has suggested that the attempt to achieve composure –
both in terms of 'composing' the narrative and of finding a 'sense of
composure' by constituting oneself as the subject of one's own account –
is at the heart of personal narratives. For interviewees, the composition
of an account that draws on existing cultural models and hence fits
established notions of identity and behaviour is essential in achieving
composure.[28] In lesbian personal narratives, the importance accorded to
openness in post-Stonewall or Gay Liberation politics has been traced back
into the pre-Stonewall era through oral histories, prompting lesbian interviewees to construct a personal narrative based around a visible, explicit
lesbian identity.

This is apparent in the narratives produced for the Hall Carpenter Oral
History Archive, which tend to focus on those aspects of the narrators'

experience which were more compatible with the expression of an explicit lesbian identity. Thus women's participation in lesbian communities such as those located in the bar culture or around the magazine *Arena Three* were frequently discussed at length, while attempts to build relationships and patterns of home life in the absence of any language of lesbian domesticity were downplayed. However, while the search for 'composure' has meant that certain common themes have emerged from lesbian personal narratives in the post-Stonewall era, the individuality of each account is equally apparent. Penny Summerfield, in her work on women's 'wartime lives', noted that her interviewees produced two types of account, presenting themselves as either heroically overcoming adversity or as 'making do' with difficulties.[29] A similar distinction emerged from the Hall Carpenter accounts, in which women appropriated the dominant narrative of self-discovery culminating in a visible identity in different ways. While some women represented themselves as actively engaging in a heroic quest for liberation, others constituted themselves within a more stoic narrative of struggle against oppression. However, as Summerfield points out, these categories were not discrete: women frequently moved between the two models at different stages in their account and, at others, failed to achieve 'composure' at all. When contemporary interpretations of an event did not allow for the articulation of a lesbian identity or when individual women did not possess a coherent understanding of their own sexuality as 'lesbian' at a given point in their past, interviewees were unable to produce a coherent lesbian narrative and suffered discomposure. In individual interviews, these moments of 'discomposure' were expressed in a variety of ways: through emotion, contradiction and, frequently, silence. However, when analysed alongside contemporary accounts provided by archives such as *Arena Three*, these moments of slippage or dislocation in a narrative can be of particular value to the lesbian historian. Contradictory passages, or moments of silence in an account, can point to those aspects of women's experience which have not fitted easily into a coherent post-Stonewall emphasis on visibility and thus provide evidence of the more fractured and less explicit meanings of lesbianism in the pre-Stonewall era.

The focus of this book is inevitably shaped by the stories which lesbians told about themselves, both at the time and subsequently. *Tomboys and Bachelor Girls* is a history of lesbians in Britain, but, like *Arena Three* and the Hall Carpenter Oral History Archive, it is dominated by the south of England and, in particular, London. Of the four key women who set up the magazine in 1964, all were based in the capital. Julie Switsur grew up in the London suburb of Twickenham; Cynthia Reid moved to London after leaving college; Diana Chapman grew up in Bristol but moved to London in her early twenties and Esme Langley was a resident of West London. Similarly, the Hall Carpenter Oral History Archive was dominated by Londoners. Its project organiser, Margot Farnham, was based in the capital and, of the twenty-three women referred to in this book, sixteen had lived for the majority of their lives in the city. Mary Wilkins, one exception, was born and lived in Warwickshire, while Margaret Cranch lived in Plymouth, before going to Cyprus with the WRAC and then moving to London. Helen Lilly, from Newcastle, was the only interviewee from the north of England, while Gilli Salvat and Elsa Beckett, from India and Southern Rhodesia respectively, were the only women to be born outside Britain: both ultimately moved to London. While in many respects, such as in their encounters with medical, educational and media characterisations of lesbianism, these women's experiences will have been representative of lesbians across the country, in other respects, such as their access to the metropolitan bar culture and the personal networks which supported *Arena Three*, their experiences must have been specific.

Tomboys and Bachelor Girls is not a book about elite women but the majority of the women referred to might be described as middle class. Rene Sawyer was the daughter of a miner and a maid and lived in a basement in Ealing and Angela Chilton was the daughter of a manual worker and grew up in a flat in Islington. However, Jackie Forster's childhood as the daughter of a colonial army doctor and her schooling at Wycombe Abbey were more representative of the group's background as a whole. *Arena Three* was established by four professional women and criticised in its early years for having a narrowly middle-class focus.

The book focuses on the years between 1945 and 1971. 1971 was in many ways a turning point in British lesbian history. The first meetings of the British Gay Liberation Front were held in London in the autumn of 1970, initiating a new, influential form of lesbian and gay politics. *Arena Three* ceased publication in 1971 and was replaced by a new magazine, *Sappho*. The decades between the end of the Second World War and 1971 witnessed significant developments in the formation of collective lesbian identities in Britain. They were also crucial years for the Hall Carpenter interviewees. Many of the narrators were born in the late 1920s and 1930s and were therefore reaching adulthood in the 1940s and 50s. It was in these decades that Cynthia Reid and Julie Switsur, Diana Chapman and Sharley McLean were making sense of their same-sex desires and striving to establish lesbian networks. Mabel Hills and Mary Wilkins were exceptions who, having been born in 1905 and 1907 respectively were already nearing forty when the war came to a close. Sandy Martin and Angela Chilton were part of a younger generation who went to school in the 1950s and emerged into a lesbian social scene at the end of our period, in time to join the wave of new political groups and nightclubs which were established in the late 1960s and early 1970s.

Tomboys and Bachelor Girls broadly reflects the life cycle of lesbian narrators, mapping individual women's journeys from childhood to adulthood and individual interpretations of sexuality to collective models of lesbian identity, onto a broader account of post-war lesbian history. Chapter 1 therefore explores attitudes toward the development of sexual identities and childhood sexuality in the post-war period, through an examination of educational and medico-scientific notions of lesbianism. Focusing on the interpretation of crushes and concerns about the seduction of young women by older, confirmed lesbians, Chapter 1 examines the contradictions in post-war attitudes to schoolgirl sexuality and the ways in which individual girls were able to make sense of and act out their own same-sex desires in the context of these debates. Chapters 2 and 3 trace the opportunities for articulating a lesbian identity in adulthood, exploring, in Chapter 2, the career paths open to lesbians in the post-war decades and examining the significance of specific occupations in providing an environment conducive to the expression of a lesbian identity. Chapter 3 explores lesbians' relationships and domestic experiences in the context of the post-war cultural prioritisation of women's domestic role, demonstrating the ways in which women struggled with the limited visibility of single women and lesbians to forge alternative patterns of relationships and domesticity.

Chapters 4 and 5 move on from this discussion of individual experience to an examination of the social spaces available to lesbians in the post-war period. Mapping lesbian socialising onto the broader entertainment districts of London's West End, Chapter 4 suggests that, while lesbians had mixed with male homosexuals, prostitutes and other marginal figures in the growing bar and nightclub scene from the 1920s onward, in the 1950s and 60s, a specifically lesbian subculture began to emerge in the residential districts of West London. Chapter 5 examines the emergence, in the early 1960s, of the lesbian organisation the Minorities Research Group and its magazine, *Arena Three*. The first specifically lesbian magazine to be produced in the UK, *Arena Three* offered women a forum to present their own understandings of homosexuality, and the dialogues they opened up with the medical profession and the media point to the dominance of these professions in shaping attitudes toward this issue in the 1950s and 1960s. However, the regular features of the magazine also offer an account of the construction of a unique lesbian community and point to the conflicts in contemporary ideas of lesbian identity in this period.

Notes

1 National Sound Archive, British Library, London (hereinafter NSA), Hall Carpenter Collection (hereinafter HCC), (C456), F1359–F1360, Margaret Cranch; NSA, HCC (C456), F2088, Diana Chapman.
2 Laura Doan, *Fashioning Sapphism: The Origins of a Modern English Lesbian Culture* (New York: Columbia University Press, 2001); James Vernon, '"For some queer reason ..." The trials and tribulations of Colonel Barker's masquerade in interwar Britain', *Signs* 26:1 (2000); Alison Oram, '"Embittered, sexless or homosexual": Attacks on spinster teachers 1918–1939', in Lesbian History Group (ed.), *Not a Passing Phase: Reclaiming Lesbians in History 1840–1985* (London: The Women's Press, 1989); Leigh Gilmore, 'Obscenity, modernity, identity: Legalizing "The Well of Loneliness" and "Nightwood"', *Journal of the History of Sexuality* 4:4 (1994); Sonja Ruehl, 'Inverts and experts: Radclyffe Hall and the lesbian identity', in Rosalind Brunt and Caroline Rowan (eds), *Feminism, Culture and Politics* (London: Lawrence Wishart, 1982); Esther Newton, 'The mythic mannish lesbian: Radclyffe Hall and the New Woman', in M. Duberman, M. Vicinus and G. Chauncey (eds), *Hidden from History: Reclaiming the Gay and Lesbian Past* (New York: Penguin, 1989).
3 Michel Foucault, *The History of Sexuality, Vol. 1: An Introduction* (Harmondsworth: Penguin, 1978), p. 101.
4 Joan Scott, 'The evidence of experience', *Critical Inquiry* 17 (1991).
5 Judith Butler, *Gender Trouble: Feminism and the Subversion of Identity* (London: Routledge, 1990).
6 Teresa de Lauretis, 'Queer theory: Lesbian and gay sexualities. An introduction', *differences: A Journal of Feminist Cultural Studies* 3:2 (1991), p. iii; Judith Butler, *Bodies That Matter: On the Discursive Limits of 'Sex'* (London: Routledge, 1993); Lisa Duggan, 'Making it perfectly queer', *Socialist Review* 22 (1992); Elisa Glick, 'Sex positive: Feminism, queer theory, and politics of transgression', *Feminist Review* 64 (2000); Sheila Jeffreys, 'The queer disappearance of lesbian sexuality in the academy', *Women's Studies International Forum* 17:5 (1994).
7 Frank Mort, 'Mapping sexual London: The Wolfenden Committee on Homosexual Offences and Prostitution 1954–57', *New Formations* 37 (1999); David Higgs (ed.), *Queer Sites: Gay Urban Histories Since 1600* (London: Routledge, 1999); Stephen Inwood, 'Policing London's morals: the Metropolitan Police and popular culture', *London Journal* (1990); Matt Houlbrook, *Queer London: Perils and Pleasures in the Sexual Metropolis, 1918–1957* (Chicago: University of Chicago Press, 2005); Judith Walkowitz, *City of Dreadful Delight: Narratives of Sexual Danger in Late-Victorian London* (London: Virago, 1992).
8 The link between narratives of modernity and urban space has been extensively explored in Miles Ogborn, *Spaces of Modernity: London's Geographies*

1680–1780 (London: The Guilford Press, 1998); Rob Shields, *Places on the Margin: Alternative Geographies of Modernity* (London: Routledge, 1991); Anthony Vidler, 'Bodies in space/subjects in the city: Psychopathologies of modern urbanism', *differences* 5:3 (1993); Mary Poovey, *Making a Social Body: British Cultural Formation, 1830–1864* (Chicago: University of Chicago Press, 1995); David Harvey, *Consciousness and the Urban Experience* (Oxford: Blackwell, 1985); David Harvey, *The Condition of Postmodernity* (Oxford, Blackwell, 1989); Edward W. Soja, *Postmodern Geographies* (London: Verso, 1989).

9 David Bell and Gill Valentine (eds), *Mapping Desires: Geographies of Sexualities* (London: Routledge, 1995); Gordon Brent Ingram, Anna-Marie Bouthillette and Yolanda Retter (eds), *Queers in Space: Communities; Public Places; Sites of Resistance* (Washington: Bay Press, 1997); Annamarie Jagose, 'Way out: The category "lesbian" and the fantasy of the utopic space', *Journal of the History of Sexuality* 4:2 (1993); Gill Valentine (ed.), *From Nowhere to Everywhere: Lesbian Geographies* (New York: Harrington Park Press, 2000).

10 See Leonore Davidoff and Catherine Hall, *Family Fortunes: Men and Women of the English Middle Class, 1780–1850* (Chicago: University of Chicago Press, 1987); Leonore Davidoff, *Worlds Between: Historical Perspectives on Gender and Class* (Cambridge: Polity, 1995); Catherine Hall, 'The early formation of Victorian domestic ideology', in Sandra Burman (ed.), *Fit Work for Women* (London: Croom Helm, 1992); Amanda Vickery, 'Golden age to separate spheres? A review of the categories and chronology of English women's history', *The Historical Journal* 36:2 (1993); Martha Vicinus (ed.), *Suffer and be Still: Women in the Victorian Age* (Bloomington: Indiana University Press, 1972).

11 Manuel Castells, *The City and the Grassroots: A Cross-Cultural Theory of Urban Social Movements* (Berkeley: University of California Press, 1983).

12 Gill Valentine, '(Hetero)Sexing space: Lesbian perceptions and experiences of everyday spaces', *Environment and Planning D: Society and Space* 11 (1993); Gill Valentine, 'Desperately seeking Susan: A geography of lesbian friendships', *Area* 25 (1993); Sy Adler and Johanna Brenner, 'Gender and space: Lesbians and gay men in the city', *International Journal of Urban and Regional Research* 16:1 (1992).

13 This is a rapidly expanding field, some of the central works being: Daphne Spain, *Gendered Spaces* (Chapel Hill: University of North Carolina Press, 1992); Kerstin Shands, *Embracing Space: Spatial Metaphors in Feminist Discourse* (London: Greenwood Press, 1999); Doreen Massey, *Space, Place and Gender* (Cambridge: Polity Press, 1994); Linda McDowell and Joanne P. Sharp (eds), *Space, Gender, Knowledge: Feminist Readings* (London: Arnold, 1997); Linda McDowell, 'Towards an understanding of the gender division of urban space', *Environment and Planning D: Society and Space* 1 (1983); Elizabeth Grosz, *Space, Time and Perversion: Essays on the Politics of Bodies* (London: Routledge, 1995); Sally R. Munt, *Heroic Desire: Lesbian Identity and Cultural Space* (London: Cassell, 1998).

14 See, for example, Jenny Ryan and Hilary Fitzpatrick, 'The space that difference makes: Negotiation and urban identities through consumption practices', in Justin O'Connor and Derek Wynne (eds), *From the Margins to the Centre: Cultural Production and Consumption in the Post-industrial City* (Aldershot: Arena, 1996).

15 NSA, HCC, (C456), F2499-F2501, Nina Jenkins.

16 NSA, HCC, (C456), F2499-F2501, Nina Jenkins.

17 Emily Hamer, *Britannia's Glory: A History of Twentieth Century Lesbianism* (London: Cassell, 1996); Jill Gardiner, *From the Closet to the Screen: Women at the Gateways Club, 1945–85* (London: Pandora, 2003). American historians, Madeline Davis and Elizabeth Lapovsky Kennedy, have researched the lesbian bar community of Buffalo, New York, in the 1940s and 1950s, building on a growing scholarly interest in post-war US lesbian culture and butch/femme, and their work remains the definitive empirical work on lesbian social interaction in pre-Liberation movement America. Madeline Davis and Elizabeth Lapovsky Kennedy, *Boots of Leather, Slippers of Gold: The History of a Lesbian Community* (London: Routledge, 1993).

18 Doan, *Fashioning Sapphism*.

19 Lisa Power, *No Bath But Plenty of Bubbles: An Oral History of the Gay Liberation Front* (London: Cassell, 1995); Sarah Green, *Urban Amazons: Lesbian Feminism and Beyond in the Gender, Sexuality and Identity Battles of London* (Basingstoke: Macmillan, 1997).

20 Eve Kosofsky Sedgwick, *Epistemology of the Closet* (London: Harvester Wheatsheaf, 1991).

21 Elizabeth Lapovsky Kennedy, 'Telling tales: Oral history and the construction of pre-Stonewall lesbian history', *Radical History Review* 62 (1995), p. 66.

22 Davis and Kennedy, *Boots of Leather, Slippers of Gold*, pp. 1–2.

23 In doing so, Davis and Kennedy draw on John D'Emilio's argument that US homophile movements laid the groundwork for the lesbian and gay politics of the late 1960s and early 1970s. John D'Emilio, *Sexual Politics, Sexual Communities: The Making of a Homosexual Minority in the United States, 1940–1970* (Chicago: University of Chicago Press, 1983). Davis and Kennedy, *Boots of Leather, Slippers of Gold*, p. 29.

24 Leila J. Rupp, *A Desired Past: A Short History of Same-Sex Love in America* (Chicago: University of Chicago Press, 1999).

25 Kennedy, 'Telling tales', p. 61.

26 Bonnie Zimmerman, 'The politics of transliteration: Lesbian personal narratives', *Signs: Journal of Women in Culture and Society* 9:4 (1984), p. 672.

27 Biddy Martin, 'Lesbian identity and autobiographical difference[s]', in Bella Brodzki and Celeste Schenck (eds), *Life/Lines: Theorizing Women's Autobiography* (London: Cornell University Press, 1988), p. 83.

28 Graham Dawson, *Soldier Heroes: British Adventure, Empire and the Imagining of Masculinities* (London: Routledge, 1994).

29 Penny Summerfield, *Reconstructing Women's Wartime Lives: Discourse and Subjectivity in Oral Histories of the Second World War* (Manchester: Manchester University Press, 1998).

1

Tomboys, crushes and the construction of adolescent lesbian identities

Reflecting on the sexual culture at Colston's Girls School in Bristol in the 1940s, Diana Chapman gave the following account of her own sexual awakening:

> And it was quite the thing there in some weird way, for all the girls to be in love with each other, at least in love with the senior girls and the staff. It wasn't thought peculiar, and when I was twelve I think I was standing on the edge of a – or walking along the edge of a swimming pool and there was a tall dark and handsome girl called Eleanor Ackroyd and she smiled at me. I fell in love passionately. And that was sort of the age of about twelve. My passionate adoration of Eleanor Ackroyd was the beginning of my emotional life.[1]

She recalled, with vivid detail, her first encounter with the 'tall, dark and handsome' Eleanor Ackroyd. At the age of twelve, this was her first love and she 'fell in love passionately'. However, Diana Chapman's opening comment that crushes were 'quite the thing' at Colston's simultaneously establishes her experience within a broader narrative of normative sexual culture in post-war girls' schools. 'All the girls' were in love, if not with each other, then with older girls or teachers and thus the account she provides of falling in love with Eleanor Ackroyd can also be interpreted as one example of a wider culture. It is only with her closing statement, that this crush was 'the beginning of my emotional life', that Diana Chapman offers an alternative interpretation of the encounter, seeking to establish the episode as the first stage in the development of an inevitable lesbian identity. Her use of language in describing the school's sexual culture reflects the ambiguous interpretations she offers: the widespread practice of crushes was 'weird', in retrospect, but at the time was 'not thought peculiar'. Same-sex emotional attachments might be interpreted simultaneously as both deviant and normative.

Diana Chapman's description of her schoolgirl sexuality is indicative of a fundamental ambiguity in post-war accounts of adolescent same-sex desire. An extensive literature on schoolgirl psychology and sexuality had developed by the 1940s, but thinking remained confused. Crushes were recognised as an important aspect of the culture in post-war girls' schools, reflected in the range of terms, from 'raves' to 'G.P.s' (Grand Passions) and 'pashes', that were used to describe them. However, educational commentators were ambiguous in their approach to this phenomenon, often viewing it simultaneously as a harmless phase in sexual development and a sinister indication of lesbian sexuality. This confusion was exacerbated at the level of individual schools, which were frequently resistant to the notion of pupils as sexual beings and remained reluctant to offer formal sex education. Lesbian narratives of childhood sexuality in the post-war decades, such as Diana Chapman's, reflect this uncertainty, representing childhood crushes as both common aspects of schoolgirl culture and the forerunner of adult lesbian sexuality.

By the 1940s, the meaning and significance of crushes and other indications of intense relationships between girls had been the subject of intense debate for more than half a century. From the late nineteenth century onward, cultural commentators were expressing concerns regarding the danger of lesbianism in women-only educational environments. The feminist campaign for greater access to education for women in the late nineteenth and early twentieth centuries had prompted opponents of women's rights to depict women's educational establishments as dominated by man-hating feminists. Martha Vicinus has argued that, as a result, intense friendships between girls or women, which had been common in boarding schools and colleges up to the late nineteenth century, now became suspect and accompanied by a new self-consciousness.[2] With the popularisation of the works of Sigmund Freud, these concerns developed further into the suggestion that such environments fostered not just feminism but lesbianism and were reinforced by research such as Katherine Bement Davis' survey of US college women which found that over a quarter of the sample had experienced intense emotional relationships with other women.[3] Lillian Faderman has highlighted two specific areas of concern regarding the dangers faced by adolescent girls in schools and colleges in the decades before and after the First World War. The first related to the education itself, which was perceived to harm the girl, developing her physical and rational capacities to a 'masculine' level and thus unfitting her to the role of companion to a man, while the second characterised the single-sex environment as one which encouraged stronger girls to prey upon weaker ones and thus fostered homosexuality.[4]

The origins of women's formal education in late-nineteenth-century feminist campaigns for sexual equality meant that girls' education often aimed to closely mirror that of boys. This was particularly apparent through a prioritising of values such as collective spirit and loyalty – as demonstrated in personal friendships and an encouragement of admiration for teachers and older students – and physical strength and courage as demonstrated on the sports field. The argument that excessive physical activity could be potentially harmful and defeminising for girls was a longstanding one, but from the inter-war years onward, these dangers were increasingly linked with lesbianism. Medical discourses of sexuality, which were becoming increasingly influential in the 1920s and 1930s, emphasised masculinity and a propensity for physical activity as indicators of lesbianism and implied a link between sexual and gender identity. Edward Carpenter's notion of a third sex was in part prompted by observation of an increasingly masculine temperament in some women, while both Havelock Ellis and Stella Browne incorporated ideas of gender inversion into their notions of sexual inversion. Doan and Waters claim, 'While Ellis sometimes challenged the equation of effeminacy and male homosexuality, he was by and large committed to the belief that lesbianism was accompanied by a recognizable mannishness'.[5] Jeffrey Weeks has argued that the characterisation of lesbians in masculine terms should be seen as both a reversal of the argument for male homosexuals and a way of explaining lesbianism in the wider context of a belief in female sexual passivity.[6]

Lesbian narratives indicate that this association of lesbianism with masculinity persisted into the post-war period. Narrators overwhelmingly constructed their childhood selves as physically active and 'tomboyish', reflecting the common theme in medical case histories. Rene Sawyer recalled being 'one of the boys' in a gang on her street in the 1940s and described her resentment at having to replace her boy's bib and braces with a top to cover her breasts as she grew older.[7] A decade later, Nina Jenkins was also part of a boys' street gang and recalled tearing her dress while attempting to climb trees. This common account of tomboyish tendencies in childhood was reinforced in many stories by a more literal affinity with boys and many interviewees tended to gravitate toward boys rather than girls as playmates. Angela Chilton articulated the reasons for this, claiming that she spent little time with girls as a teenager because 'their conversation was boring – it was all about fashion and lipstick colours – and they had pictures of Elvis and Cliff Richard on the walls, and Rock Hudson and Dirk Bogarde'. The boys, on the other hand, talked about sport and cars, topics which were much more interesting to her.[8]

Angela Chilton identified sport as her favourite subject in senior school in the late 1950s, where she played hockey, rounders and tennis, as well as boxing in a local club after school.[9] She recalls being in trouble at school for not being sufficiently 'lady-like' in the way in which she played sport, reflecting a common educational concern that participation in sport might result in 'masculine' and potentially lesbian tendencies. In 1935, the *Daily Herald* had reported that such concerns had been expressed by Dr Williams, a speaker at an education conference:

> Dr Williams had dealt with the effect on the temperament of the ductless glands, and said that games such as hockey and lacrosse develop that part of the suprarenal gland which presides over the combative element of a person's character. 'You cannot confine the desire and aptitude for combat to cricket and football,' he said. 'They inevitably appear in the whole character, and what was originally a gentle, feminine girl becomes harsh and bellicose in all relations to life. The women who have the responsibility of teaching these girls are, many of them themselves embittered, sexless or homosexual hoydens who try to mould the girls into their own pattern.'[10]

In suggesting that competitive sports could have the effect of masculinising girls and encouraging sexual deviance, Dr Williams was contributing to a much broader debate regarding the gendering of the curriculum, which continued throughout much of the twentieth century. Prevailing cultural attitudes regarding gender differentiation prompted many such commentators to challenge the principle of sexual equality in education and argue for a specifically 'feminine' curriculum. Carol Dyhouse has argued that an emphasis on the domestic role of women prompted educational authorities, from the late nineteenth century until the 1960s, to value domestic science and other subjects, which were perceived as training girls for their futures as wives and mothers, above more 'academic' subjects such as maths and science.[11] In 1923, the Board of Education's Consultative Committee Report on gender differentiation in the secondary school curriculum had argued that it was time to move beyond the feminist argument for sex equality and accept that boys and girls had different roles to play in society. The Committee stressed the apparent cognitive, emotional and physiological differences between boys and girls and argued that the curriculum should reflect these differences and prepare boys and girls for the different roles they were to undertake in society.[12] By the time the Norwood Committee published its findings in 1943, official views had altered slightly. While the Report assumed that girls and boys had different 'natural interests' in marriage and motherhood or jobs and careers, it was no longer felt that these differences should be automatically built into the curriculum.[13] Nevertheless, despite widespread post-war educational reforms and an expansion in women's education, this longstanding conflict appears to have continued into the post-war period. The educationalist, John Newsom, claimed in 1949 that 'the future of women's education lies not in attempting to iron out their differences from men, to reduce them to neuters, but to teach girls how to grow into women and to relearn the graces which so many have forgotten in the past thirty years'.[14] His views apparently enjoyed considerable public support and Jenni Murray has commented that *Women's Hour* programmes in the 1950s reflected a similar belief that education and femininity were incompatible and that women's education would be a disservice in the marriage market.[15]

A second area of concern regarding girls' education centred on the single-sex environment as one which could potentially foster homosexuality.[16] These anxieties coalesced around the phenomenon of the schoolgirl crush, which was the focus of considerable attention in a broad range of literature, produced by educational commentators, head teachers, youth workers and medical professionals as well as novelists. Alison Oram and Annmarie Turnbull have argued that there was 'a well-established nineteenth-century debate about the emotional significance of crushes and how to contain their disruptive nature, which was later joined by a variety of medical and psychological approaches discussing them in more sexualised terms'.[17] They have suggested that these anxieties reached a height in the inter-war period. This is supported by Rosemary Auchmuty in her work on literary representations of girls' schools, who has argued that, while crushes on other girls and teachers were a normal part of life for fictional schoolgirls in the 1920s, a change in emphasis occurred from 1928 onwards, in the wake of publicity surrounding the obscenity trial of Radclyffe Hall's *The Well of Loneliness*.[18] Girls' school stories had emerged as a popular genre of fiction in the wake of the late-nineteenth and early-twentieth-century expansion in girls' education, reaching their heyday in the 1920s and 30s, and continued to be produced into the 1940s and 50s. Prolific storywriters such as Angela Brazil, Elsie J. Oxenham and Elinor M. Brent-Dyer followed the lives of fictional schoolgirls and their friendships, often in series based on the same groups of friends. Modelled on middle-class girls' public schools such as Roedean, Cheltenham and Wycombe Abbey, the stories idealised such values as loyalty, team spirit, romantic love and respect for authority and brought them to a wide audience drawn from the working class as well as the middle and upper classes, and adults as well as children. Rosemary Auchmuty has suggested that, while heterosexual love is ostensibly held up as the ideal goal of all women and most characters do ultimately marry, it is the friendships between the girls and women that actually form the emotional centre of these novels. Men are frequently dismissed as a hindrance to the enjoyable business of spending time with women and it is negotiating the often painful but rewarding experiences of love and affection for other girls that determine the plot. However, she argues that the redefinition of lesbianism and female friend-ships more generally which occurred in the aftermath of *The Well of Loneli-ness* trial, and the increasing cultural emphasis on domesticity and heterosexual love in the 1940s and 50s, were reflected in the schoolgirl story genre. Behaviour, such as kissing and bed-sharing, which had been regarded as a normal aspect of female friendship in the 1920s, was no longer exhibited by the schoolgirl characters of the post-war period, and while the girls continued to exhibit signs of admiration for each other in childhood, from adolescence onward their attentions became much more strongly focused on marriage and men.

Nevertheless, lesbian narratives suggest that schoolgirl crushes contin-ued to be commonplace experiences in the post-war period. Pat Arrow-smith explained that, although she had 'had a pash' on a number of girls at her school in the early 1940s, 'crushes were quite normal at Stover [school]'. Julie Switsur echoed this interpretation, describing herself as having had crushes on one or two older girls at her Twickenham convent school, but observing that this 'was the done thing in the '50s'.[19] Active debate about the schoolgirl crush continued in educational literature into the post-war decades, reflecting this continued prevalence of crushes as an aspect of school culture.

While crushes were increasingly discussed in sexualised terms from the inter-war period onward, commentators were divided as to whether they should be understood as harmless phases in adolescent sexual devel-opment or dangerous incidences of lesbian desire. In 1927, Lilian Faith-full, former Principal of Cheltenham Ladies College, had published a series of talks which she had given to the school on a range of topics, from 'slang' to 'friendship', followed by a commentary on the letters she had received from pupils in response to her talks. In a chapter entitled, 'Real and Counterfeit Friendships', she made a sharp distinction between raves, which she regarded as both 'futile' and 'mischievous', and hero-worship, which she believed to be 'healthy and natural':

> I learn from various letters that I am quite wrong in stating that a girl is limited to one rave at once. It seems that you can have as many as seven-teen, and that at any rate three is quite usual! We must be talking of differ-ent things. For experiences that you can duplicate over and over again like this are perfectly futile, – without meaning or value in your life. This absurd kind of rave is just a matter of fashion, and you adopt it because you want

to be in the fashion. But it is distinctly mischievous, and you must be warned against it, and urged to give it up. It will give you a habit of spurious forced emotion, which is exceedingly silly, and which you may find that you cannot get rid of easily. Indulgence in these false emotions may be the prelude to flirtation later on.

... A really honest devotion to someone of fine character, who is however rather remote from you, is healthy and natural. Its influence may be altogether good, if the person who experiences it has perception delicate enough to know that her feeling must be purged of everything silly to be worthy of so fine an object. We miss a great incentive in life if we have no capacity for hero-worship.[20]

Faithfull's comments indicate that, although she clearly regarded raves – as distinct from hero-worship – in sexualised terms, potentially leading to flirtation in adulthood, they did not apparently suggest to her the possibility of lesbianism. By the 1940s, however, under the influence of psychoanalytic ideas about sexual development, crushes were being described in more explicitly sexual terms alongside discussions of homosexuality. Josephine Macalister Brew, a youth leader in the 1940s and 50s, made the following comments in a 1945 issue of *Club News*, the journal of the National Association of Girls' Clubs and Mixed Clubs:

In the next stage of development, there is an increasing interest in the same sex ...

Often during this period in which boys and girls are interested in their own sex, instead of these attachments to older persons they develop a very close friendship with someone of their own age. We are all familiar with the type of girl in the Club world who says, 'I'll do it if my friend does' and with the boy who is always telling you what 'the fellow he knows at work' says about this, that and the other. Here again you have a violent friendship which is very touching in its loyalty and which one need not concern oneself with very much ...

Many people get worried about various difficulties, such as masturbation and homo-sexuality. On the whole there is no need for the average person to be concerned with this unduly; both things are evidences of incomplete stages of development. In some cases, it is true that they block the natural development of the individual and this is partly the reason for the disapproval, both religious and social, with which they have always been regarded. For most people, both boys and girls, masturbation and homo-sexuality is a phase through which they may pass and has no deep significance.[21]

Macalister Brew's comments suggest an understanding of crushes as a common stage in adolescent sexual development. She is careful to advise readers that it is only in a limited number of cases that such behaviour might be taken to indicate homosexuality; for the majority, it is clearly a passing phase. In his 1945 manual on sex education, aimed at 'parents, teachers and youth leaders', Cyril Bibby also discussed both homosexuality and crushes as 'sex problems in the school'. Identifying single-sex boarding schools as the most common site of homosexuality in schools, he focused much of his discussion of homosexuality on boys, referring to crushes as an issue confined to girls' schools. Bibby similarly considered intense emotional friendships between pupils generally harmless, only prompting 'serious concern' in the rare cases 'when they lead to definite love-play and mutual masturbation'.[22]

However, this notion of crushes as primarily emotional appears to have given way to increasingly sexual interpretations by the late 1960s. Helen Richardson, Deputy Headmistress at Shaw Classifying School, made a familiar distinction, in her 1969 work on approved schoolgirls, between 'crushes' and overt lesbianism. She claimed that:

> Staff did not hide from the problems of homosexuality. They were aware of the 'crushes' girls had for members of staff, which could drive the girl to excesses of showing off and jealousy, and which were generally handled with sympathy and realism (avoiding, for instance, situations where compromise was possible). They were aware of 'crushes' on other girls, and recognized the exaggerated male or female hair styles or gait or other gestures involved. They were alert to the possibility of bed-sharing, but avoided drawing attention (or those who were wise did) in a shocked way, since this would have made the practice more interesting … They believed the problem of homosexuality was kept within safety limits in the school.[23]

Richardson, however, makes a new distinction between girls' crushes on teachers, which she appears to regard simply as a form of attention-seeking behaviour, and crushes on other girls, which are more explicitly lesbian in their manifestations of butch/femme roles and are potentially sexual. Moreover, her comments on bed-sharing highlight a practical issue which may have influenced different institutions' attitudes toward the possibility of lesbianism.

Lesbian sexual activity was apparently perceived as a more tangible possibility in residential institutions such as boarding schools, approved schools and remand homes. Longstanding concerns about single-sex environments had been fuelled since the inter-war period by a proliferation of literary portrayals of lesbianism in girls' boarding schools. Clemence Dane's *Regiment of Women*, published in 1917, centred on a woman teacher, Clare Hartill, who preyed on the youth of her pupils in a stifling girls' boarding school, while Christa Winsloe's *The Child Manuela*, published in 1934, depicting the relationship between a female pupil and teacher at a girls' seminary, was also produced as a film, *Madchen in Uniform*. A growing self-consciousness about lesbianism in women's colleges and institutions can be found in the lesbian-themed pulp fiction that was emerging as a significant new paperback market in the 1940s and 50s. This genre of lesbian fiction was dominated by representations of lesbian activity in same-sex environments, with popular titles including *Women's Barracks*, *Dormitory Women*, *Female Convict*, *Nurses Quarters* and *Girls Dormitory*. The plotlines of lesbian pulp fiction novels were often highly formulaic and Jaye Zimet, in her work on American pulp fiction, has noted that the figure of the predatory lesbian played a key role in the narrative.

> Two of the frequently exploited clichés were that when women were without men, they were bound to be turned into lesbians or that one dyke alone could corrupt any number of innocent young girls. Publishers and cover artists delighted in the depictions of lesbians in prison, in sororities, in dormitories and in reform schools, all waiting to seduce the latest addition.[24]

In post-war institutions attempts to control sexual behaviour tended to be concentrated on the dormitory environment. Angela Chilton provided an indication of such a policy in an account of her experience in a remand home in the late 1950s. Angela entered the home at the age of fifteen, but was surrounded by older girls of about seventeen. She described being given the job of 'dormitory duty', and explained that the rules stated that girls must undertake this task in groups of three. While Angela claimed not to have understood the significance of this rule at the time, she commented that the other girls used to sit her down outside the dormitory with a pile of comics and instructions to whistle if she heard anyone coming. She told her interviewer that she had subsequently realised why the girls always took so long to make the beds, suggesting that the older girls understood both the purpose of the rule and how to flout it.[25] The spatial dimension of lesbian activity was likely to be much more complex than these rules implied, however. Attempts to suppress transgressive sexual activity in institutions had long been concentrated on dormitory and sleeping quarters, but it is unlikely that sexual encounters were confined to these spaces. The open-plan layout and multiple occupancy of dormitories established an environment of mutual surveillance which could often inhibit sexual expression and lesbian accounts suggest that other locations, such as lavatories, cupboards or school grounds were often considered to offer greater protection from discovery. Rene Sawyer, who claimed that she had 'always wanted to be physically close to girls. I found out at an early age that I could kiss girls and they liked it', conducted this activity in the school toilets, where the other girls would apparently queue up to be kissed.[26] Rosanna Hibbert recounted a similar experience with a girl she had fallen in love with at school in the 1940s. Rosanna wrote love letters to the girl, and again, used the school toilet block as a location for hugging and kissing.[27]

However, it is also possible that longstanding notions of a link between delinquency and sexual deviance or, at least, an actively sexual identity, may have exacerbated fears of lesbianism in approved schools, remand homes and other correctional institutions, such as those described by Helen Richardson at Shaw Classifying School and Angela Chilton. This connection is echoed in an article concerning borstals for girls in The Lancet in 1951, in which borstal girls were characterised as sexually active to the point of deviance.[28] Drawing on a study of 300 borstal girls by Dr Phyllis Epps, the author listed the offences for which Epps' borstal girls were committed, before commenting that: 'Only 9 girls in the series had been charged for sexual offences, but in fact most had had sexual experience, and 102 could be regarded as prostitutes. There had been 67 pregnancies, 7 legitimate and 47 illegitimate births, and 13 miscarriages, among 59 girls.' This perception of 'delinquent' girls as sexually experienced inevitably shaped expectations about their behaviour within the borstal. Thus Epps commented that the borstal environment was likely to teach a girl about deviant sexual behaviour.

> Not only can she learn more of acquisitive crime from her more experi-
> enced fellow trainees, but she can learn more of sexual deviations. Sex,
> sport and crime, in that order, form 74% of the main subjects of conversa-
> tion in boys' borstals (Leitch) and certainly sex and crime appear to be the
> most popular topics among girls.[29]

While these accounts suggest an increasing tendency to interpret crushes as sexual and potentially lesbian in the post-war decades, concerns were exacerbated by attitudes toward the sexuality of older girls and single woman teachers. In his 1945 work on sex education, Cyril Bibby charac-terised crushes directed by pupils at their teachers as potentially much more serious than those on other girls. In an obscure reference to the possibility of lesbianism in the older woman, Bibby warned:

> We may not lose sight of the fact that the teacher, deprived as she often is
> by the unbelievably foolish marriage bar of the satisfaction of having
> husband and children of her own, may, albeit unconsciously, achieve a good
> deal of personal gratification from the relationship. Unless very wisely
> handled by the older partner, such 'G.P's' may have a permanent effect on
> the girls' development, hindering considerably the attainment of emotional
> maturity.[30]

Bibby's characterisation of single women teachers as a potential threat to female pupils echoed a common inter-war theme in educational literature. Alison Oram's work on spinster teachers in the decades between the wars has highlighted the impact of notions of the predatory lesbian on attitudes toward unmarried teachers in this period.[31] The growth of teaching into one of the key professional occupations open to women in the late nineteenth and early twentieth centuries, and the close links between many of the early women teachers and feminism, had, by the inter-war period, positioned women teachers at the forefront of political debates about women and employment. Tensions within the teaching profession over issues such as equal pay, equal promotion prospects and the marriage bar were largely split along gender lines and, just after the First World War, the majority of women teachers left the main teaching union, the National Union of Teachers (NUT), to form their own union. The status of school teaching in this period as the only profession in which it was possible for women to earn a salary much above subsistence level, combined with the introduction of regulations, requiring women teachers to resign on marriage, by many local authorities in the early 1920s, meant that approximately 85 per cent of women teachers in the 1920s and 30s were single women.

In the context of these political conflicts, spinster teachers were particularly vulnerable to accusations of lesbianism. The figure of the predatory lesbian, a manifestation of the 'true invert', who was responsible for seducing the weaker or 'pseudo' invert, had been familiar to medical discourses on lesbianism since the nineteenth century. Laura Doan has drawn attention to the prevalence of this theme in sexological writings in her work on attempts to legislate against lesbian activity in 1921.[32] She cites August Forel's claim to 'have known several women of this kind, who held veritable orgies and induced a whole series of young girls to become their lovers'. Forel further asserted that 'when a woman invert wishes to seduce a normal girl, it is easy for her to do so'.[33] This idea, Doan observes, recurs in the writings of Albert Moll who stated that 'many women inflicted with sexual inversion practice masturbation ... Those who masturbate themselves think of young girls during the act ... There seem to be women of homosexual tendencies who desire young immature girls'.[34] Sexological ideas were influential in allowing critics to characterise single women teachers as 'embittered, thwarted, sexually frustrated or deviant' women, and, by the 1930s, Oram argues, feelings had reached such a height that it was possible to explicitly accuse single teachers of lesbianism in the national press. Harold Smith supports a similar interpretation in his research into debates surrounding the marriage bar in teaching in the inter-war period. He has suggested that fears that single women teachers exerted an unhealthy influence on their pupils, and could potentially seduce their female pupils into lesbianism, played a significant role in the decision to lift the marriage bar in teaching in 1944.[35]

These attitudes continued to be voiced in the post-war period in the writings of educationalists such as Cyril Bibby and medical literature on lesbianism. In 1947, Albertine Winner, Medical Officer to the Auxiliary Territorial Service (ATS) during the war, drew on the notion of the older, predatory lesbian in her characterisation of adult lesbian identity. She made a (hierarchical) distinction between two distinct lesbian types: the first, a woman whose primary emotional attachments were with women, and whose relationships were sincere, faithful and might or might not have been sexual. This first type of lesbian, who embodied the key post-war feminine ideals of domesticity and monogamy, was described as 'harmless' except insofar as her relationships rendered both women sterile. The second, 'more dangerous', type was the 'promiscuous Lesbian', whose aim was presented as primarily sexual. 'Such women', Winner claimed, 'are usually dominant and forceful personalities and may often seduce weaker and more pliable women who are otherwise perfectly normal heterosexuals'.[36] In this characterisation, Winner reproduced a classic distinction between the more active, sexual lesbian seducer and the passive, heterosexual object of her advances. However, in a specific reference to pupil-teacher relationships, Winner asserted that, while schoolgirl crushes aimed at teachers were commonplace, cases in which the teacher reciprocated these feelings were extremely rare:

> Though the schoolgirl 'crush' is very common and may lead to the tragic situations described in 'Madchen in Uniform' and 'Regiment of Women,' what may be described as the 'Choir-boy Syndrome' is practically non-existent. Little girls fortunately do not seem to have the attraction for their own sex that little boys do.[37]

With the lifting of the marriage bar in teaching at the end of the war, a gradual shift began to take place in attitudes toward lesbianism in female educational establishments. While crushes continued to be regarded as a common aspect of adolescent sexual development in girls, the sexuality of female teachers was less likely to be viewed with suspicion. In addition, by the mid-twentieth century, progressive educationalists were increasingly advocating co-educational schools as a further solution to the problem of homosexuality. A. S. Neill, head teacher of the co-educational public school, Summerhill, argued in 1945:

The school of tomorrow will be co-educational. Our segregated schools are clearly wrong in that they separate boys and girls from the opposite sex in an unnatural and dangerous way … The segregated school is fundamentally a funk hole made by parents and teachers who fear sex and too often hate it. They are ready to face the evil that youthful sex, when denied a natural outlet, tends to become homosexual, apparently thinking that, of the two, homosexuality is less objectionable than heterosexuality. The conspiracy of silence about homosexual practices at public schools is a well-preserved one, and only a fraction of public school products will admit that homo-sexual affairs took place in their schooldays. Just as silent is the conspiracy to hide the fact that boarding school girls get passions on bigger girls and mistresses, a fact that must throw some light on the prevalence of frigidity among many middle- and upper-class women.[38]

Despite the suggestion by progressives such as Neill that a 'conspiracy' of silence about homosexuality in single-sex establishments was potentially unhealthy, in the immediate post-war decades, open discussion of sexual matters was extremely limited in schools. Contradictory understandings of the schoolgirl crush, and tensions between the liberal and feminist desire to provide full education to girls and the cultural emphasis on women's maternal and domestic roles in this period, rendered any discus-sion of sexuality problematic in girls' educational establishments.

The continued dominance of ideals of gender equality and academic achievement, particularly in private and grammar schools, meant that few girls at school in the 1940s, 50s and 60s were exposed to any discussion of sexuality, heterosexual or otherwise. Felicia Lamb and Helen Pickthorn, in their survey of post-war girls' education, claim that the prioritising of public boys' school values continued to occur in girls' private schools immediately after the war:

Years later [the ex-pupils] were to complain not just of the gaps in their education – their lack of general knowledge, modern history, economics; not just that cooking had been for dimwits and science had never included domestic electricity; not even that so much time had gone on team games but that there was no positive feminine ideal put in front of them. They were not actually exhorted that strength and manly fortitude were the most important qualities in life, but the character moulds designed by Arnold of Rugby were still in use in girls' public schools in 1950.[39]

Mary Evans, in her semi-autobiographical account of girls' grammar schools in the 1950s, has argued that any acknowledgement of the contemporary feminine roles of marriage and motherhood would have been fundamentally incompatible with the prevailing feminist emphasis on academic achievement. She observes: 'If we had cheerfully expressed no interest in education and its rewards for girls – and said instead that

meeting a husband with a substantial income was a much more important goal – then we would have left the school, and its teachers, with little
rationale for their existence.'[40]

The consequent insistence on the essentially asexual nature of schoolgirls emerges clearly from many of the post-war surveys of girls' schools
and colleges. In Mallory Wober's survey of twenty-three girls' boarding
schools, conducted in the late 1960s for the Boarding Schools Research
Unit at Kings College, Cambridge, he presents little evidence of any overt
sexual culture in girls' boarding schools of this period. Wober distributed
questionnaires to both the staff and pupils of each school and found a
tension between the priorities of teachers and those of pupils. While
members of staff placed little importance on matters concerning the girls'
bodies or emotional experiences, the girls objected 'that not much is
being done ... about preparing them to deal with the roles of wife and
mother, or to help them in their relationships with boys'.[41] In the context
of boarding schools, these complaints appear to have focused on a lack of
contact with boys, and a perception that the school was failing to take the
initiative in organising joint events with boys' schools in the area. For day-
school girls, conflict centred on the lack of discussion of sexual matters.
Sex education in most girls' schools of the period appears to have been
confined to a brief discussion of menstruation – sometimes taking the
form of a letter to parents asking them to raise the subject with their
daughters – and an analysis of animal reproduction as a part of the
biology syllabus. Lesley Hall has pointed to the haphazard application of
sex education in the 1940s, observing:

> While sex education of the young was said to be desirable, and sex
> educator Cyril Bibby was appointed a special advisor to the Department of
> Education, there was no requirement that it be included in the curriculum
> and the decision as to whether it should take place, and of what it should
> consist, rested largely on decisions of individual head teachers or boards of
> school governors.[42]

Teachers were unlikely to have received any formal instruction in such
matters themselves and it was often widely assumed that parents would
undertake the task of informing their children on this subject.[43] It was not
until the mid-1960s, Hall argues, that any serious attempts to increase the
provision of sex education in schools were made, when the Family Planning Association undertook an education programme directed at educa-
tors and health workers. Nevertheless, sex education provision continued
to be random and subject to local variation.

Outside the classroom, schoolgirls' own attitudes reflected this confusion and lack of explicit information. The playground provided a forum

for abstract debates about popular idols but often little more and Mary Evans complained that, even amongst pupils in her girls' grammar school in the 1950s, 'Being interested in boys was generally thought vulgar, being not interested in boys was regarded as peculiar'.[44] The lack of explicit discussion of sexuality in post-war girls' schools and the ambivalent understandings of teenage crushes as both potentially lesbian and as a commonplace aspect of normative sexual development meant that many schoolgirls were apparently unaware of the deviant sexual identities associated with same-sex desire and lesbianism. Jackie Forster, a pupil at Wycombe Abbey in the 1940s, described her childhood confusion regarding the sexual culture at her boarding school:

> Well, in Wycombe, there were enormously emotional relationships going on with women and we used to hear about girls being expelled because they were found together – we never quite knew what being found together meant. But I certainly remember – because I was sleeping in a dorm – and there was a woman there who had the most amazing boobs for her age and I remember she used to come into my cubicle and let these boobs hang over me and get into bed with me and I adored it. But we didn't actually kiss – we sort of cuddled and things. And I thought 'Why me?', you know, 'why does she pick on me?' And then she'd sort of say 'I must go now', and go back to her bed and I knew, obviously, this wasn't the done thing to do. And I had tremendous crushes on older women and would write passionate letters and hang around in the corridors. But there was never any mention of lesbianism connected with it, you know, it was just passion.[45]

This account indicates a complex understanding of the emotional relationships which the girls in her peer group experienced with each other. Her opening discussion of girls 'being found together' suggests that an interpretation of certain forms of behaviour as lesbian was in operation at her school. However, as a child, Jackie Forster clearly had an extremely limited understanding of the meanings which were ascribed to such behaviour and did not associate it with her own dormitory experiences – although on some level she was aware that it was 'not the done thing'. Her comment that crushes were 'just passion' suggests that within her own childhood understanding of sexuality, and the wider sexual culture of the school, the practice of crushes afforded a considerable space for the expression of same-sex desire outside the discourse of explicitly lesbian sexuality. Jackie Forster's account echoed the experience of Myrtle Solomon, a decade earlier, who 'hopped from passion to passion' at school, and, wanting to establish a proper relationship with the people she liked, always 'declared her love for people quite early on'. When she embarked on a three-year sexual relationship with a German refugee girl who came to live with her family as a teenager, she again had little awareness of people's potential reactions. She observed that while she 'was afraid of being found doing something naughty', she had 'no real sense that lesbianism was wrong'.[46]

Social taboos inhibiting the discussion of homosexuality meant that girls and young women attempting to make sense of same-sex attraction in the 1940s and 50s had limited resources available to them. Fears concerning a potential lesbian presence in same-sex institutions, expressed in educational literature, were occasionally made apparent through school policy, but these concerns were unlikely to be communicated to the girls themselves in a period when sex education of any kind remained highly controversial. Lesbianism, which had been touched upon in some serious literature in the inter-war period, became an increasingly popular theme in the pulp fiction which was being produced on a mass scale in the US and UK after the war, but these works were unlikely to be available in lending libraries or other venues accessible to young people. Films examining the subject did not start to appear until the 1960s.[47] Radclyffe Hall's iconic inter-war lesbian novel, The Well of Loneliness, republished in 1949 after its initial prohibition, remained the most well-known and accessible literary treatment of the subject. For many girls attempting to make sense of same-sex desire in the post-war decades, reading the novel represented a rite of passage, providing a coherent model of lesbian identity. Eileen Carty, writing in to the lesbian magazine, Arena Three, in 1967, claimed: 'The Well will always be my vade mecum: it explained 'me' to me in the far off days when the subject was very taboo, and there were certainly no books easily come by.' Miss C. M. W., in the same issue, echoed this theme, explaining: 'I have a French edition, and ever since I first read it, in the greatest secrecy, at 18, I regard it as my bible. Stephen Gordon may not seem "with it" to the 1967 Lesbian, but her code of honour is an outstanding example to each and every one of us.'[48] For Diana Chapman at the age of twenty-one, reading The Well of Loneliness for the first time in the year it was republished, the experience was highly emotional:

> I had a dentist's appointment and that particular dentist always kept you waiting for at least an hour and a half, and so by the time I got into his chair I'd read about a third of the book. I was shattered. I was hit for six. I thought, this is me, this is what it's all about. I wept copiously, I went about in a daze. I read it at the dentist and then I went home to my digs and sort of just sat there glued for the rest of the evening, you see ... Well I think I remember these terrible feelings that this woman Stephen has and all her frustrations because she's not a man and because she loves a woman and yet all her finest feelings, all her love, everything is just dirty and desecrated and

she can't talk about it and it's secret and I thought yes, this is me. This is it. And of course it also sold me the idea that all lesbians were masculine and tall and handsome and Stephenish. Well of course I should have looked at myself and realised I wasn't any of these things. I didn't think of lesbians as being, sort of ordinary women – I thought they were all very masculine.[49]

For other young women, however, the novel failed to offer them a lesbian identity which they could relate to. Rosanna Hibbert, who read *The Well of Loneliness* as an adult, later in life, thought it 'a pretty awful book', which didn't teach her anything about lesbianism because Stephen was 'so grotesquely male'. Mrs P. K. responded to a 1967 letter in *Arena Three*, which had described a woman's experiences smuggling a French edition of *The Well* into the UK in 1938. In her letter, she provided an account of her schoolgirl experiences with the book, commenting:

> I was vastly amused by your adventures in smuggling The Well into the country. In that same year I was locked in a school loo with four other girls – also reading The Well, but in English, thank goodness!
>
> In those days, one wasn't considered at all with it unless one had read Lady Chatterley and The Well, and the loo was the only safe place to catch up with our reading. All I remember of those far off days is that we thought Lady Chatterley screamingly funny, and The Well interminable. As I recall, we never survived Stephen's dreary childhood ... not surprising, as we had only 15 minutes' break morning and afternoon, and were restricted to the pace of the slowest reader.
>
> Many years and a World War later, I finally caught up with The Well, and I must agree, the style is abominable! I also realised that not one of us had understood a flaming word of it, though we would never have admitted that. We read it because it was forbidden fruit. If it had not been banned, would it have sunk unnoticed?[50]

Such accounts suggest that while *The Well of Loneliness* was significant for some women in the post-war years, offering a masculine version of lesbian identity, others found both the style and the central character, Stephen, difficult to relate to. Nevertheless, the novel's apparent accessibility to girls and young women in this period rendered it a rare literary introduction to ideas about lesbianism.

While some girls drew on literary models as a source of information, others were introduced to the notion of lesbianism by members of their peer group or older girls at school. Margaret Cranch described an encounter with a lesbian couple at grammar school in the 1950s as her first explicit confrontation with a lesbian identity. She recalled a girl in the sixth form, who would arrive at school accompanied by a woman in trousers and short hair, as being an object of particular fascination for herself and her friends. Margaret recounted an exchange, after she and her friends had been following this couple around for some time, in which the two overt lesbians confronted the younger girls and told them that the reason for their fascination was that they too were lesbians. Although the younger girls were apparently pleased to have a name for their feelings, they had a very limited understanding of what this meant. Margaret Cranch recalled how she and her friends had subsequently used the term 'lesby' to each other, shouting the word out on the school hockey pitch, unaware that the term might have any meaning for others who heard it.[51] The lack of a clear understanding of the meanings which were ascribed to same-sex desire was a theme which many narrators echoed. Cynthia Reid maintained that she did not think of the full physical relationship she had with another girl at college 'in terms of homosexuality'. She explained:

> When I confided the nature of the relationship with a mutual close friend at the college, she said in surprise, 'But you're clearly the most obvious lesbian I've ever seen'. And my response was, 'The most obvious what?' I'd never heard the word; I didn't know what she was talking about. She said, 'Well, women who fall in love with other women'. And for the first time in my life, I had to sort of sit back and think, 'Oh, there's a word for something that I must be'.[52]

For many girls, feelings of same-sex desire were experienced as increasingly problematic with the onset of puberty and their teenage years. The ambiguous representation of crushes as both a potential signifier of same-sex desire and as a stage in a normative progression to heterosexuality prompted a number of women subsequently to engage in heterosexual relationships. Cynthia Reid explained that she regarded her crushes on women as 'completely separate' from her expectations of marriage and children, and had in fact had two relationships with boys while at school.[53] Nina Jenkins echoed this. Despite having 'fallen passionately in love' with the female hockey captain at her school, she observed:

> All my sexual adventures were with boys and I don't think – it had never occurred to me that it could be any other way. As so many young women at that time I don't think sexuality had actually crossed my mind – I was very innocent about that kind of thing. I thought I had to have boyfriends, and I liked some boys and when they got to all the kissing and cuddling bits it was mostly a bore but I put up with it and until I fancied the hockey/ swimming captain I really wasn't interested in women either.[54]

Jackie Forster's childhood experiences of same-sex desire and sexuality did not prevent her from having a range of sexual experience with men and getting married, before beginning a lesbian relationship later in life.[55]

For others who continued to express desire for other girls and women, the late teenage years were a particularly problematic period, as they became increasingly aware that their same-sex desires were no longer regarded as 'normal'. Pat Arrowsmith recalled approaching a sex-education teacher at the end of a lecture in the final years of her school career, concerned at the fact that she 'fancied' her best friend. The woman told her to 'quell' her feelings. Rene Sawyer also sought advice at the age of sixteen when her girlfriend told her that their relationship had to end because she was not a boy.[56] Such experiences point to puberty as a moment of crisis and increasing clarity in understandings of lesbian identity.

This emphasis on puberty as a key moment in sexual development was the product of a medical discourse on lesbianism and female sexual development, which had dominated thinking about sexuality since the nineteenth century and became an important point of reference for youth workers and young women themselves in the post-war decades. Chris Waters has argued that the hostility of the British medical establishment toward any discussion of sexual matters, and the reluctance of British Freudians to dwell on Freud's ideas about sexuality at the possible expense of the wider applications of psychoanalysis, combined to delay the reception of Freud's sexological work in the UK, but that, 'psychoanalytic accounts of the aetiology of homosexuality had, by the 1950s, come to dominate much "official" thinking on the subject'.[57] With the advent of Freudian psychoanalytic approaches to sexual development, earlier notions of the homosexual as a special category of person were replaced with a theory of universal infant bisexuality.[58] Thus homosexuality, like heterosexuality, came to be regarded as a possible outcome of any individual's sexual development, and was explained as the result of an inhibition of the 'normal process' occurring at puberty, which could be sparked off by the child's environment. Eustace Chesser, a Harley Street psychiatrist and gynaecologist and a prolific author of popular sex manuals in the post-war years, drew heavily on Freud's explanation of lesbian sexuality in his early discussions of the subject. Assuming a psychoanalytic model of sexual development, he asserted three causes of lesbianism: firstly, that by remaining in the clitoral phase and thus failing to solve penis envy, the girl remains attached to the mother; secondly, that the formation of an excessive attachment to her father prevents the adult woman from finding another man to replace him and thus denies her sex instinct a normal outlet; and thirdly, that hatred of the father, as a result of childhood trauma, causes the woman to consider all men hateful and untrustworthy. While all three were drawn directly from Freud's theories, Chesser favoured the first with more detailed explication, linking failure to resolve

penis envy with the dominance of masculine traits, exhibited in tomboyish behaviour as a child and in an undue emphasis on careers in adulthood.

> It has been suggested by some psychologists that an undue delay at the
> clitoral stage is a factor in female homosexuality. As long as the girl thinks
> of her clitoris as a penis, however rudimentary, her attitude tends to be
> masculine. She is aggressive and boyish in her play ...
>
> As her sexual impulses strengthen they still remain focused upon the
> parent of her own sex. Provided they can be sublimated there is no great
> harm done. She will probably grow into what is termed 'the career woman'.
> But if her personality is not strong enough to sublimate her instinct in this
> way she may become homosexual by inclination if not in practice.[59]

In this explanatory model, the key moment in development was puberty.
While a masculine aggressiveness and tomboyishness were apparently
acceptable aspects of 'normal' development up to puberty, their persist-
ence beyond that point would, Chesser argued, indicate a disposition
toward homosexuality. The strengthening of sexual desire with age would
confirm this predisposition. Thus, for Chesser, once puberty had been
passed, no external forces were required to push the child into lesbianism:
the natural strengthening of her sexual impulses would complete the
process unassisted.

Albertine Winner, giving the first post-war scientific paper on the
subject of homosexuality in women to the Psychiatry Section of the Royal
Society of Medicine in 1947, similarly favoured a psychoanalytic model.[60]
A physician rather than a psychiatrist, Winner drew on her experience as
Medical Officer in the ATS during the war, supplemented by her reading
of the existing literature on the subject, in making her observations.
Winner reiterated the emphasis on adolescence as the defining moment in
the formation of a lesbian identity, commenting that:

> In dealing with large numbers of Lesbians one of the most striking
> things is the recurrent traits of immaturity, mainly emotional, but showing
> themselves in many unexpected ways, that one meets in women of high
> intellectual or artistic development. This certainly bears out the view that
> the homosexual relation is an immature one, an arrest of normal sexual
> development at an adolescent stage.[61]

Winner draws an interesting connection here between her apparent observation of lesbians as 'emotionally immature' and the psychoanalytic argument that homosexuality emerged as a result of incomplete sexual
development. She seems to be arguing a quite literal interpretation of the
notion of arrested development, applied to emotional development as
much as sexual development, so that adult lesbians, in her view, remain

permanently in a state of quasi-adolescence. In this model, there is apparently no distinction to be made between the adolescent lesbian and the 'immature' adult lesbian.

Winner's paper was followed by a small number of further studies in the late 1940s and 1950s. J. Tudor Rees and Harvey V. Usill's *They Stand Apart: A Critical Survey of the Problems of Homosexuality* included a chapter on homosexuality in women in a section dealing with medical aspects of homosexuality, but offered little more than an overview of existing literature. The author, W. Lindsay Neustatter, M.D., admitted to having few case histories of lesbians to draw upon and ultimately only reproduced one as 'quite representative'. The history focused largely upon the subject's relationship with her parents and her tomboyish behaviour and reflected late-nineteenth century sexological methods and approaches.[62] The sexological project in the late nineteenth and early twentieth century had undertaken two fundamental aims: that of explaining the appearance of the homosexual phenomenon in certain individuals and that of defining the central characteristics of the homosexual. Laura Doan and Chris Waters have argued that the publication of Havelock Ellis' work, *Sexual Inversion*, in 1896, in which he explained what he termed 'sexual inversion' as a 'congenital anomaly', constituted a first significant challenge to the established consensus that homosexuality was an acquired condition.[63] The German lawyer, Karl Heinrich Ulrichs, whose work was circularised in Britain by Edward Carpenter, added to the congenital argument with his 'third sex' model of homosexuality. Ulrichs claimed that sexual orientation was innate in members of the 'third sex', explaining that 'the 'germ' of same-sex desire is implanted *ab ovo* in the very physiognomy of the man-loving man', emerging at puberty.[64] This notion of lesbian identity as innate confirmed the existence of lesbianism in the subject from birth and implicitly highlighted puberty as a central moment in which sexual identity was formed. However, sexological notions of homosexuality as innate were frequently united with suggestions of the need for an external catalyst to spark the development of a lesbian identity. For Havelock Ellis, certain environmental factors external to an individual's make-up could precipitate this 'latent condition', although they did require a 'favourable organic predisposition' on which to act.[65] Stella Browne, whose writing on female sexual inversion in the inter-war period owed much to Havelock Ellis, placed greater emphasis on environmental factors. She qualified her assertions regarding the innate nature of lesbianism with the comment that homosexuality was in part a result of society's repression of the 'normal sexual impulse', and should society take a less prudish attitude toward women's sexual behaviour, the incidence of homosexuality would diminish.[66] Sexological works on female homosexuality therefore frequently relied upon case histories which emphasised both an innate homosexuality, exhibited through tomboyish tendencies and the presence of an external catalyst, such as traumatic relations with parents or a seduction by an older woman.

The publication of Dr. George W. Henry's *Sex Variants* in the UK in 1950 provided 'medical and allied professionals only' with a further body of such material. Henry's research, conducted in conjunction with the American organisation, the Committee for the Study of Sex Variants, remained staunchly within this sexological tradition of cataloguing sexual abnormalities. His two-volume collection of 'Homosexual Cases' began with brief summaries of the women he had interviewed in the course of his research, outlining parental background, childhood development and adult sexual experience. Henry then reproduced these case histories in full, apparently in the interviewee's voice, with opening and closing comments of his own. Interviewees were encouraged to emphasise poor relationships with their parents, histories of mental instability in the family, tomboyish or sporty behaviour in childhood and current sexual relations.[67] In 1957, Frank Caprio's book-length study of homosexuality in women in the US and Europe was published in Britain, drawing on a combination of early sexological and later psychoanalytic approaches.[68] Although writing from a medical background, Caprio's work offered few new conclusions. His opening section reviewing the existing scientific literature on homosexuality was followed by a discussion of the 'lesbian theme' in history and literature and an outline of the place of the lesbian in contemporary society, in the prison population and amongst prostitutes. Influenced by psychoanalytic studies, Caprio argued that the theory of universal infant bisexuality meant that lesbians could be 'cured' by simply uncovering their repressed heterosexuality but in defining the contributing factors to lesbianism, he drew on classic sexological explanatory models which focused on parental influences, psychic traumas, alcoholism and seductions by older women.

Medical science remained one of the most influential forces explaining the aetiology and characteristics of female homosexuality in the post-war decades. In a field dominated by psychoanalytic interpretative models, but still influenced by earlier thinking, the figure of the lesbian was constructed as immature and unfulfilled, neurotic and jealous, a sexual predator and a naïve, passive victim. This literature, and the medical practitioners who applied it, constituted an important point of reference for many young women. Medical discourse offered an interpretative model within which women could make sense of, and label, their same-sex desires. While much of the literature on lesbianism in the post-war decades was clearly intended for a 'professional' readership, lesbian accounts suggest that encounters with medical thinking, either through the literature itself or through contact with doctors and psychiatrists, frequently played a key role in women's development of a sense of lesbian identity. Diana Chapman described her engagement with the medical literature in the late 1940s and early 1950s as a negative experience. Having already decided that she was a lesbian, Diana did not find her reading encouraging:

> Yes, I thought I was a lesbian. But then, I thought that it was ridiculous and awful and every book on psychology I ever read – and I had a stack of those blue pelicans – told me that it was immature and that I should really get my act together and reconcile myself to my femininity and find myself a good man and have children. And so I thought, 'This is ridiculous, I must try to simply get on with being a normal woman', which I tried to do without very much success.[69]

Julie Switsur, who worked in a library after leaving school in 1957, came across a number of references to homosexuality and similarly decided that homosexuals were 'a dreadful lot'. However, when she fell in love with her female boss, she started seriously searching out such literature. Like Diana Chapman, Julie did not respond positively to the books she read, explaining, 'mostly they were dreadful psychoanalytic things – awful'. Poor communication and a lack of understanding meant that, for some women, personal encounters with the medical profession were equally unproductive. Rene Sawyer visited her doctor in 1952 when, at the age of sixteen, her girlfriend told her that the relationship had to end because Rene was not a boy. Faced with the possibility that she was not like other girls, Rene decided she would tell the doctor that she was changing into a boy. He sent her to a psychiatrist: an encounter which Rene experienced as both frightening and confusing. This was the first time she had heard the words 'lesbian' and 'homosexual' and did not understand what the psychiatrists were talking about.[70]

However, lesbian accounts suggest that, while medical literature throughout the period continued to rely on pre-war interpretative models in their approach to lesbianism, a shift had occurred by the 1960s in the approaches taken by medical practitioners. In the early 1960s, Julie Switsur's experience with medical practitioners was more positive than that of Rene Sawyer a decade earlier. Despite her limited success with the published literature, Julie apparently regarded the medical profession as the primary source of information on this subject and some years later, still unclear as to whether or not she was a lesbian, but wanting to resolve the issue, Julie Switsur wrote to a counsellor she knew of, asking for a referral to a psychiatrist. Her contact wrote back inviting her to come to him, and, as she felt they got on well, she embarked on a course of 'sex counselling' with him. Switsur describes a process in which the counsellor discussed sex with her, showed her pictures of female genitalia and finally arranged for her to have sex, blindfolded, with another of his 'lesbian' patients. The experience, she claimed, 'gave [her] the certain knowledge that [she] was gay'.[71] While psychiatrists frequently played a role in confirming women's sexual identity and giving a name to their same-sex desires, accounts of therapeutic intervention are rare. In contrast to the extensive research and apparatus aimed at curing male homosexuality in the 1950s and 60s, the absence of legal sanctions against lesbians appears to have rendered a therapeutic solution less urgent for women. Many women who sought medical assistance regarding their lesbianism in this period were advised simply to 'adjust' to their sexual identity. Pat Arrowsmith, who was put in touch with an analyst when she became concerned that her lesbianism would hinder her work as a social worker, was told that there was no point having analysis unless she felt 'out of accord with herself' on account of being a lesbian. Sandy Martin, who, as a teenager in the early 1960s, was taken by a social worker to see a psychiatrist, received a similar response. Martin explained that she had come to see him because she was a lesbian, adding, 'I think I'm supposed to be cured or something'. His reply, she recalled, was, 'Well, it's more about accepting who you are really'.[72]

The medical profession and psychiatric literature offered one avenue through which teenagers and young women in the post-war period were able to identify and interpret their same-sex desires. For others, the onset of adulthood meant the beginning of a new struggle to conform to social expectations of heterosexual femininity and marriage and many women spent much of their lives attempting to resolve these conflicts. The contradictory representation of schoolgirl sexuality in educational and medical literature in the 1940s and 50s afforded considerable flexibility for the expression of female same-sex desire in adolescence. Ambiguous characterisations of the schoolgirl crush as both a passing phase in normal sexual development and an indicator of an innate lesbian sexuality, combined with an established culture of intense emotional relationships between younger and older girls and teachers, offered a degree of license for the expression of same-sex desire. Reluctance to acknowledge girls' sexual identities or to consider their potential futures as wives and mothers, produced a culture of silence around schoolgirl sexuality which facilitated the development of same-sex relationships. However, these opportunities

were limited to a brief period of adolescence and on reaching maturity
young women had to negotiate new roles, centred on work, the home and
the social sphere, which offered different opportunities and limitations in
the expression of lesbian sexuality.

Notes

1 NSA, HCC (C456), F2088, Diana Chapman.
2 Martha Vicinus, 'Distance and desire: English boarding-school friendships,
   1870–1920', *Signs* 9:4 (1984), pp. 618–19.
3 Katherine Bement Davis, *Factors in the Sex Life of Twenty-Two Hundred Women*
   (London: Harper and Brothers, 1929).
4 Lillian Faderman, *Surpassing the Love of Men: Romantic Friendship and Love Between Women
   from the Renaissance to the Present* (London: The Women's Press, 1985).
5 Laura Doan and Chris Waters, 'Introduction: Homosexualities', in Lucy Bland
   and Laura Doan (eds), *Sexology Uncensored: The Documents of Sexual Science* (Chicago:
   University of Chicago Press, 1998), p. 43.
6 Jeffrey Weeks, *Sex, Politics and Society: The Regulation of Sexuality Since 1800* (London:
   Longman, 1981).
7 NSA, HCC (C456), F1328-F1330, Rene Sawyer.
8 NSA, HCC (C456), F1622-F1624, Angela Chilton.
9 NSA, HCC (C456), F1622-F1624, Angela Chilton.
10 *Daily Herald* (5 September 1935), in Alison Oram and Annmarie Turnbull, *The
   Lesbian History Sourcebook* (London: Routledge, 2001), p. 145.
11 Carol Dyhouse, 'Towards a "feminine" curriculum for English schoolgirls:
   The demands of ideology 1870–1963', *Women's Studies International Quarterly* 1
   (1978).
12 Board of Education, *Report of Consultative Committee on Differentiation of the Curriculum
   for Boys and Girls Respectively in Secondary Schools* (London: HMSO, 1923).
13 *Curriculum and Examinations in Secondary Schools: Report of the Committee of the Secondary
   School Examinations Council appointed by the president of the Board of Education* (London:
   HMSO, 1943) [The Norwood Report]. Ministry of Education, *Report of the
   Central Advisory Council for Education '15–18': The Crowther Report* (London: HMSO,
   1959) observed that while there was little room in the curriculum of 'more
   able girls' for matters related to their 'special needs as women', schools
   should discuss these issues with 'less able' girls.
14 John Newsom, *The Education of Girls* (London: Faber and Faber, 1948). For a
   discussion of Newsom, see Tessa Blackstone, 'The education of girls today', in
   Juliet Mitchell and Ann Oakley (eds), *The Rights and Wrongs of Women*
   (Harmondsworth: Penguin, 1976).
15 Jenni Murray, *The Woman's Hour: Fifty Years of Women in Britain* (London: BBC Books,
   1996).
16 Faderman, *Surpassing the Love of Men*.
17 Oram and Turnbull, *The Lesbian History Sourcebook*, p. 130.
18 Rosemary Auchmuty, '"You're a dyke, Angela!" Elsie J. Oxenham and the rise
   and fall of the schoolgirl story', in Lesbian History Group (ed.), *Not a Passing*

   Phase: Reclaiming Lesbians in History 1840–1985 (London: The Women's Press, 1989); Rosemary Auchmuty, *The World of Girls* (London: The Women's Press, 1992); Rosemary Auchmuty, *The World of Women: Growing Up in the Girls' School Story* (London: The Women's Press, 1999).

19 NSA, HCC (C456), F1326–F1327, Pat Arrowsmith; NSA, HCC (C456), F2108, Julie Switsur.

20 L. M. Faithfull, *You and I, Saturday Talks at Cheltenham* (Chatto & Windus, 1927), pp. 118–19.

21 J. Macalister Brew, 'How the mind works', *Club News* (January 1945), p. 2.

22 Cyril Bibby, *Sex Education* (London: Macmillan, 1945), p. 114.

23 Helen Richardson, *Adolescent Girls in Approved Schools* (London: Routledge & Kegan Paul, 1969), p. 50.

24 Jaye Zimet, *Strange Sisters: The Art of Lesbian Pulp Fiction 1949–69* (London: Penguin, 1999), p. 24.

25 NSA, HCC (C456), F1622–F1624, Angela Chilton.

26 NSA, HCC (C456), F1328–F1330, Rene Sawyer.

27 NSA, HCC (C456), F1328–F1330, Rosanna Hibbert.

28 *The Lancet* (3 March 1951), p. 519.

29 Dr Phyllis Epps, *British Journal of Delinquency* (January 1951), p. 187.

30 Bibby, *Sex Education*, p. 114.

31 Oram, 'Embittered, sexless or homosexual'. Also see her *Women Teachers and Feminist Politics, 1900–1939* (Manchester: Manchester University Press, 1996).

32 Laura Doan, '"Acts of female indecency": Sexology's intervention in legislating lesbianism', in Lucy Bland and Laura Doan (eds), *Sexology in Culture: Labelling Bodies and Desires* (Cambridge: Polity Press, 1998).

33 August Forel, *The Sexual Question: A Scientific, Psychological, Hygienic and Sociological Study for the Cultured Classes* (London: Heinemann, 1906), p. 252.

34 Albert Moll, *Perversions of the Sex Instinct: A Study of Sexual Inversion* (Newark: Julian Press, 1931) [1891], pp. 231, 233.

35 Harold L. Smith, 'The womanpower problem in Britain during the Second World War', *The Historical Journal* 27:4 (1984). The National Archive, London (hereafter TNA), ED 136/467, Education Act 1944: Suggested amendments; TNA: ED 136/480, Education Act 1944: Committee stage.

36 Albertine Winner, 'Homosexuality in Women', *Medical Press and Circular* (September 3 1947), p. 219.

37 Winner, 'Homosexuality in Women', p. 220.

38 A. S. Neill, *Hearts Not Heads in the School* (Herbert Jenkins, 1945), pp. 78–9.

39 Felicia Lamb and Helen Pickthorn, *Locked-Up Daughters: A Parent's Look at Girls' Education and Schools* (London: Hodder and Stoughton, 1968), p. 78.

40 Mary Evans, *A Good School: Life at a Girls' Grammar School in the 1950s* (London: Women's Press, 1991), p. 40.

41 Mallory Wober, *English Girls' Boarding Schools* (London: Allen Lane, 1971), p. 16.

42 Lesley Hall, *Sex, Gender and Social Change in Britain since 1880* (Basingstoke: Macmillan, 2000), p. 148. Also, see Paul Ferris, *Sex and the British: A Twentieth Century History* (London: Mandarin, 1994); Dorothy M. Dallas, *Sex Education in School and Society* (London: National Foundation for Education Research in England and Wales, 1972).

43 Theodore F. Tucker, *Parents' Problems and Sex Education* (London: The Bodley Head, 1948); Cecilia Mireio Legge and Fred Frankiand Rigby, *Life and Growth* (London: Faber and Faber, 1950).

44 Evans, *A Good School*, p. 44.

45 NSA, HCC (C456), F1607–F1612, Jackie Forster.

46 NSA, HCC (C456), F2082–F2083, Myrtle Soloman.

47 *The Children's Hour* (US, 1961; Released as *The Loudest Whisper* in UK); *Les Biches* (France, 1968); *The Killing of Sister George* (US, 1968). See Stephen Bourne, *Brief Encounters: Lesbians and Gays in British Cinema 1930–1971* (London: Cassell, 1996).

48 *Arena Three* 4:10 (October 1967), pp. 10–11.

49 NSA, HCC (C456), F2088, Diana Chapman.

50 *Arena Three* 4:10 (October 1967), pp. 10–11.

51 NSA, HCC (C456), F1359–F1360, Margaret Cranch.

52 NSA, HCC (C456), F2109, Cynthia Reid.

53 NSA, HCC (C456), F2109, Cynthia Reid.

54 NSA, HCC (C456), F2499–F2501, Nina Jenkins.

55 NSA, HCC (C456), F1607–F1612, Jackie Forster.

56 NSA, HCC (C456), F1326–F1327, Pat Arrowsmith; NSA, HCC (C456), F1328-F1330, Rene Sawyer.

57 Chris Waters, 'Havelock Ellis, Sigmund Freud and the state: Discourses of homosexual identity in interwar England', in Bland and Doan (eds), *Sexology in Culture*, p. 165.

58 Sigmund Freud, *The Standard Edition of the Complete Psychological Works of Sigmund Freud*, 24 vols., trans. James Strachey et al. (London: Hogarth Press, 1961), vol XIX.

59 Eustace Chesser, *Odd Man Out: Homosexuality in Men and Women* (London: Victor Gollancz, 1959), pp. 96–7.

60 Winner, 'Homosexuality in Women', p. 219.

61 Winner, 'Homosexuality in Women', p. 219.

62 J. Tudor Rees and Harvey V. Usill (eds), *They Stand Apart: A Critical Survey of the Problems of Homosexuality* (London: Heinemann, 1955).

63 Doan and Waters, 'Introduction: Homosexualities', p. 42.

64 Karl Heinrich Ulrichs, *The Riddle of 'Man-Manly' Love: The Pioneering Work on Male Homosexuality*, 2 vols, trans. Michael A. Lombardi-Nash (Buffalo, NY: Prometheus Books, 1994 [1864–1880]), p. 35.

65 Havelock Ellis, *Studies in the Psychology of Sex, Complete in Two Volumes* (New York: Random, 1942 [1902]).

66 Stella Browne, 'Studies in feminine inversion', *Journal of Sexology and Psychoanalysis* (1923).

67 Dr. George W. Henry, *Sex Variants: A Study of Homosexual Patterns* (London: Cassell, 1950 [1941]).

68 Frank Caprio, M.D., *Female Homosexuality: A Psychodynamic Study of Lesbianism* (London: Peter Owen, 1957).

69 NSA, HCC (C456), F2088, Diana Chapman.

70 NSA, HCC (C456), F1328–F1330, Rene Sawyer.

71 NSA, HCC (C456), F2108, Julie Switsur.

72 NSA, HCC (C456), F2483–F2487, Sandy Martin.

2

The 'all-out career woman' and narratives of lesbianism at work

In 1964, *The Times* published an article entitled 'Bachelor Girl', describing the plight of the young unmarried woman in her late twenties with nothing to occupy herself but her career. 'Feminists and writers in the more sophisticated magazines', the correspondent explained, 'may argue persuasively about the superior position of the bachelor girl ... How much more exciting life can be for the bachelor girl, they say, than for married couples like themselves, weighed down with families. Think of the opportunities for travel and an uninterrupted career!' However, in the correspondent's view, no family wanted a bachelor girl for a daughter and such women were continually accused of subjecting themselves to unnecessary social and economic hardship or of trying to avoid their fundamental responsibilities as women. The reality, the correspondent suggested, was somewhere between the two: the bachelor girl was not a social rebel but someone with a deep fear of commitment in personal relationships. 'What such a girl needs most are tact, tolerance and under-standing. She wants to feel that parents and relatives are with her, not against her, that they can help her to come to terms with her emotional problems, or that at least they have the imagination to realize that she is not simply being a rebel.'[1]

In the post-war period, ambivalence regarding women and paid employment meant that women's experience of work was construed simultaneously as a wilful dereliction of woman's social and biological responsibilities as wives and mothers; a useful forum in which young women could potentially meet future husbands and married women could learn skills beneficial to domestic harmony; and an outlet for the suppressed energies of those ill-suited by nature to marriage and mother-hood. While certain occupations, conventionally defined as appropriate for women, lent themselves to a construction of the woman worker as 'feminine' and potentially heterosexual, others, perceived to be more masculine and active, resulted in a construction of female workers as ambitious, career-oriented and possibly sexually deviant. Conventionally feminine occupations tended to encourage women workers to project a heterosexual identity at work and were therefore environments which proved insignificant to and problematic for the construction of a lesbian identity. For those employed in masculine-gendered occupations, their experience of work may have played a more significant part in the construction of their lesbian identity and was therefore an aspect of their lives which they emphasised in a lesbian life-history interview.

In the aftermath of the Second World War, a proliferation of advice books aimed at assisting girls and young women in the choice of a career indi- cated a changing attitude toward women and work and an increasing expectation that girls would leave school with the skills and intention to join the labour force.[2] Women's work, as the authors of these career manuals perceived it, was no longer simply a temporary measure to supplement a family income or acquire pin-money for a wife, it was a long-term commitment requiring forethought and choice. In a speech opening the Schoolgirls' Exhibition in 1949, Dame Mary Tyrwhitt, Direc- tor of the Women's Royal Army Corps, advised girls to consider the issue of a career. *The Times* reported:

> Dame Mary Tyrwhitt said present-day statistics showed that many women would not have a chance to marry, and, therefore, all must be prepared to adopt some other career. In choosing a career, the individual had to consider personal interest, ability, work which would allow scope for devel- opment and also be of benefit to the community. If later she married, the fact that she had done a job of work, and made a success of it, would, by broadening her interest and outlook, make her a better citizen and a more interesting and capable wife and mother.[3]

Population imbalances and economic uncertainty in the aftermath of two world wars prompted an increasing perception that women should possess the ability to support themselves, in the event that they were not supported by a husband. However, it was the increasing choice in occupa- tions which the authors of career manuals emphasised in justifying their guides. In 1944 Ursula Bloom, a journalist with *Woman's Own*, observed in her career guide:

> [N]ever before will women have had such a wide field in which to compete. The last war was the beginning. Until then nobody was anything save a domestic servant, a companion, or a governess. A few of them were

nurses, but not very many, and it was frowned upon that a girl should want to earn her living. The 1914–18 war stopped that, and made it possible for every girl to earn in a very large number of spheres. But the 1939–(Heaven knows what) war is making it possible for every girl to earn her living in every sphere, and that is why it is so increasingly difficult to choose.[4]

Careers manuals for girls in the 1940s and 50s portrayed a world of employment filled with a bewildering choice of occupations. Girls were presumed to have an extremely limited conception of the types of work open to them and it was this need for direction which the manuals sought to answer. Career guides provided directories of possible occupations, with information on the skills and training required and the organisations which girls should contact for assistance.

This emergence of the notion of 'careers' for women in the 1940s and 50s reflected changing experiences of work for women in the first half of the century. Penny Tinkler has defined the term 'careers' in this context as 'occupations which required training and which offered prospects for advancement.'[5] As such, this concept was largely class specific in this period, related to the late-nineteenth and early-twentieth-century expansion in educational opportunities for middle-class girls. The emergence of girls' public schools and access to higher education for women enabled middle-class girls to pursue professional training for the first time. Perhaps more significantly, this expansion in educational opportunities fostered a new ideal, so that 'many secondary school headmistresses ... whilst not dismissing marriage as a legitimate goal, promoted a liberal education for their pupils followed ideally by a university education or teacher training and a professional career'.[6] The opening up of previously male occupations before and during the First World War meant that an increasing number of professional occupations were available to educated middle class women in the inter-war period, while wider labour market conditions facilitated the emergence of the career for middle-class women in the mid-twentieth century. Elizabeth Wilson has argued that, in the inter-war period, middle-class women were enabled by the continued availability of domestic servants to combine the domestic responsibilities of marriage with a career.[7] Although numbers of domestic servants declined rapidly during and after the Second World War, post-war labour shortages encouraged many women to remain in, or return to, the workforce in the 1940s and 50s.

The post-war proliferation of girls' career manuals reflected this wider preoccupation with women and work, as did other literature directed at young women. Penny Tinkler's analysis of girls' magazines in the period 1920–50 has tracked a similar development in the representation of work for women in this increasingly popular medium. Magazines addressed to secondary school, and thus predominantly middle-class girls, such as *Miss Modern* and the *Girls' Own Paper*, she comments, placed considerable emphasis on their readers' careers.[8] Tinkler argues that a growing perception that work was not incompatible with femininity and a realisation that many middle-class women might be called upon to support either themselves or an incapacitated or unemployed husband at some stage in their lives, led to 'an increased acceptance of professional employment for middle-class girls'.[9] Magazines responded to this situation by offering advice to their readers on the types of career open to them and the training necessary to pursue them. One of the longest running features was 'Carol's Career Corner' in the *Girls' Own Paper*, which in 1943 discussed medicine and veterinary science as possible professions for women.[10] Magazines targeted at a more working-class audience proved much more reluctant to discuss work, however, reflecting the still limited and monotonous work options open to their readers. While editors could not afford to completely ignore an important aspect of many readers' lives, work themes were largely confined to fictional representations that gave scope for more fantastical and exciting portrayals of the workplace. Hence, Tinkler argues:

> Career girls did appear in the fiction of these papers but portraits of heroines as detectives, circus performers and actresses were glamorous and far removed from the realities of the labour market. The fictional representation of acting, for instance, was merely an attempt by editors to pander to their readers' fantasies to ensure that their paper sold.[11]

In place of realistic portrayals of work experiences, these magazines continued to focus firmly on marriage and motherhood as the life ambition of their readers and to portray work as a stop-gap before marriage. Pearl Jephcott, author of a survey of 103 'ordinary' girls, published in 1948, confirmed this view. She observed:

> It is rare to meet a girl who is excited or enthusiastic about the actual work she performs. She may talk of the liveliness of the workplace, or the good money she earns, or 'the best boss in the world'; but she seldom indicates anything approaching enthusiasm for what she has been doing from 8 a.m. to 5.30 p.m. for perhaps the last five years.[12]

Instead, the girls she questioned focused their attention on social lives conducted outside of working hours and on marriage prospects.

Despite the increasing perception that women should be capable of working to support themselves, attitudes toward women and work throughout this period continued to be dominated by concerns about the perceived threat to women's domestic role. With increasing numbers of

married women entering the labour force in the 1940s and 50s, much of
the debate focused on the relationship between women's employment and
marriage. Official messages regarding the place of the married woman in
the workforce were mixed. Post-war labour shortages forced the government to explore new sources of labour in the 1940s and 50s and, with 92
per cent of single women already employed in 1947, married women
provided one of the few remaining untapped options.[13] However, Wendy
Webster argues, the married women's recruitment campaign initiated
through the Factories (Evening Employment) Order of 1950 'exemplified
both the characteristic view that employment was peripheral to a woman's
main activities and the development of patterns of feminized work
which ensured that employment could be fitted in around the needs of
families'.[14] At the same time, the post-war Labour government sought to
promote a domestic ideal for women, striving to lessen the domestic
burden for the housewife through proposed interventionist policies, and
reconstructing the role of 'homemaking' as a career. Throughout the
1950s and 1960s, organisations and cultural commentators continued to
express the view that women's work should take second place to marriage.
In the 1964 edition of their careers guide, the Women's Employment
Federation observed:

> Many girls feel – and their parents too sometimes – that with the likelihood
> of early marriage, it is not worth the time, trouble and financial sacrifices
> to take a long training for work which they will do, perhaps, for a few years
> only.[15]

Despite arguing that girls should take a longer term view and equip themselves for work later in life, after raising a family, the comments reflected
an assumption that women would leave the workforce in the first years of
marriage. Women's magazines demonstrated a similar presumption. In
contrast to girls' magazines, they made little reference to work, assuming
that employment was a concern merely for young, single women and
representing working wives as 'bad' wives.[16]

Ambivalent views on married women working were complicated by
increasingly negative attitudes toward working mothers in the post-war
period in the context of growing concern over the falling birth-rate.
Nikolas Rose has traced the development of the notion of the juvenile
delinquent from the nineteenth into the twentieth centuries, arguing that
delinquency was increasingly conflated with neglect of children after the
Second World War, so that the emotional economy of the family came to
be regarded as critical in the shaping of the child's psyche. He argues:

It was in the two decades following the end of the war that this vision of the child and its family was generalized. The group life of the family, its relational economy, the dependencies, frustrations, jealousies, attachments, rivalries, and frustrations that traversed it, became both the means of explanation of the troubles of childhood and the means of construing the ideal family.[17]

Wartime conditions enabled psychiatrists and social workers such as Anna Freud and John Bowlby to conduct research into the impact of childhood separation from the family in nurseries and urban evacuation. John Bowlby emphasised the mother-child bond as particularly important, claiming in 1952 that 'the prolonged deprivation of the young child of maternal care may have grave and far-reaching effects on his character and on the whole of his future life'.[18] These ideas gained new currency in the post-war period and became quickly absorbed into debates about women's employment. Although the government closed over half of its wartime nurseries following the Armistice, and devolved responsibility for their maintenance to local authorities, the provision of nurseries for the children of working mothers remained a controversial issue in the 1940s and 50s.[19] In his 1949 study of sexual behaviour, the popular psychiatrist Eustace Chesser argued:

> We find a growing tendency for the state to assume that children can be as well cared for in nurseries conducted by local authorities as by their own mothers; that it is desirable to enrol as many married women as possible in industry, and that it is in the national interest for women to perform tasks similar to those of men …
>
> These disturbing tendencies reveal plainly the influence of the propaganda in favour of complete equality between the sexes … Yet if, casting aside all sex prejudice, we regard objectively the whole matter of the relative value of the sexes, we can find little to account for the tendency to turn against women's fundamental biological role.[20]

This notion that feminism, by urging mothers into the workplace, had encouraged women to reject their 'natural', biological function, was commonplace in the 1940s and 50s.[21] Such views continued to be voiced throughout the period and, as late as 1965, the Countess of Dartmouth told the National Association of Round Tables annual conference that:

> Women today have gilded fetters but millions are chained to the treadmill of job, home, husband, children, until they drop with exhaustion …
>
> Women have lost their mystery and their glamour. They have therefore killed romance. Instead we have sex in its most revolting forms.

> Filthy books, filthy plays, filthy magazines are currently glorified, and
> there are the same kind of perversions and homosexuality that marked the
> decline and fall of the Roman Empire.[22]

Despite the lurid prose, the speech echoed an enduring belief that
employment for married women threatened the family and thus the roots
of British society.

In the context of these debates, and despite increasing numbers of
married women and mothers in the workplace, the figure of the working
woman in the post-war period was inevitably construed as the antithesis
of the domestic ideal. In her discussion of the construction of women
workers in the Report of the Royal Commission on Equal Pay in 1946,
Elizabeth Wilson claims:

> Work and marriage were still understood as alternatives. The Report
> assumed in fact that there were two kinds of women. You could either be a
> wife and mother or a single career woman. To a certain extent this division
> corresponded to a (perceived) class division among women in relation to
> their work. It was assumed that the majority of those who chose to work
> belonged in the more interesting fields; in the professions, in the Civil
> Service, or in teaching. The rest were, as workers, transient, less highly
> skilled, inferior in class and status.[23]

This binary opposition between the domestically oriented and perhaps
casually employed wife and mother and the career-oriented single woman
resulted in a negative definition of the career woman as the inverse of the
domestic ideal. Obscure references to the 'all-out careerist' implied a
deviant figure whose desire for career success fundamentally de-feminised
her. Psychoanalytic approaches to sexual development prompted medical
theorists to portray the career woman as the victim of arrested development. In a conflation of the patterns of development of the lesbian and the
career woman, both were women who had failed to develop a maternal
instinct and thus mature beyond the adolescent phase of homosexuality.
Drawing on this explanatory model, Eustace Chesser observed in 1949
that: 'Some there will always be who are emotionally unfitted to perform
the role of mothers; they will find their best opportunities for self-
expression outside of the home.'[24] However, for the majority of women
the role of unmarried career woman was assumed to be a failure rather
than a deliberate choice on the part of the woman.

Post-war accounts pathologised the single woman either for her failure
to fulfil woman's primary roles of marriage and motherhood or for the
inevitable decline which would result from this deprivation. Robert Latou
Dickinson and Lura Beam had established in their 1934 medical analysis

of 600 single women that the idleness or disuse of a woman's sexual and reproductive organs would almost certainly cause an array of serious diseases including fibroid growths and cancers of the female organs.[25] For those single women who did not succumb to terminal diseases of the reproductive organs in middle age, characterisations of the spinster as 'neurotic, prudish, dowdy', frustrated and depressed, offered little hope. In 1951 Marie Blanche Smith gave a depressing account of the decline faced by the single woman:

> Leaving out the under-sexed woman and the all-out careerist, this business of facing life without a man is very difficult for most women. Some of them crack under the nervous strain and find themselves in mental homes, or suffering from psychosomatic illness of some kind; others suffer agonies of guilt from secret love affairs; others' masochism seems inexhaustible; others when in the society of those who are married have a ghastly sense of inferiority which hurts and even maims; others take to drugs or become 'good-time' drinking girls, hanging around pubs and 'clubs'; others drink in secret. Quite often these women have come from the ranks of girls with fine principles, from good homes and respected professions. Loneliness and despair work havoc with them, and they clutch at anything that relieve these. Ultimately, a section of them give way to the temptations of prostitution.[26]

Despite an increasing number of books directed at single women by medical professionals, clergymen and counselling organisations in the post-war period, few solutions were offered to the supposed difficulties of the single woman. Identifying loneliness and the frustration of woman's 'natural' sexual and maternal instincts as the primary concerns of single women, this material frequently offered paid employment as a 'second-best' option for women who had failed to marry. In her popular advice book, reissued in a new version in 1960, Laura Hutton portrayed work as a solution to the problems of the single woman:

> There is no doubt that an immense amount of useful sublimation of sexual energy is carried out by the majority of single women. Work, professional interests and recreations are often their salvation. The very fact that most of them have to work is a boon to them. Such things fill their lives and use up their energies in ways that are pleasant and profitable to themselves and to others.[27]

Paid employment, in Hutton's view, was a useful outlet to frustrated energies for those women who found themselves unable to fulfil woman's natural role. However, it was clearly not ideal:

> For an unmarried woman, though her professional work may satisfy many
> needs of her nature, it can never be her natural fulfilment, day by day, as
> marriage and children are. Nor has she the man's incentive to work, the
> maintenance of his family.[28]

Employment could alleviate much of the suffering experienced by the
single woman, but was not to be regarded as a rewarding option for
women.

In the context of these conflicting attitudes toward women and work,
cultural constructions of specific occupations were central to the ways in
which individual women were perceived. Women's employment opportunities had, throughout the century, been dictated by long-standing
notions of gender difference which characterised women as passive, irra-
tional and nurturing. Such notions had confined women primarily to the
sectors of education, health or domestic service, expanding only to admit
women to clerical and light industrial occupations in the inter-war period.
This gender segregation in the workplace was largely predicated upon the
long-standing ideology of separate spheres, so that women's roles in the
public sphere of the workplace were justified as an extension of the roles
they had traditionally performed in the private sphere of the home.

Despite the important challenge posed to gendered notions of employment by women's introduction into traditionally male spheres during the
Second World War, the majority of women's opportunities in the post-war
labour market remained constrained within conventionally feminine
occupations. Pat Thane has claimed that women workers were concentrated in lower status, white-collar, service and industrial occupations.
Although the majority of women worked in the private sector, the number
of women in the professions increased marginally in this period and
recruitment to administer the newly constituted Welfare State meant that
women comprised 47.5 per cent of 'social welfare and related workers' by
1961.[29] Moreover, even in these arenas, clear distinctions were made
between occupations which were acceptable for women, or for which
women were 'naturally' suited, and those that were not. In her 1957
career manual, Mary Bolton advised those readers who were considering
a career in dentistry:

> Physical fitness is essential, as is first class eyesight. A calm approach to life
> is necessary, together with the ability to deal efficiently with emergencies
> as and when they arise. Manual dexterity is more essential than great
> strength and it is for this reason that women make such excellent dentists.

It is a fallacy to suppose it needs a man's strength to draw teeth, in fact a
woman's knack is more often than not more successful.[30]

Here Bolton drew upon long-standing arguments that women workers
possessed greater manual dexterity than their male counterparts to
identify dentistry as particularly appropriate work for women. However,
those occupations which continued to be regarded as most suitable for
women in the post-war period were those which drew upon notions of
women as naturally caring and nurturing and suited to working with
families and children.

The conflict in post-war government policy between promoting
women's primary role as wives and mothers, and the need for women to
fill increasing labour shortages, had resulted in large numbers of single
women – amongst them lesbians – being employed in conventionally
feminine roles in the expanding health care and social work sectors.
Newly identified 'failing families' became a particular object of concern to
the recently formed Welfare State and many lesbians employed in social
work found themselves in the anomalous position of intervening in, and
giving advice on child-care and other domestic issues. Pat Arrowsmith was
employed as a social worker in the 1950s and found her role to be highly
problematic. After four months working with 'problem families' in Liverpool, she embarked on a social science course, but was unable to resolve
a perceived conflict between her lesbianism and the role of social worker.
She claimed that she saw her lesbianism 'as a flaw and didn't feel qualified
to do in depth psychological work trying to "mend" families when [she]
was flawed [herself]'. While colleagues, who were aware of Pat Arrowsmith's sexual identity, and an analyst, with whom she was put in touch,
did not regard her lesbianism as an obstacle to her work, she remained
uncomfortable in her role and ultimately left the profession a year after
finishing the course.[31] Elizabeth Wilson experienced similar discomfort in
her work in the child guidance movement in the 1960s. 'As defined by my
colleagues', she claimed, 'my work was to help women to be better
mothers – not an aim with which I had much sympathy, or for which I
was appropriately equipped.'[32]

The traditionally female occupation of teaching proved equally problematic for many lesbians in the post-war period. While the role of
providing guidance and education for children had conventionally marked
out teaching as an appropriate occupation for women, inter-war debates
about spinster teachers continued to overshadow perceptions of single
women in the profession after the war. The influence of medical
discourses characterising lesbians as emotionally abnormal and potentially
predatory, meant that single women teachers were increasingly regarded

as poor role models for girls. By the mid-century, growing public awareness of lesbianism meant that many commentators were making explicit
links between the potential homosexuality of single teachers and their
harmful effect on pupils. The influential educationalist, John Newsom,
commented in 1948:

> The woman who is unhappily married should be kept out of the schools,
> for she is apt to be bitter and resentful ...
>
> The same thing is true of persons with strong homo-sexual impulses –
> or perhaps it would be better to say, persons in whom their homo-sexual
> impulses have distorted their attitude towards the opposite sex. They should
> not be in a position to influence children over the age of eleven. Between
> eleven and fourteen feelings of love and admiration are normally directed
> upon persons of one's own sex. If children of this age take for their models
> adults who have not progressed beyond this stage, or who have reverted to
> it, they may themselves become incapable of healthy growth ... This danger
> ... is greatest in girls' schools because, contrary to the general belief, the
> effects of homo-sexuality are even more serious in women than in men.[33]

Newsom argued that, even in cases where the teacher exercised complete
self-control or was unaware of her own abnormal state, she nevertheless
represented a poor example for adolescent girls. Other objections,
centring on a concern that lesbian teachers might attempt to seduce their
female pupils, continued to be voiced in the post-war decades, although
with less conviction than during the inter-war period. In a 1966 summary
of popular attitudes toward lesbians and work, journalist Bryan Magee
commented:

> The other fear – that lesbians will seduce and corrupt people with whom
> they come in contact in the course of their work – I find it hard to take
> seriously ...
>
> One aspect of the question remains in a separate category, and that is
> when children are involved. The sexual exploitation of children is wicked.
> The only profession in which one might expect it to be a danger is the
> teaching profession. Even here, fears are exaggerated.[34]

Despite popular attitudes, the continued popularity of teaching as an
acceptable occupation for women meant that many lesbians worked in the
profession throughout the post-war period. Rosanna Hibbert recalled
there being 'something suspect' in the relationship between the matron
and the head of her house at her boarding school in the 1940s, while
Jackie Forster assumed that many of her teachers, who had 'Eton crops and
flat shoes' and were called 'mannish', 'must have been lesbians'.[35] When
the lesbian magazine, *Arena Three*, conducted a survey of its readers in 1965,
teachers and nurses were identified as the 'strongest contingents'.[36]

However, widely expressed fears concerning the dangers of lesbians in schools undoubtedly had an impact on many teachers' behaviour. Miss L. W. Marlow wrote in to *Arena Three* in 1967 to explain why, as a teacher, she felt unable to declare her lesbianism at work:

> This may be cowardice. I am happy in my job and would hate to put it in jeopardy. I am well aware that, while men and women – whether psychologically suited to the job or not – are eagerly accepted as teachers of children of the opposite sex, a homosexual in a corresponding position is automatically considered dangerous. – (Of course … we're all sex maniacs!) – and unfit to deal with children of either sex – (it might be contagious!) This mainly is why we hesitate to declare ourselves in relation to our work.[37]

A year later, these views were echoed by Hester Caulton from Staffordshire, who wrote:

> I am in charge of a happy, progressive school. I love the children dearly; standards are high and comments from Inspectors very favourable. Yet, may I assure Jane Marshall [a previous correspondent] – in spite of all these facts, if the parents of the children of my school learned that I am a Lesbian, and happy to be, their immediate reaction would be one of disgust. In fairly small communities such as this, scandal runs like a flame through straw. Despite my sincere efforts to give all that is best to my pupils, parents would believe that I would 'contaminate' their children, or teach them 'dirty habits', or educate them to be 'not nice'.[38]

Assumptions that certain occupations, such as teaching and clerical work, were intrinsically better suited to women facilitated constructions of women who worked in these occupations as feminine and heterosexually attractive. Sandy Martin, who qualified as a shorthand typist in the early 1960s, described her work environment as one which was dominated by notions of femininity, complaining that 'the women I knew at work bored me to tears, talking about domesticity all the time – knitting and babies and the price of margarine'.[39] Career manuals reinforced this picture in an attempt to define marriage and paid employment as mutually complementary. Ursula Bloom touched upon this theme repeatedly in her overview of the types of jobs available to women in the post-war years. While unremitting in her insistence that the 'modern' woman must be focused and determined in her pursuit of the ideal career, she nevertheless conceded:

> You have got to realize that, even though you hate saying it, the goal of most women's existence is marriage. At the back of her mind every girl is old-fashioned enough to admit that she wants to taste the sweetest experience of all; she wants a man, and a home, and perhaps a child or two. She cannot

have any of these things unless she lives a life which gives her the opportunity to *meet* suitable people. Half the old maids in this world came, not
because they were niched 'old maid' from the start, but because they never
had the chance to meet the right man.[40]

Throughout her manual, Bloom outlined the opportunities that innumer-
able feminine occupations, ranging from shop buyers to domestic service,
would offer for meeting suitable husbands. Others developed this argument further, suggesting that certain occupations provided women with
invaluable training and skills that would enable them to build and maintain the perfect marriage. Angela Holdsworth has argued that secretarial
work was seen as particularly useful in this regard. The experience of
being responsible for assisting a male employer was represented as useful
preparation for assisting a husband, while the opportunity to observe the
atmosphere of the office was regarded as a practical lesson in tolerance for
a fatigued and irritable husband returning home after a long day's work.[41]
Journalist Bryan Magee shared this view of the post-war workplace,
commenting:

> Every large organization employing men and women is a hive of heterosex-
> ual activity. The number of people having affairs with other people in the
> same office or factory – one thinks for example of secretaries and their
> bosses – must run into hundreds of thousands. It is an utter commonplace
> of life, and no realistic person would expect to eliminate it.[42]

The characterisation of mixed workplaces as explicitly heterosexual arenas
placed non-heterosexual women in a difficult position. Rosanna Hibbert,
who worked in an office as a copy-writer in the 1950s, described her
experience as emotionally oppressive to the extent that she was forced to
leave her job. Her difficulties came to a head when she fell in love with a
woman in her office: although they had a brief sexual affair, Hibbert's
colleague, whom she described as 'very flirtatious', then embarked on
another affair with a male colleague. Rosanna Hibbert recalled the distress
the spectacle of this heterosexual affair had caused her in the face of her
own desires, ultimately prompting her to resign.[43] However, for many
women, unwanted attentions from male colleagues were the cause of
greatest difficulty. In 1964, *Arena Three* featured an article entitled, 'Managing Men', advising its readers on how to respond when invited out for a
drink by a man from work, suggesting that this was a common
dilemma.[44]

The issue of appropriate clothing and appearance in the workplace was
one of the central difficulties faced by women who found conventionally
feminine roles uncomfortable. Many occupations, particularly in the
clerical and professional sectors, carried with them an assumption that

women workers would conform to contemporary ideals of feminine dress. *Arena Three* again offered advice to readers on how to deal with this expectation:

> For my money the Lesbian who errs a trifle on the conservative side looks a whole lot better than the one who goes about looking like a send-up of a male impersonator (if you get the idea). Better look female than funny, as one of the wiser ones once remarked.
>
> What to wear in working hours depends enormously, of course, on what you do. A professional or executive job, or one involving a lot of contact with public, demands some concessions to convention ... The good plain suit, the classic overcoat – these may be expensive, but they are always right and never let you down.[45]

Many women undoubtedly attempted to follow this advice, often conforming to feminine fashions in the workplace, and assuming a more masculine image in their leisure time. On a visit to the lesbian nightclub the Gateways in the 1960s, Bryan Magee noted that most of the butch lesbians he consulted in his research claimed to adopt a more feminine persona for the workplace:

> Most of these extreme butch types live double lives. During the day, at their jobs, they are normal-seeming girls: at nights and weekends they become boys. At work they wear feminine clothes, make-up, and sometimes even look rather pretty; then at night they go home, wash off their make-up, put on men's clothes and are indistinguishable from men ... I once asked such a girl ... 'What about your hair? You're wearing a haircut like mine – how can this possibly look feminine during the day?' She simply smiled, and with an obviously practised gesture put her hands to her neck behind her ears, pushed her fingers up into her hair and over her head as if pushing off a helmet – and the hair which had been lying back flat and masculine swept up and over and forward and suddenly looked feminine and pretty, like a black chrysanthemum.[46]

Whether such versatile hairstyles represented a unique approach or a common practice, this account suggests that women were acutely aware of the possibilities of performing a range of identities in the workplace and the nightclub.

Much of the research undertaken by lesbian and gay theorists into the issue of sexual identities in the workplace has represented the workplace as a site in which a lesbian identity must be suppressed. The geographer, Gill Valentine, in her consideration of lesbians' experience of the workplace, has represented this arena as a hostile public environment structured according to heterosexual norms.[47] She draws attention to the impact which gender coding of certain tasks, expectations about

appearance, and even office gossip about home life, have in characterising
the workplace as heterosexual. Valentine argues that, in such an atmosphere, lesbians have often felt compelled to conceal their sexual identity
and evade personal conversations thus isolating them from heterosexual
and lesbian colleagues alike. While Valentine's analysis offers a sympathetic
interpretation of the lesbian at work, focusing on the oppressive structures
of the work environment, the emphasis on visibility as an individual's
contribution to minority politics has led many theorists to view those
who pass, or conceal their sexual identity, as cowardly and passive victims
of oppression. In 1980, Adrienne Rich argued of passing, that: 'The retreat
into sameness – assimilation for those who can manage it – is the most
passive and debilitating of responses to political repression, economic
insecurity, and a renewed open season on difference'. Claudia Card echoed
this interpretation, claiming that, 'Successful passing hides one's status as
a target of oppression'.[48] In both interpretations, the lesbian's interaction
with her work environment is defined by her need to conceal an innate
identity and draws upon political conceptions of sexual identity as either
closeted or visible, oppressed or liberated. Viewed in the specific historical context of the post-war workplace, however, a much more complex
picture emerges of the lesbian at work. The ambivalent contemporary attitudes to employment for women rendered all women workers potentially
suspect. While it was increasingly regarded as acceptable for women to
work before marriage and after their children had grown up, those
women who failed to conform to the heterosexual ideal of the married
woman were often perceived, not as single heterosexual women, but as
'career women'. Women who utilised the dubious identity of the 'bachelor girl' or career woman in the post-war period drew on a model of femininity which was constructed as at best asexual and potentially deviant.

The anomalous position of such women in the post-war workplace is
apparent from lesbian accounts of working in feminine occupations.
Cultural constructions of the woman worker in a conventionally female
occupation as overwhelmingly heterosexual rendered the projection of a
lesbian identity in the post-war workplace highly problematic and
personal narratives frequently demonstrate the insignificance of the workplace as an arena for the articulation of a lesbian identity. A number of
women interviewed for the Hall Carpenter Oral History Archive did not
offer any detailed description of what their work might have entailed, or
identify their experiences of work as significant or positive through
expressions of interest or enthusiasm for it. Sandy Martin never explicitly
stated what type of employment she had undertaken, while Cynthia Reid
offered no further details than the information that she had worked 'in

computers'.[49] Other women articulated a sense of distance between their working and 'lesbian' lives very clearly in life history interviews. Mary Wilkins, who came of age in the inter-war years and worked as an optician from the 1930s onwards, commented that she had always felt her sexuality to be completely separate from every other aspect of her life. Other people, she believed, viewed her as 'a successful professional woman' in a generation of women who were 'very dedicated to their work'.[50] Diana Chapman echoed this view, commenting of her work as a dentist in the 1950s and 60s:

> But when it came to work, it always seemed to me that you appeared to live in a vacuum. I mean, if you were straight say, you might come into the office, or the surgery or whatever, on Monday morning and say, 'Oh yes, I went to a party on Saturday and oh, you know, wonderful men, or horrible men, or something', whereas if you're a lesbian, you don't say anything like that. You give the appearance of being a very lonely person having no social life at all because you can't talk about it.[51]

Diana Chapman's account of the issues raised by not conforming to a heterosexual ideal can be examined in the light of Sherrie Inness' notion of 'partial passing' as a strategy in which the lesbian attempts to avoid any overt signifiers either of homo or heterosexuality.[52] Inness suggests that this variation on passing can be unexpectedly problematic as the woman 'does not try to appear as heterosexual as possible but instead provides an opaque surface on which viewers can inscribe lesbianism or heterosexuality'.[53] The failure to project a heterosexual identity can, in itself, distance the subject from colleagues. She argues:

> Partial passing does not allow the heterosexual viewing audience the secure sense that the lesbian is 'one of them'. Quite to the contrary, partial passing actually might accentuate a lesbian's otherness, because of the ways that she fails to adhere to societal gender norms. The lesbian who partially passes is not invisible. She stands out from the crowd in many ways. She does not adopt overt signifiers of heterosexual identification … This positioning of the partial passer, rather than being a sign of weakness, actually can be a sign of strength, since she does not accept the security offered by full passing.[54]

Inness's performative approach is helpful in making sense of Diana Chapman's account of the workplace, in which she identified her sense of isolation from colleagues as deriving from her inability to perform either a lesbian identity or a heterosexual one.

By the 1960s, however, the emergence of lesbian communities and politics which defined lesbian identity in explicit, visible terms meant that many women were considering the declaration of a lesbian identity as a

solution to these difficulties. When Julie Switsur confided in a work
colleague at Twickenham Library in the mid-60s, the woman appeared
shocked and thought it 'was wrong'. However, by the end of the decade,
when a forthcoming article about her lesbianism in the *News of the World*
prompted Julie to tell her new boss in computing, she received a more
positive reaction. 'He just put his arm round me and said "I hope you
make a nice lot of money", which I thought was a very odd reaction but
I liked it.' Angela Chilton, who worked in a variety of temporary jobs
throughout the 1960s, including a pickle factory in Peckham, before
taking a permanent position with a firm of solicitors, commented that she
was always open with employers, to avoid any danger of blackmail, and
never experienced any problems.[55] The idea of declaring a lesbian identity
at work appeared much more problematic to other women, however. In
1968, *Arena Three* published an interview with 'Helen B. of County Down',
in which Helen described her experience working for the civil service.
Helen had been employed as a civil servant for fifteen months when she
informed an older woman at work that she was a lesbian. The woman
responded supportively and Helen subsequently felt encouraged to write
to a colleague, with whom she had become close, expressing her friendship. She received no immediate reaction, but some time later was ordered
to report to a departmental official, who told her that he had 'been
hearing things' about her and asked her to resign.[56] Subsequent issues of
Arena Three carried a number of letters from readers in response to this
interview, all of whom felt that Helen should have been more discrete.
Miss F. R. from London wrote: 'It doesn't need the "Round the Horne"
BBC radio show to illustrate that the Service is famed for its "pooves" and
"leses". But they do not attract undue attention unless their behaviour is
out of the ordinary. Their private lives are their own concern so long as
they don't offend public taste.' Miss C. H. asked 'why did poor Helen B.
have to put her foot in it?' and a civil servant of eighteen and a half years'
standing commented: 'When I first read it, I was disgusted that such a
thing could happen. Then I read it again, and thought: "Well, she did ask
for it."'[57]

A small number of less conventionally female occupations, such as the
police force and the women's armed services, leant themselves to very
different models of the working woman. The women's services and police
were particularly distinctive occupations for women in the immediate
post-war period in that they combined a rare opportunity for women to
undertake physically active roles and develop independent careers within

a single-sex working environment. Cultural associations of masculinity and women-only environments with lesbianism meant that the women employed in such workplaces were constructed as potentially sexually deviant. These environments provided women in the post-war decades with a rare public forum in which they could articulate a certain type of lesbian identity, one which was defined by the perception of a lesbian threat. This explicit construction of the police or service woman as physically active and potentially lesbian was inevitably more compatible with the development of a lesbian identity and as such these career choices constitute a central theme in personal narratives of lesbians who had worked in these professions.

The women's services and police had been contentious since their establishment during the First World War, but their expansion in the 1950s and 60s increased women's visibility in these occupations. The numbers of women police rose from 246 in 1939 to four times that in 1949. By 1963, their numbers had grown to just over 3000.[58] Philippa Levine, in her study of the origins of women in the police force, draws attention to a number of conflicts in the role of the early policewoman.[59] Although initially employed in response to pressure from suffrage, social purity, and other women's campaigners to protect the rights of women in the criminal justice system, early policewomen soon found themselves patrolling in the neighbourhood of military camps and in other public areas to prevent women from engaging in illicit sexual encounters. Levine argues that these women police had to maintain a delicate balance, in justifying their existence, between pointing to their special female empathy with other women and yet demonstrating their ability to meet the requirements of their new policing role. Levine suggests that at the heart of this conflict was a sense that women police had crossed a boundary by undertaking work in the public sphere of the street. Laura Doan picks up on this conflict in her discussion of the Women Police Service (WPS) in the inter-war years.[60] Under the leadership of Margaret Damer Dawson and Mary Allen, both of whom were lesbians, the WPS made an important contribution to women's policing during the First World War. However, Doan has argued, their former connections with the militant suffrage movement, and their unconventional gender and sexual identities meant that, when the Metropolitan Police decided to establish their own women's police service, the WPS were largely excluded and increasingly came into conflict with the Met during the 1920s.

> The final irony perhaps is that a predominantly lesbian WPS leadership ... who wanted the power to police heterosexual behaviour – patrolling parks to disrupt activities of heterosexual couples, assisting in raids on brothels,

preventing loitering and solicitation by prostitutes, and aiding women and children who had been indecently assaulted – were, as a result of the Met's campaign, constituted as the impure. While in the public sphere WPS were 'enforcing norms of sexual morality', in their private lives they rejected the dominant culture's valorization of femininity and family and preferred not to marry or take up conventionally feminine occupations.[61]

While the conflict between the Met and the WPS constructed the official Metropolitan Women Police Patrols as the acceptable and sanctioned face of women policing, with the gradual demise of the WPS in the late 1920s, many of the concerns regarding women police became focused on female members of the official force.

The Second World War and consequent mobilisation of men consti-tuted a turning point for women's opportunities in both the police force and services. Women were not only in greater demand, but were expected to perform duties previously reserved to men. While this was considered justifiable in the unusual conditions of wartime, such a position was harder to maintain in the very different climate of the post-war years. Despite considerable expansion in the numbers of women police in the post-war years, both the police and military authorities were careful to make clear distinctions between the roles performed by their male and female employees. Policewomen were not admitted to the Police Federation until 1949, while servicewomen were confined to non-combatant roles. Women police were still largely expected to specialise in areas involving women and children. They arrested or moved on prostitutes, picked up missing girls and approved school absconders, as well as occasionally intervening in domestic disputes. However, this work inevitably brought women into a highly visible and often threatening public arena and thus posed a challenge to notions of appropriate gendered and sexual behaviour. The services, although equally gendered, used women in a wider variety of functions, ranging from engineering and communications to physical training.

In a period when cultural media tended to emphasise women's presumed physiological weakness and their solely domestic outlook, women who undertook more active and public roles were inevitably regarded with some suspicion. Turn of the century sexologists had posited a link between lesbianism and active, masculine roles and post-war commentators echoed this theme, positing a 'natural' sympathy between lesbians and masculine physicality. Bryan Magee, writing about lesbians and work in the mid-1960s, commented that:

There is a marginal tendency for lesbians to go into the women's services, partly again because of the grease and overalls, partly because of the feeling of living a rough, tough, down-to-earth sort of life, and the unfemininity of it all, even to the uniform; and partly because of the rich opportunities provided for homosexual activity in all-female camps, barracks and so on.[62]

In her 1971 psychiatric survey of lesbianism, Charlotte Wolff referred to a lesbian she had interviewed about her previous service in the Women's Royal Air Force (WRAF) Police, who apparently claimed to have specifically chosen the WRAF because of the type of work involved: 'I chose the air force as I am fascinated by anything mechanical, especially cars and planes, and the prospect of flying added incentive.'[63] Wolff developed this argument further, asserting that, for some women, the fact that such work was conventionally defined as 'masculine' provided a further incentive. By performing their job to a high standard, the women were able to demonstrate that they were as capable, if not more so, than their male counterparts. Quoting a second woman, Charlotte Wolff asserted that this was the interviewee's primary source of satisfaction when she served in the Women's Royal Naval Service (WRNS) during the war. In response to an enquiry about what aspects of her service she enjoyed, she had answered:

> I loved wearing uniform to start with. And I liked the idea of duty. I became an officer. I think that the war gave me an opportunity to show that I am as good as a man, or better. I love to compete with men. My greatest moment was when an admiral told me, and other people in the services too, that I was just as good as a man.[64]

Eustace Chesser similarly attributed lesbians with a desire to compete with men. Observing that lesbians were most likely to be found in 'masculine' occupations such as the police, prison work, the services and a variety of outdoor occupations, he claimed:

> The overt Lesbian suffers from a basic insecurity and a constant fear that the loved one is seduced into heterosexuality. She enters into competition with men and often compensates for her sense of inferiority by imitating the dress and mannerisms of men. The persistence of an infantile male genital envy leads some to go to the length of employing an artificial penis.[65]

For Chesser, this association of lesbianism with masculine roles was therefore the result of sexual jealousy.

Tessa Stone has identified a similar concern regarding the subversive potential of women's assumption of male roles in her research into the Women's Auxiliary Air Force (WAAF) during the Second World War. She found a clear differentiation in discussions of WAAF substitution between the more active 'male' tasks performed by the Royal Air Force (RAF) servicemen, and the less active jobs undertaken by their female counterparts. Thus, while the servicewomen were praised for fulfilling their tasks as well as the men, this approbation was limited by the understanding that other jobs existed which only the men could undertake. Stone qualifies this argument, however, with the finding that for the servicewomen themselves, distinctions between the different jobs performed by the WAAF were made on the basis, not of how 'active' and 'masculine' they were, but on proximity to the centre of operations and hence perceptions of how important they were to the war effort.[66]

Concerns regarding the challenge posed to established gender and sexual norms by women's appropriation of male roles frequently centred on the defeminising effect of uniforms. Laura Doan has argued that it is not insignificant that the dispute between the Metropolitan Police and the independent Women Police Service in the 1920s focused on the issue of the uniforms worn by the WPS. The uniform was regarded as an inherently masculine form of attire, both in its associations with certain 'masculine' occupations and in the defeminising effect which its straight and unwomanly cut had upon the wearer. The wearing of the uniform, she suggests, could be interpreted as a visual indication of the female wearer's desire to assume male roles and thus constituted a rejection of conventional femininity and potentially heterosexuality. She claims:

> For the individual wearer the WPS uniform may have represented police power and perhaps gentleman-like chivalry, but to many outsiders the garb was the symbolic representation of a bizarre claim to masculinity itself. The uniform did not transform WPS officers into men but into mannish women, and perhaps for the most astute observer, female sexual inverts. The uniform embodied empowerment and masculine authority and also expressed (or allowed members to express) sexual identity.[67]

While Doan's comments focus on concerns about the uniform worn by the WPS as a symbol of wider anxieties regarding the unofficial nature of WPS work, the politically radical politics of many of its leaders, and the unconventional gender and sexual identities of some officers, such anxieties were clearly felt with regard to all women in uniform. Lilian Wyles, the first policewoman to be attached to CID, recalled the public reaction to policewomen in the 1920s and 30s in her memoir:

> The advent of women in police uniform on the streets caused much curiosity. For a short time we were one of the sights of London, along with the Tower and Westminster Abbey. It became a trifle embarrassing when people stopped in front of us, saying to each other in voices nicely pitched to reach our ears, 'How queer', 'How unwomanly', 'Not quite nice, do you think?' or else, 'Some of Fred Karno's girls – what?' Fred Karno, I believe, was a comedian who staged extremely comic turns.[68]

Although Lilian Wyles claims that the public soon became accustomed to the sight of uniformed policewomen, women's uniforms continued to be regarded as culturally disruptive. Historians of the women's services have drawn attention to a widespread practice by servicewomen during the Second World War of altering uniforms or complementing them with 'feminine' underwear or cosmetics in an attempt to render them more feminine.[69] However, the suspicion with which women in uniforms were regarded clearly also offered opportunities for women to employ them as a signifier of a deviant sexual identity. Pat James, who wore a uniform when working in the ambulance service in the late 1930s, offered an account of the impact her appearance had on another woman:

> So at seventeen, I was driving an ambulance, and I had to go to dinner one night with friends. There was a woman there, an artist's model, one of the notorious Augustus John's. When we were leaving, she said, 'I'll drop you home'. I said yes, and we caught a taxi. The taxi had to turn round in the road and I fell over and ended up in her arms, it sounds incredible but she started kissing me. And at that time I had my ambulance uniform on – a collar and tie and also my hair was short – that's just because of being on twenty-four hour duty and ready to go out at a minute's notice. I think because of how I looked, she felt she could be attracted to me.[70]

Pat James' account suggests that she regarded her uniform as a visual indicator of a lesbian identity and that this was a message which at least one woman had understood.

Leisa Meyer, in her study of sexuality in the US Women's Army Corps (WAC) during the Second World War, has argued that uniforms and visible manifestations of gender identity were central to the attitude of the military authorities toward lesbianism in the ranks.[71] Claiming that 'In contrast [to male GIs], accusations of lesbianism within the WAC were the apotheosis of cultural anxieties over women's entrance into the military, the seeming renunciation of feminine values for the embrace of the masculine', she argues that 'WAC leaders created a framework in which masculine appearance and behavior, not only sexual acts between women, were the key criteria for defining the 'lesbian threat' within the corps'.[72] In other words, in a culture that linked 'masculine' image and behaviour with lesbianism, all women who chose to enter the women's services were considered suspect. In order to protect themselves from such accusations, the leaders of the WAC punished the visible cultural signs of lesbianism as severely as lesbian sexual activity itself. British lesbian accounts similarly emphasised the significance of a masculine image as an indication of potential sexual deviance in the services.

Margaret Cranch's experience of being accused of tomboyish tendencies during her basic training as a WRAC cadet in the late 1950s suggests that the British women's services were equally concerned to foster a feminine image.[73]

The single-sex environment that characterised these workplaces fuelled concerns about the possible presence of lesbianism in these occupations. These particular work environments were unusual in that they both incorporated an overlap between living and working space. In the women's services, the military camp comprised the entire world of the service-woman; in the police force, the relationship between the two varied. While all new police recruits were sent to live-in training schools, active policewomen were divided between police section houses and private accommodation, depending upon availability and personal preference. Women in the services were accommodated either in purpose-built housing or in blocks with members of other services, but always in military camps on a single-sex basis.[74] Fears that female and male single-sex environments encouraged homosexuality by depriving their inhabitants of contact with members of the opposite sex had been growing since the late nineteenth century. Such concerns had focused particularly on the public school and wider education system, where, for women, suspicions about all-female establishments were exacerbated by associations with feminism and concern that academic life and professional employment defeminised women.

Tessa Stone has argued that associations between all-female establishments, and in particular girls' schools, and lesbianism played a key role in shaping WAAF policy toward lesbianism. The WAAF directorate, she claims, drew on the language of schoolgirl crushes and immaturity to express their 'uncompromising approach to lesbianism':

> The directorate's policy regarding 'WAAF with lesbian tendencies' was exemplified by their choice of 'password' in mixed discussion – 'Misfit' – and by the comparison of the WAAF with 'large girls' schools'. Thus women who even gave the impression of being lesbians were to be treated as schoolgirls. They should be interviewed by a senior WAAF officer, and told that 'grown-up women do not usually indulge in these silly "schoolgirl crazes" … which most sensible people learn to despise as they grow older and more sensible'.[75]

In more serious cases, women accused of lesbian activity were either separated from each other by being transferred to different posts, or were discharged from the services. However, such a course of action was presented as a last resort and each case was dealt with on an individual basis. Dorothy Sheridan has demonstrated that in the Auxiliary

Territorial Service (ATS), although a document outlining official policy on lesbianism was available, copies were retained by the medical officer and only sent to officers on application when a relevant case arose.[75]

The possibility of illicit homo- or mono- sexual acts does to some extent seem to have preoccupied those responsible for the design and policing of women's dormitories in the post-war period. However, while the military authorities, at least, were actively attempting to stamp out public displays of affection between women, sources from both the police and military authorities in the 1940s and 50s suggest a much greater preoccupation with preventing illicit heterosexual encounters. That practical considerations were at the heart of measures controlling male access to female accommodation is apparent from the language used by the military authorities. Reports on the women's services include detailed statistics on so-called 'wastage' due to pregnancy. The services were apparently keen to avoid losing trained female personnel to marital and maternal obligations.[77] This perception that heterosexual encounters posed the greater threat is apparent in the layout of the accommodation. In the majority of women's police section houses, the accommodation seems to have been based on two women sharing a room and as such provided an unintentionally favourable environment in which to conduct a lesbian relationship. One of the most popular London section houses, Peto House, in Pembridge Square, had formerly functioned as a hotel, and therefore comprised self-contained single or twin bedrooms, possibly with locking doors.[78] Personal accounts suggest it was even possible to put in a request for a specific room-mate, if a suitable reason could be offered.[79] This was not the case in all women-only living spaces. Accommodation in the services was more varied and, as a rule, less private. An individual usually had to reach the rank of officer before being entitled to a private room and for most women, on first joining the services, the large open-plan dormitory seems to have been the likely accommodation.[80]

The extent to which women were able to negotiate these obstacles is difficult to establish. Rene Sawyer, describing her experience upon joining the WRAC in 1954, referred to the presence of so many women in one dormitory as both inhibiting and liberating:

> Of course, this was a great opportunity for me to strike up quite nice relationships with different girls that I found attractive and quite frankly there was quite a few girls that found me attractive. We were having little liaisons, but there was nothing sexual because one couldn't do this – not in a barracks with thirty women all sleeping together. Because it would've been rather difficult. So it was just sort of at the kissing, cuddling stages and of course we were working so hard training.[81]

While the spectacle of large numbers of women sleeping in the same room represented unlimited opportunities for lesbian sexuality, Sawyer experienced the practical realities rather differently. Some interviewees claimed to have conducted their lesbian affairs during leave with women in other camps. Officially organised social events, such as sporting competitions, allowed women from different camps to meet and identify each other during work hours, but any sexual encounters occurred off-duty and away from at least one of the women's home base.[82] Tensions regarding the possibility of lesbianism informed the location of lesbian encounters, but did not prevent its occurrence and lesbian accounts for both the police and the services suggest that lesbian sexual encounters proliferated in this environment.[83]

Fears regarding the potential threat of lesbianism in the police force and women's services were reflected and reinforced by the police and military authorities in their recruitment and public relations drives. Joan Lock, in her history of the British policewoman, commented that, in the late 1940s, 'everything the Metropolitan women did was news, particularly any arrests, attempted arrests or signs of toughness. Strength and femininity were the two requirements always juxtaposed.' She quotes one headline as saying: 'Must be pretty – and tough.'[84] A *Times* article of 1956 echoed this message. Quoting Chief Superintendent Elizabeth Bather, head of the Metropolitan Women Police, it noted: 'We don't want "tough" women,' she says, 'this is a woman's job as a woman. And we don't want Olga the beautiful spy.'[85] Such statements illustrate the conflicting aims of police recruitment drives. While the job clearly required 'tough' women who were capable of undertaking arduous physical work, concerns about lesbianism prompted the police authorities to emphasise femininity as an equally important attribute.

A more explicit approach was taken by the women's services, in which lesbianism was a disciplinary offence. In contrast to official sources, which claimed that disciplinary action was only taken against lesbians as a last resort, lesbian accounts of the disciplinary process suggest that it was low profile but vigilant. Nina Jenkins, when asked what life was like for lesbians in the WRAF in the mid-1960s, replied:

> Absolutely awful ... I was embroiled in another world that didn't really have words even, it was just understood as things were in those days – nobody actually sat down and talked about it, but things were understood. It was all a nod and a wink and any one didn't know about lesbians who ever got found out, because anybody who ever got found out got the bums rush so fast – there were rumours about people who had been thrown out in the past. You would hear about somebody who had been very famous for something – captain of the WRAF hockey team for years – and you'd say

'What happened to so-and-so?' and a veil would be drawn over it and you'd sort of be left to *assume* that she might have been one of *those*.[86]

Margaret Cranch reinforced this picture of the constant threat of detection under which lesbian servicewomen lived. She claimed:

> What happens is, they might get caught with their lover, I mean they might only be holding hands and gave someone a little kiss perhaps, but someone was seen doing it and they were immediately brought up before the commanding officer and discharged.[87]

She went on to describe in some detail the implications of such a discharge, emphasising that it was a 'dishonourable discharge' and that the bad reference it carried made it extremely difficult for women to obtain employment afterwards.

The punitive stance adopted by the services offered an ambiguous message, indicating both that the military authorities were committed to eradicating the threat of lesbianism in their ranks, but also explicitly drawing attention to the presence of a perceived lesbian threat. During and immediately after the Second World War, popular fears concerning the deviant sexuality of women who joined the army rendered the recruitment of servicewomen difficult.[88] This problem was sufficiently serious, particularly during the war, to prompt many branches of the women's services to employ public relations officers in an attempt to counter these negative messages. Nancy Spain, assistant to the WRNS Press Officer during the war, described her role as a combination of strategy and damage limitation:

> Our business was (occasionally) to write features about WRNS activities and feed them out to the Press. More often, however, news would break about Wrens and we would then have to restrain the National Press from saying anything that would affect our dignity.[89]

At the same time, statements issued by the women's services attempted to downplay the significance of their anti-lesbian policy, arguing that it rarely needed to be brought into force. Albertine Winner, a Medical Officer in the ATS during the war, claimed in 1947 that:

> Lesbianism was not an important problem in the Women's Services. The problem was dealt with in a very sensible way and every effort was made to avoid magnifying it, for gossip and scare-mongering are far more dangerous than the unfortunate Lesbians themselves … A very small number indeed of serious cases came to light, mostly centring round a promiscuous psychopath, and, in the same Service, only some half-dozen women had to be discharged on these grounds out of nearly a quarter of a million who passed through our hands. This is a very remarkable record and

I want to emphasise that it was not due to ignorance of the possibilities, though there certainly was a very sensible awareness of when action was and was not required.[90]

Winner, although careful to stress the very small numbers of lesbians in the ATS, reinforced the notion that lesbianism was an ever-present danger within the women's services, requiring constant vigilance on the part of the authorities. Her description of a lesbian as 'a promiscuous psychopath' constructed the lesbian servicewoman as both sexually active and emotionally unstable, an identity which reinforced the power of the lesbian as a predatory and disruptive force.

Constructions of the women who worked in the police force and women's services as unfeminine and suspect, evident in the defensiveness and unease of police and military publicity, represented such occupations as conducive to women who felt uncomfortable with more conventional feminine roles. Some women, such as Margaret Cranch, were drawn to the services by the expectation of meeting other lesbians there, while others were attracted by less explicit cultural links between active work, uniforms and women-only environments and lesbianism. Nina Jenkins claimed:

I felt that I wanted to do something exciting, and the services were really the only exciting careers for women ... The Royal Air Force is actually one entity – women join the Royal Air Force same as the men and they can be posted to all the same places as the men and they can do the same jobs so it seemed to me that that was going to offer me the most adventure.[91]

For Nina Jenkins it was the association of men's jobs with 'adventure' and 'excitement' which prompted her to join the RAF. Having embarked on a career in the services or police, however, many women found themselves in a culture which enabled them to develop a more explicit lesbian identity. Janine, a new recruit to the WRAC in the early 1960s, described how a friend had first told her about lesbians in the services:

We were on Black Rock, one of the beaches at Black Rock, one day after I'd decided to go into the WRAC, on the pebbles, and [my friend] said, 'Janine, there is something that I must tell you, if you're going to join the WRAC. There are these women, called 'lesbians'. It was very easy to be gay. It wasn't a hassle or a problem, certainly not at the age of sixteen and a half going into the WRAC, where practically everybody was gay. I mean all the women were gay.[92]

On joining the services, many women found themselves drawn into a lesbian social circle. Vick Robson described a thriving lesbian social scene in the WAAF:

We were sent to Ullsworth to do a bit of training on some naval aircraft, stripping them down, you know and building them up. I got in with some girls stationed there, and they said 'Are you like us?' So it started off again and I thought 'Oh, I'm back on Cloud Nine again'. Then I was sent up to Scotland; we went to do our training for seven months as an electrician and we all passed out as first-class air women.[93]

Barbara Bell offered a similar account of the police force, commenting:

There were quite a few lesbians in the police circle ... I'd made great friends with a woman called Tonks. She was brought in as a rookie and I had to carry her round the beat ... There were another two I used to visit quite frequently ... We used to meet up after work, sometimes a little gang of us, which was super.[94]

Such accounts suggest that these environments fostered the emergence of specific work-based models of lesbian identity and offered access to small social circles defined by same-sex desire.

In contrast to the feminine, heterosexual identity constituted in conventionally female occupations, these relatively new roles in the police and women's services enabled the expression of an unconventional and potentially lesbian identity. Occupations such as teaching and social work, which drew on notions of women as naturally caring and nurturing, proved problematic for many lesbians in the post-war period, requiring women to perform an identity based on heterosexual availability and feminine dress. Other women were able to draw on the ambiguous gender and sexual coding of unconventional occupations in the police and women's services to articulate a coherent model of lesbian identity. However, the binary opposition between the domestically oriented wife and mother and the career-oriented single woman in post-war ideology meant that broader work-based identities such as 'career women' and 'bachelor girls' offered lesbians an escape from the problematic emphasis on heterosexual domestic roles for women in this period.

Notes

1 'Bachelor girl', *The Times* (13 January 1964), p. 11.
2 Ursula Bloom, *Me − After the War: A Book for Girls Considering the Future* (London: John Gifford, 1944); Mabel Esther Allan, *Here We Go Round: A Career Story for Girls* (London: Heinemann, 1954); Mary Bolton, *Modern Careers for Girls* (London: W. Foulsham and Co., 1957); *I Want to be ... A 'Girl' Book of Careers* (Watford: Hulton Press, 1957); Women's Employment Federation, *Careers: A Memorandum on Openings and Trainings for Girls and Women* (London: Women's Employment Federation, 1964).

3 'Career or marriage: Advice to women', *The Times* (6 August 1949), p. 3. The Schoolgirls' Exhibition was a week-long careers fair, with stands on nursing, cookery, nursery training and floristry, in addition to the women's services and secretarial training.

4 Bloom, *Me – After the War*, p. 1.

5 Penny Tinkler, *Constructing Girlhood: Popular Magazines for Girls Growing Up in England 1920–1950* (London: Taylor and Francis, 1995), p. 97.

6 Tinkler, *Constructing Girlhood*, p. 91.

7 Elizabeth Wilson, *Only Halfway to Paradise: Women in Post-war Britain 1945–1968* (London: Tavistock, 1980).

8 Girls' cartoon series on careers proved so popular that the magazine released a separate book on careers which included descriptions of various professions alongside reproductions of the cartoons. *I Want to be* ....

9 Tinkler, *Constructing Girlhood*, p. 97.

10 Tinkler, *Constructing Girlhood*, p. 101.

11 Tinkler, *Constructing Girlhood*, p. 93.

12 Pearl Jephcott, *Rising Twenty: Notes on Some Ordinary Girls* (London: Faber and Faber, 1948), pp. 120–1.

13 Alva Myrdal and Viola Klein, *Women's Two Roles* (London: Routledge & Kegan Paul, 1956), p. 54.

14 Wendy Webster, *Imagining Home: Gender, Race and National Identity 1945–64* (London: UCL Press, 1998), p. 132.

15 Women's Employment Federation, *Careers*, p. 5.

16 Marjorie Ferguson, *Forever Feminine: Women's Magazines and the Cult of Femininity* (London: Heinemann, 1983).

17 Nikolas Rose, *Governing the Soul: The Shaping of the Private Self* (London: Routledge, 1990) p. 156.

18 John Bowlby, *Maternal Care and Mental Health: A Report Prepared on Behalf of the World Health Organisation* (Geneva: World Health Organisation, 1952), p. 46.

19 See Denise Riley, *War in the Nursery: Theories of the Child and Mother* (London: Virago, 1983).

20 Dr Eustace Chesser, *Sexual Behaviour: Normal and Abnormal* (London: Medical Publications, 1949), pp. 79–80.

21 Elizabeth Wilson discusses this argument in her *Only Halfway to Paradise*, p. 27.

22 'Women: Mystery and glamour lost', *News Letter: Belfast* (14 May 1965).

23 Wilson, *Only Halfway to Paradise*, p. 45.

24 Chesser, *Sexual Behaviour*, p. 70.

25 Robert Latou Dickinson and Lura Beam, *The Single Woman* (London: Williams and Norgate, 1934).

26 Marie Blanche Smith, *The Single Woman of Today: Her Problems and Adjustment* (London: Watts and Co., 1951), p. 23.

27 Laura Hutton, *The Single Woman: Her Adjustment to Life and Love* (London: Barrie and Rockliff, 1960), p. 52. This replaced her earlier work, *The Single Woman and her Emotional Problems* (London: Bailliere, Tindall and Cox, 1937).

28 Hutton, *The Single Woman* (1960), p. 5.

29 Pat Thane, 'Women since 1945', in Paul Johnson (ed.), *Twentieth Century Britain: Economic, Social and Cultural Change* (London: Longman, 1994).

30 Bolton, *Modern Careers for Girls*, p. 54.

31 NSA, HCA (C456), F1326-F1327, Pat Arrowsmith.

32 Elizabeth Wilson, 'Memoirs of an anti-heroine', in Bob Cant and Susan Hemmings (eds), *Radical Records: Thirty Years of Lesbian and Gay History* (London: Routledge, 1988), p. 44.

33 Newsom, *The Education of Girls*, p. 149.

34 Bryan Magee, *One in Twenty: A Study of Homosexuality in Men and Women* (London: Secker and Warburg, 1966), p. 162.

35 NSA, HCA (C456), F2095-F2096, Rosanna Hibbert; NSA, HCA (C456), F1607-F1612, Jackie Forster.

36 *Arena Three* 2:2 (February 1965), pp. 8–9.

37 *Arena Three* 4:7 (July 1967), pp. 10–11.

38 *Arena Three* 5:8 (August 1968), pp. 10–11.

39 NSA, HCA (C456), F2483-F2487, Sandy Martin.

40 Bloom, *Me – After the War*, p. 6.

41 Angela Holdsworth, *Out of the Doll's House: The Story of Women in the Twentieth Century* (London: BBC Books, 1988).

42 Magee, *One in Twenty*, p. 162

43 NSA, HCA (C456), F2095-F2096, Rosanna Hibbert.

44 'Managing men', *Arena Three* 1:8 (August 1964), pp. 6–7.

45 *Arena Three* 1:6 (June 1964), p. 3.

46 Magee, *One in Twenty*, p. 156.

47 Valentine, '(Hetero)Sexing space'.

48 Adrienne Rich, *Compulsory Heterosexuality and Lesbian Existence* (London: Onlywoman Press, 1981), p. 204; Claudia Card, *Lesbian Choices* (New York: Columbia University Press, 1995), p. 198.

49 NSA, HCA (C456), F2483-F2487, Sandy Martin; NSA, HCA (C456), F2109, Cynthia Reid.

50 NSA, HCA (C456), F1325, Mary Wilkins.

51 NSA, HCA (C456), F2088, Diana Chapman.

52 Sherrie A. Inness, *The Lesbian Menace: Ideology, Identity and the Representation of Lesbian Life* (Amherst: University of Massachusetts Press, 1997).

53 Inness, *The Lesbian Menace* p. 168.

54 Inness, *The Lesbian Menace*, p. 169.

55 NSA, HCA (C456), F2108, Julie Switsur; NSA, HCA (C456), F1622-F1624, Angela Chilton.

56 *Arena Three* 5:10 (October 1968), pp. 4–5.

57 *Arena Three* 5:11 (November 1968), pp. 5–6.

58 Joan Lock, *The British Policewoman: Her Story* (London: Robert Hale, 1979).

59 Philippa Levine, '"Walking the streets in a way no decent woman should": Women police in World War I', *Journal of Modern History* 66 (1994).

60 Doan, *Fashioning Sapphism*.

61 Doan, *Fashioning Sapphism*, p. 49.

62 Magee, *One in Twenty*, p. 160.

63 Unnamed lesbian's autobiography, reproduced in Charlotte Wolff, *Love Between Women* (London: Gerald Duckworth and Co., 1971) p. 196–7.

64 Second unnamed lesbian's autobiography, reproduced in Wolff, *Love Between Women*, p. 111.
65 Chesser, *Odd Man Out*, pp. 102–3 and pp. 114–15.
66 Tessa Stone, '"Creating a (gendered?) military identity": The Women's Auxiliary Air Force in Great Britain in the Second World War', *Women's History Review* 8:4 (1999).
67 Doan, *Fashioning Sapphism*, p. 75.
68 Lilian Wyles, *A Woman at Scotland Yard* (London: Faber and Faber, 1952), p. 45.
69 Gerard de Groot, 'Lipstick on her nipples, cordite in her hair: Sex and romance among British servicewomen during the Second World War', in Gerard de Groot and Corinna Peniston-Bird (eds), *A Soldier and a Woman: Sexual Integration in the Military* (Harlow: Pearson Education, 2000); Dorothy Sheridan, 'ATS Women: Challenge and Containment in Women's Lives in the Military During the Second World War' (MLitt dissertation, University of Sussex, 1988).
70 Pat James, quoted in Suzanne Neild and Rosalind Pearson (eds), *Women Like Us* (London: The Women's Press, 1992), pp. 57–8.
71 Leisa D. Meyer, *Creating GI Jane: Sexuality and Power in the Women's Army Corps During World War II* (New York: Columbia University Press, 1996).
72 Meyer, *Creating GI Jane*, p. 149.
73 NSA, HCA (C456), F1359–F1360, Margaret Cranch, see p. 1.
74 TNA, ADM 1/ 21067, WRNS accommodation; TNA, MEPO 2/8231, Memorandum from Superintendent Gargrave A4 Branch to D.I., 29 August 1962; TNA, MEPO 2/6158, Section House accommodation for women police; TNA, MEPO 5/518, Pembridge Hall Section House for Women Police.
75 Tessa Stone, 'The integration of women into a military service': The WAAF in the Second World War' (PhD dissertation, University of Cambridge, 1998), p. 170.
76 Sheridan, 'ATS Women: Challenge and Containment', p. 65.
77 TNA, AIR 20/10864, WRAF: moral welfare 1960–1968.
78 TNA, MEPO 2/8231, Memorandum from Superintendent Gargrave A4 Branch to D.I., 29 August 1962; TNA, MEPO 2/6158, Section House accommodation for women police; TNA, MEPO 5/518, Pembridge Hall Section House for Women Police.
79 Barbara Bell, *Just Take Your Frock Off: A Lesbian Life* (Brighton: Ourstory Books, 1999).
80 TNA, ADM 1/ 21067, WRNS accommodation.
81 NSA, HCC (C456), F1328–F1330, Rene Sawyer.
82 NSA, HCC (C456), F2499–F2501, Nina Jenkins.
83 Janine, quoted in Brighton Ourstory Project, *Daring Hearts: Lesbian and Gay Lives of 50s and 60s Brighton* (Brighton: QueenSpark Books, 1992), p. 19; Sheila, quoted in Brighton Ourstory Project, *Daring Hearts*, p. 20; Bell, *Just Take Your Frock Off*, p. 59.
84 Lock, *The British Policewoman*, p. 187.
85 'P.C. II9 will be on duty', *The Times* (24 December 1956), p. 9.
86 NSA, HCC (C456), F2499–F2501, Nina Jenkins.

87 NSA, HCC (C456), F1359–F1360, Margaret Cranch. See also Pat James, quoted in Neild and Pearson (eds), *Women Like Us*, p. 59; Gill, quoted in Brighton Ourstory Project, *Daring Hearts*, p. 32.

88 In 1941, the Markham Committee was established to investigate rumours of sexual immorality in the women's services.

89 Nancy Spain, *Why I'm Not a Millionaire: An Autobiography* (London: Hutchinson, 1956), p. 49.

90 Winner, 'Homosexuality in Women', p. 220.

91 NSA, HCC (C456), F1359-F1360, Margaret Cranch; NSA, HCC (C456), F2499–F2501, Nina Jenkins.

92 Janine, quoted in Brighton Ourstory Project, *Daring Hearts*, p. 19.

93 Vick Robson, quoted in Neild & Pearson, *Women Like Us*, pp. 52–3.

94 Bell, *Just Take Your Frock Off*, pp. 65–6.

3

Lesbian domesticity: relationships and the home

In September 1965, an article entitled 'Myth – or unpalatable fact?' appeared in the lesbian magazine, *Arena Three.* The author, calling themselves 'Commutator', cited a statistic from a recent television programme which had claimed that 93 per cent of marriages remained intact. Reflecting on whether the same could be said of lesbian relationships, 'Commutator' asked:

> Wouldn't you say … that the 'average' lesbian is – if you want to compare her with the heterosexual world – most closely similar to the het[erosexual] adolescent, the teenager who shops around from one to t'other, dropping this one, picking up that one – until he or she attains social, emotional and sexual maturity, wants to 'settle down', raise a family, take on responsibilities, buy a house, make a real home with a permanent partner – a life-long permanent partner, not just bed-and-board companion for a 'permanency' lasting maybe two, three or five years at the outside?'[1]

In characterising lesbian relationships as immature and short-lived, Commutator drew on a familiar post-war theme in medical and popular literature. Contemporary representations of lesbians as urbane, sexually promiscuous career women contrasted starkly with women's conventional roles as wives and mothers in the post-war decades.

In the historical imagination, it is the figure of the housewife who has come to symbolise British cultural imperatives in the late 1940s and, in particular, the 1950s. The Second World War had signalled a new and closer relationship between the state and its civilian population, prompting Alison Light to observe that: 'the First World War belonged to Tommy Atkins but the true heroics of the Second were to be found in the actions of "ordinary people" on "the Home Front".'[2] In the aftermath of war, new state practices of interventionism became embedded in the framing of the Welfare State. Through state provision of health care, education and financial assistance for parents in the form of the Family Allowance, the state assumed a paternalistic right to intervene in its citizens' domestic affairs. Women, in their roles as wives and mothers, were identified as central figures in this new society and 'their' concerns – those of the family and the home – acquired a high profile on the post-war political agenda. The dominant discourse of feminine domesticity was, however, framed in overwhelmingly heterosexual terms and the experiences of single women and lesbians were conspicuous by their absence. Medical and self-help literature constructed the home as a place of isolation and failure for the single woman, while literary texts represented the lesbian as a sexually sophisticated, urban figure, the antithesis of the post-war housewife. These discourses distanced lesbians from narratives of feminine domesticity current in the 1940s and 1950s and many women struggled with limited housing options and the absence of positive relationship models in an attempt to forge lesbian forms of domesticity.

Aspirations of marriage and the creation of a 'home' as the feminine ideal became a central cornerstone of post-war ideology. Women's magazines, which were becoming increasingly popular in the post-war decades, played a key role in propagating this culture of feminine domesticity. Martin Pugh has demonstrated that a new wave of women's magazines, including *Woman's Own*, *Woman* and *Woman's Illustrated*, emerged in the 1930s which promoted the domestic ideal for working class and middle-class women. He claims: 'Perhaps the best example of a magazine which actively campaigned for domesticity was *Woman's Own*, which from the outset devoted itself to the belief that marriage was the best job for a woman.'[3] In her analysis of *Woman*, *Woman's Own* and *Woman's Weekly* in the period 1949 to 1974, Marjorie Ferguson identified marriage and domesticity as dominant themes. The two primary themes, 'Getting and keeping your man' – which accounted for 59 per cent of all non-beauty themes in this period – and 'The happy family', promoted the ideals of romantic love within marriage and family solidarity and stability. Heterosexual love either leading to, or within, marriage, was represented as a basic precondition for femininity and prompted much debate on the nature of 'true love'.[4] For Pugh, this emphasis on marriage and domesticity was not imposed on the readership but coincided with, and was even encouraged by reader's views. Rare attempts by women's magazines to 'venture beyond the staple fare into articles on social problems were rewarded only by a prompt drop in sales'.[5]

This cultural prioritising of the family and the home was emblematic of a widespread perception of the nuclear family as the 'building block of society' in the post-war decades. Children were increasingly regarded as a national resource, and became a focal point of the work of the Welfare State. Continuing wartime habits of interventionism, the government sought to ensure basic levels of nutrition and health for children through such policies as free milk and orange juice, and free doctor's visits under the newly instituted National Health Service.[6] Women, in their capacity as mothers, benefited too, receiving free vitamins and prioritised milk rations during pregnancy; child psychologists, such as John Bowlby, located the mother at the heart of family and domestic life by emphasising the importance of the mother-child relationship in child development.[7] These ideas were translated into official practice when the Family Allowance, introduced in August 1946, was paid to the mothers – as principal carers – of two or more children.[8]

The growing emphasis on the importance of women's role as mothers prompted increasing concern about their domestic burdens. Elizabeth Wilson has argued that, in this period, social democrats, such as Beveridge, employed the language and imagery of the factory and the battlefield in their descriptions of housework, in an attempt to give dignity to women's labour. She claims that 'the theme of "the housewife's home is her factory" was part of the broader theme of "homemaking as a career" so popular after the war'.[9] Educational debates reinforced such arguments, encouraging girls to study domestic science as part of a wider commitment to the 'professionalisation' of housework. While these concerns about the housewife's burden had first emerged as part of a wider discourse of the domestic in the inter-war period, they were given renewed impetus by the near disappearance of domestic service after the Second World War.[10] The demise of domestic service meant that, for the first time, middle-class women had to shoulder the entire burden of housework and child-care without any form of outside assistance. While the Welfare State sought to alleviate their burden, private enterprise increasingly directed its attention to the tools of the modern housewife. The housewife became a primary consumer in the so-called 'affluent' post-war society, the target of advertising campaigns which marketed a range of labour-saving devices from the tin-opener to the vacuum cleaner.[11] For some post-war social and cultural critics, women were to blame for what they regarded as a culture of competitive acquisitiveness, emerging on the new post-war housing estates.[12] However, Judy Giles has argued that an examination of working-class women's experience of this culture demonstrates that the trend toward domestic consumerism represented a more complex set of ideologies than the contemporary critique implied. 'Understanding what being a housewife meant to these women,' she claims, 'requires focusing on material things – a house, a three-piece suite, a sewing machine – not simply as objects of status or acquisitiveness, nor for their labour saving potential, although these factors are present, but for their meaning as icons of a longed for and deeply desired better future.'[13] A range of commercial media therefore combined with educational and social commentators in the immediate post-war decades to promote marriage and domesticity as aspirational goals for women.

The influence of post-war domestic ideology on women is evident from the number of women who later identified as lesbian that chose to marry and start a family in this period, despite feelings of same-sex desire. Sharley McLean, who recalled having been 'aware of lesbian feelings' as a teenager, nevertheless had no conscious understanding of homosexuality in women. She married her husband, Alan, after the war and had a son, Michael, in 1949. Although Sharley had 'quite liked' Alan and 'probably thought she was in love', she 'hated being touched' and abandoned all sexual activity with Alan after Michael's birth. The marriage was not a success and Sharley ultimately attempted suicide, before a psychiatrist suggested to her that she might be lesbian. Jackie Forster married her husband, Peter, in a 'big society wedding at St James, Piccadilly' in 1958, after having had both adolescent lesbian experiences and a succession of sexual affairs with men. She was apparently content in her marriage until she met Hattie, the American Managing Editor of *Harpers Bazaar*. Visiting Hattie and her family in Georgia for Christmas, Jackie found herself in bed with her friend. The experience was 'a revelation' and, in 1961, Jackie was divorced from her husband. Sharley McLean and Jackie Forster's experiences were typical of many women who later identified as lesbian.[14] Other women felt pressured into marriage by social attitudes despite being aware that they were attracted to women. In December 1965, the Bristol *Evening Post* ran an article in its 'Taboo Subjects' series, featuring an interview with a married lesbian. Asked by the reporter, 'But how could you get married?', the woman apparently replied:

> I didn't want to. I never wanted to. But everyone pushed me into it. You people just don't know what it's like to feel different and then have everyone else pushing you into their own pattern … Oh, they kept on so! And they say the day a girl marries is the happiest day in her life. I can tell you it was the unhappiest in mine. But they all kept on so. He did too. So I just gave in and got married.[15]

Cultural prescriptions representing marriage as the ultimate goal for young women, combined with pressure from family and friends prompted many women to conform to social expectations.

In January 1965, the editor of *Arena Three* reported that she had received a large number of letters in response to a recent newspaper article about the magazine. At least 150 of these, she observed, were from married women, many of whom had a similar message:

> Dear Miss Langley,
>   At last I have found someone who will be able to understand. I got married when I was 20, in the hope that it would 'change' me, but it made not a scrap of difference ... I have never been able to speak to anyone about this before. Thank you for just being there to listen to me.
>   Mrs ...[16]

Married women clearly represented a significant minority of subscribers to *Arena Three*, and letters were regularly published from married lesbians wishing to be involved in the magazine. In 1965, Janice O'Brien explored the reasons which prompted lesbians to marry in an article on lesbian mothers. She explained:

> Many, if not most, people think it extremely odd, almost a contradiction in terms, that a woman should at the same time love her own sex and be a mother. The two states, although not mutually compatible, are not exclusive.
>   Why, being as she is, does a lesbian have children, anyway? Many reasons, some of them common to both heterosexual and homosexual women. Longing for a child can be a most intense emotion – strong enough to lead into marriage those who might otherwise remain outside it.
>   Some women have tried using marriage and motherhood as a 'cure' – mostly, as far as I have observed, unsuccessfully.
>   Others have become aware of their lesbian tendencies fully only after marriage and the birth of children. Somewhat different is the case of the marriage where both partners are homosexual or bisexual – presumably they will agree about some of the most important aspects of life.[17]

The dominance of heterosexual family-centred accounts of the domestic ideal was reinforced by characterisations of lesbianism in post-war literature as the antithesis of conventional femininity and domesticity. Representations of lesbians in medical literature and fiction overwhelmingly reinforced notions of lesbians as single, marginal figures, existing on the peripheries of society. In a number of novels, the depiction of fictional lesbian characters as distant from the conventional structure of family life was utilised to facilitate the development of intense emotional and sexual relationships. In Gale Wilhelm's 1938 novel, *Torchlight to Valhalla*, the death of Morgen's father leaves her alone in their family house, sparking an emotional and sexual journey which culminates in a lesbian love affair.[18]

Freudian medico-scientific attempts to explain the aetiology of lesbianism in terms of a breakdown in the parent-child relationship were replicated in other literary portrayals of the lesbian as the product of a broken home. This is apparent in Ann Bannon's lesbian pulp fiction of the 1950s and 60s. Written at the cusp of an explosion in paperback and 'pulp' fiction, her first novel, *Odd Girl Out*, was the second best-selling paperback of 1957 in the US. Exported to the UK, American lesbian pulp fiction proved equally popular and sold widely at railway station news-stands and stationers.[19] Laura Landon, the heroine of *Odd Girl Out*, is the child of a broken home. Her parents are recently divorced, leaving her without a stable home environment to return to in the college vacations. Largely notable by their absence, the brief references to Laura's parents suggest a difficult relationship. Occasional letters from Laura's father indicate that he is a pragmatic and unfeeling man to whom Laura reacts with frustration and tears. In *Beebo Brinker*, the second novel in Bannon's series, Beebo Brinker is driven to New York not only by the hostility of her neighbours but also by the difficulties of a troubled home life. Her mother is dead, leaving her in the care of an alcoholic father and a hostile older brother. The emotional and communication barriers between the lesbian protagonist and her family are therefore matched by the physical distance between Beebo's city life and that inhabited by her family.

The durability of nineteenth-century understandings of the private, domestic and emotional sphere as feminine, and the public, urban and rational sphere as masculine rendered the public domain a literary and cultural shorthand for deviant femininity. By the mid-twentieth century, the powerful image of the suburban housewife, established by the growth in suburban housing estates during the 1920s and 1930s, had reinforced the notion of the city as a site of masculinity and deviant femininity. Liz Heron has argued that the city can be seen as 'the site of women's most transgressive and subversive fictions throughout the [twentieth] century, as a place where family constraints can be cast off and new freedoms explored, as a place where the knowledge acquired through urban experience not only brings changed perceptions of identity, but inescapably situates the individual within the social order'.[20] This is apparent in Ann Bannon's *Beebo Brinker*, where the titular heroine first appears wandering the streets of New York's Greenwich Village. Escaping from rural Wisconsin where the hostile local inhabitants thought her queer, Beebo has come to New York in search of a job and her 'true' identity. The city, and Greenwich Village in particular, represents a place of tolerance and freedom of expression where any identity, and specifically that of the homosexual, is possible. The search for a lesbian identity is represented as a process in which the heroine must abandon such emblems of female security as family and home, embarking instead on a journey through the public spaces of the city.[21] Sally Munt has argued that the city represents a focal point in narratives of sexual identity formation, claiming, 'The utopian/dystopian paradox of hope for the city is that more pleasure is taken in the journeying towards it, as a process of desire and transformation, than in the (deferred) arrival'.[22] Examining the modernist figure of the flaneur as a potential metaphor for the lesbian's movement through public, urban space, she claims:

> Resisting the conformity of 1950s' small-town suburbia, men and women in the post-war USA were drawn to cities as a place to express their 'deviant' sexuality. Their newly-acquired gay and lesbian identities were predominantly urban, emanating from the social geographies of the streets. The anonymity of the city made a gay life realizable in a repressive era.

Lesbian novels of the period reflected this 'odyssey', depicting heroines such as Beebo Brinker as 'eroticised urban explorer[s]'.[23]

Lesbian accounts suggest that some women responded to these fantasies of the city as a place of sexual freedom. When Barbara Bell was invited to leave her home town of Blackburn in 1939 to begin training as a policewoman in London, her expectations of London were shaped by notions of the city as a site of endless possibility. She explained:

> Going to London was considered very daring [by her aunt and neighbours] and an insult to Lancashire. What was wrong with staying in Blackburn? They thought London was a wicked place. But they didn't know how wicked!
>
> I thought I'd find everything in London and I'd try to achieve my three ambitions – a flat, a profession and a girlfriend. I was sure I would find somebody in London and I instinctively knew that I would find somebody in the police.[24]

Elsa Beckett also imagined moving to London and beginning a new life with her girlfriend, Catherine, in the late 1960s, as a means of escaping a restrictive life with her family in Southern Rhodesia.[25]

While lesbians were frequently represented as distant from conventional femininity – urbane, sexually promiscuous and independent from family structures – they were also regarded as an active threat to family life. This notion of the lesbian was not new in the post-war era. In her analysis of the 1921 parliamentary debate on proposed legislation against lesbianism, Laura Doan draws attention to an argument that lesbianism undermined the institution of marriage and thus posed a threat to the continuance of civilised society and the human race. Citing two speakers who proposed this argument, she comments:

> In fact, both Macquisten and Wild describe particular cases known to them where marriages had been wrecked because the wife had been lured and corrupted by another woman. Wild cites a marriage where the 'wife had been taken from [the husband] by a young woman,' and Macquisten tells of a home ruined 'by the wiles of one abandoned female'.[26]

Although Macquisten and Wild's specific sources are unclear, the association of lesbianism with marital breakdown was relatively widespread in the inter-war and post-war years and featured as a theme in medical literature and in fictional representations of the lesbian.[27]

In the post-war decades, media representations of lesbianism also characterised lesbians as a threat to marital and family life, focusing on divorce cases and murder trials. The increased divorce rate in the late 1940s and 1950s resulted in a number of divorce cases, involving accusations of lesbianism, being widely reported in the press.[28] The divorce of Mr James Lloyd Spicer and his wife, Mrs Patricia Greville Spicer, hit the news in 1954, when he cited her lesbian relationship with a Mrs Stella Ryan as amounting to cruelty. Reporting the judge's decision in favour of the husband, The Times stated: '[Mr Justice Karminski] had had a good deal of evidence in the case that the wife admittedly formed an affection of such a kind for another woman as to give her husband grave cause for anxiety as to the precise nature of that association.'[29] In 1952, the inhabitants of Devon and Cornwall were witness to the dramatic spectacle of a twenty-year-old girl, dying of tuberculosis, facing a murder trial on a stretcher. Bertha Mary Scorse was accused of the murder of her lesbian lover, Mrs Joyce Mary Dunstan, in a fit of rage prompted by Mrs Dunstan's decision to leave Scorse.[30] In a detailed account of the two-day trial, the News of the World quoted a number of letters which Scorse had written to Dunstan at the beginning of their relationship. The two had met in a sanatorium where they were both being treated for tuberculosis, and when Scorse returned home, she received a letter from Dunstan's husband, informing her that Dunstan would soon be returning home to him. She wrote to Dunstan:

> I feel as if the bottom of my world had dropped out ... I am fed up. I hate him. He's got to see once and for all that you are through.
>   Please, Joyce, darling, for my peace of mind and happiness. He's got to accept your word as final.

While Dunstan did leave her husband to live with Scorse, their relationship lasted only two years before Dunstan left to live with her mother.

Scorse followed her there and stabbed her to death. Attempting to argue that Scorse's actions were the result of insanity, the defence counsel, John Maude QC, claimed, 'Being shut up with this illness for months, she had no hope of being loved by a man, but she wanted to be loved by somebody'. Judged on moral grounds, he suggested, the jury might say 'that the devil brought the two women together in their sickness and misery'. However, this was not their function: instead, they should listen to Dr Roy Neville Craig, specialist in mental diseases, when he claimed that 'she was a psychopath – a person with very strong anti-social trends and abnormal traits'. The judge's closing comments to the jury that, 'You may feel disgust or sorrow that this sort of thing should be, but there is no possible doubt that this girl was passionately attached to the dead woman and it would seem it had been reciprocal', gave one of the few indications of Dunstan's role in the affair. However, the *News of the World* focused almost entirely upon the pathological figure of Scorse, reinforcing fears about the threat posed to marital relationships by unbalanced lesbian seductresses.

In the post-war era negative representations of the lesbian as an external threat to family life began to acquire a new resonance with the development of fears regarding the 'problem family'. The concern of the Welfare State with 'failing' families created a new discourse linking lesbians and 'the family'. Lesbians, as single career women, had long been in the anomalous position of intervening in, and giving advice on childcare and other domestic issues. However, in the late 1960s, a new awareness of lesbianism as a social phenomenon and a growing appreciation of lesbians' experiences as wives and mothers, and not simply as single and socially marginal figures, began to emerge. A gradual shift had occurred during the decade from a characterisation of married women as victims of external lesbian seductresses, to an increasing awareness of the potential lesbianism of married women themselves. For a 1964 article entitled 'Scouting for – the public image' in *Arena Three*, Hilary Benno interviewed a range of different people about their perceptions of lesbians. She reported:

> A male night telephone operator (the father of two) told me cheerfully: 'Oh, we quite often hear them chatting on the line to one another. Married women, y'know, husband gone off for the weekend up North or somewhere … so they promptly get on the line to the old girlfriend y'know, and pass on the glad news the coast's clear.' He drank another pint of bitter and looked thoughtful. 'Though, I must say, the women are much more discreet than the male homos over the wire. Funny thing, that, when you think of it. I mean, it's the men who risk getting pinched, isn't it? But then, women just are mostly more discreet than men when it comes to love affairs and sex and all that.'[31]

Later in the decade, a number of articles in the press and women's magazines explored the issue of lesbianism and drew attention to the position
of the married lesbian. In a 1969 article in the Hemel Hempstead *Evening
Echo*, Jean Ritchie represented the idea of the married lesbian as the final
taboo: 'This is the story', she claimed, 'of two women who find themselves outside even that [lesbian] society. Lesbians are suspicious of them
– they cannot accept two married women with children in their ranks. Yet
they are lesbians, and so society at large – the society which accepts their
husbands and their children – will not tolerate them either.'[32]

This understanding of lesbians as potentially central to the nuclear
family, rather than as posing an external threat, resulted in a closer state
scrutiny of lesbian-headed households as 'problem families' in the late
1960s and early 1970s. Lesbian mothers became a new object of concern,
prompting the state to intervene in removing children from lesbian-
headed households. Such concerns impacted on a number of Hall Carpenter interviewees. Angela Chilton, who was in a relationship with a mother
of two from 1964 to 1971, recalls the effect of this new interest in lesbian
mothers. Her lover, Jean, was so concerned that her lesbianism might
cause her to lose custody of her children that she asked Angela to move
out of their shared house. In the 1960s, Rene Sawyer was involved in a
high-profile legal battle between her lover, Marion and Marion's ex-
husband over access to their children. Marion's husband had filed for
divorce, citing Rene as correspondent, and used their lesbianism as an
argument to oppose Marion's application for access.[33]

However, for many lesbians in the post-war period, the impact of the
ideological focus on married women and the family was experienced as
an erasure of the concerns of single women. Conceptions of the domestic
sphere as woman's 'natural' location – the place in which her fundamental roles were performed – were inverted by cultural commentators to
represent the single woman's home as empty and unfulfilled. Writing on
the 'loneliness of the unmarried woman' of middle age in 1963, a woman
medical correspondent observed:

> Most single women of this age group live alone in bleak bedsitters or tiny
> bachelor flats – most do their own cooking, and when they shut their front
> door after them in the evening, are alone till they leave their flat the follow-
> ing morning.[34]

While the daytime hours could be filled with work, she argued, it was the
evening at home which emphasised a single woman's isolation and social
exclusion. The depiction of the single woman as isolated was replicated by
press reports in the 1960s representing lesbians as lonely, pathetic individuals. Barbara Buchanon's 1965 article in the Bristol *Evening Post* ran under

the by-line, 'Life for these women offers no more than utter, appalling loneliness', while a *Sunday Times* feature on 'Women as Lesbians' in the same year referred to a lesbian couple who had both been 'intensely lonely' before meeting each other two years before.[35]

This conflation of cultural representations of single women and lesbians was equally apparent in a sharing of common practical difficulties. The housing situation in the post-war period reflected the ideological prioritising of the family and was therefore problematic for single women and lesbians. Despite inter-war building programmes, the destruction and damage of many houses during wartime air raids and the post-war increase in the birth-rate made the acute housing shortage a key political issue in the late 1940s. As with the aspiration of 'Homes Fit for Heroes' after the Great War, housing became a symbol of post-war social reconstruction. Wartime surveys, such as Mass Observation's 'Enquiry in People's Homes', anticipated and encouraged this debate, which received official attention in the 1944 Dudley Report, offering guidelines for public housing.[36] Alison Ravetz has argued that housing was a key issue in the 1945 general election, and that the Labour Party's promise that it would 'produce a good home in a well planned environment for every family in need' was a major contributory factor in its electoral success.[37] Ernest Bevan's ideal of mixed-class communities in new public housing estates was slow to materialise, however, in the context of limited building materials and urgent post-war housing needs. While government subsidies were provided for the restoration of older properties and the building of flats as well as houses, in reality, Alison Ravetz has maintained, most councils concentrated their resources on the construction of self-contained family houses.

Housing had historically been a problematic issue for single women who had no legal or financial identity outside of the family and marriage. Women were conventionally expected to remain living with their families until marriage and many women who did not marry continued to inhabit the parental home, or that of other family members, for much of their adult lives. This practice was widespread in the inter-war years, and continued into the 1950s and 60s, particularly for working-class women.[38] Mabel Hills, whose father died in 1915 when she was ten, lived with her mother in the family home in Forest Hill until her mother's death during the Second World War, as did her contemporary, Mary Wilkins.[39] The practical expectation that single women would continue to reside in the family home was reinforced by a widespread assumption that unmarried daughters would shoulder the responsibility of caring for ageing or sick parents or of simply providing company for a mother after the death of a father. Rene Sawyer, who left home to join the WRAC in 1953, was forced to return only a year and a half later when her mother's health deteriorated, only to leave home a second time in 1957. Similarly Sandy Martin, despite having left home at eighteen, returned to her parents' house three years later, in 1967, to help her mother care for her sick father, and the two continued to live together after her father's death.[40] That lesbian daughters were frequently expected to shoulder the burden of caring for family members is apparent from discussions in *Arena Three*. In March 1965, an article entitled 'Looking after mum' discussed the convention that unmarried daughters look after elderly and semi-dependent parents, and offered readers advice on how to cope with this situation and retain some independence.[41]

For those without dependent family members, occupational accommodation sometimes offered lesbians an alternative to the parental home. Young working-class girls had been sent away from home to work as live-in domestic servants throughout the nineteenth and early twentieth century and, in the mid-twentieth century, other occupations began to provide women workers with accommodation. The emerging women's police force offered its recruits accommodation in police section houses, while servicewomen were accommodated in designated housing belonging either to their own service or shared with other branches of the women's services. By the 1940s, the educational sector already had an established tradition of women's employment with many women teachers and university lecturers living in teacher-training colleges, schools and university college lodgings.[42] Nevertheless, the problem of accommodation for single, working women attracted the attention of welfare and women's organisations from the early twentieth century onwards. Early housing reformers and religious bodies founded hostels and sought to incorporate suitable accommodation into new model housing settlements, while philanthropic groups such as the Soroptomists used charitable funds for projects such as the construction of single women's housing.[43] The Young Women's Christian Association (YWCA) performed an important role both in providing and servicing women's hostels and in disseminating information on available housing. In London, the Sisters of the Cross and Passion operated hostels which offered individual and communal bedrooms, study sitting rooms, and shared kitchen facilities, or self-contained flatlets, for between thirty and fifty 'young civil servants, business girls and students'.[44] This type of accommodation was primarily directed toward younger women, reflecting an expectation that older women would be married and living in family housing. Rosanna Hibbert recalled her time staying at a women's hostel as the most enjoyable aspect of her life while studying at Guildhall in the early 1950s. She recalled the experience as a sociable one in which she made a number of friends, as did Pat Arrowsmith who embarked on a sexual relationship with another woman at the hostel in Chester where she lived in the mid-1950s. Boarding houses or 'private hotels' offered a similar impermanent source of housing on the private rental market, offering accommodation and often lunch and tea to their residents. While these existed across London, they were concentrated particularly in the residential areas of Bayswater, Kensington and Bloomsbury.[45] Accommodation bureaux and advisory bodies such as the YWCA offered lists of such accommodation as well as acting as a go-between in flat shares. Single women had been forging female residential communities since the 1890s, and the flat- or house-share gained further popularity as a housing solution for young women after the Second World War, catering for single working women dislocated from their home towns and families.[46]

For those who could obtain and afford them, self-contained flats and houses were available from the local authority or the private rental markets, as well as, for the lucky few, to buy. Esme Langley was able to obtain accommodation in local authority housing at Broadhurst Gardens in West Hampstead in the 1960s, perhaps as a result of having two sons.[47] However, while central and local government focused ideas and resources on the construction and restoration of family housing, the available housing stock suitable for single people remained depleted after the war. Alison Ravetz has emphasised that the building of flats has not been a part of the English housing tradition, so that purpose-built flats and maisonettes comprised only 7 per cent of housing stock in 1964. Although 'walk-up' blocks of flats, known as 'Buildings', had been built by local authorities from the 1840s onwards as part of slum clearance programmes, these were primarily occupied by white-collar workers as family homes. Similar blocks, known as 'Mansions', were built for middle-class families from the 1870s, but it was only from 1900 onwards that flats became specifically associated with single people. After 1900, new blocks of flats, known as 'Chambers' were designed for professional men and women, with small 'continental' kitchens and often communal dining rooms. Ravetz argues that this was 'a trend that was disapprovingly associated with the growing independence of the modern young woman'.[48] The increasing popularity of flats for private renting as an investment option resulted in larger numbers being built in the 1920s and 30s. Again, Ravetz has argued, although marketed as small, middle-class family homes, 'increasingly they became reserved for single childless or retired people'.[49]

The failure of local authorities to incorporate single-occupancy housing into their post-World War Two building programmes meant that this earlier housing formed the bulk of available housing stock for single women in the 1950s and 60s. While the wealthier lesbian could join the growing number of owner-occupiers in the post-war decades, the majority were drawn to the private rental housing located in less affluent neighbourhoods. In his 1958 *Penguin Guide to London*, F. R. Banks commented:

> Residential Hotels or blocks of flats, with suites of furnished apartments, and in some cases restaurants and room attendance ('service flats'), have sprung up in many quarters of London. The most palatial (and most expensive) are in Kensington and Bayswater; in less exclusive quarters charges are proportionately less.[50]

Lesbian residential patterns tended to follow this concentration of suitable housing in West London.[51] Hall Carpenter interviewee, Olive Ager, visited her girlfriend in Kensington in 1964, and Rene Sawyer, who also moved to the area in the mid-1960s, described the area around North Kensington and Ladbroke Grove as having a strong gay presence. Comparing it to the community atmosphere of the East End, she remembered a large number of lesbians and gay men living in the area and forming a close-knit community. When *Arena Three* began to hold social meetings in different areas of London, the West London group covering Kew, Kensington and Richmond was among the largest and most vibrant.[52]

Just as housing options for unmarried women were restricted in the post-war years, women embarking on a lesbian relationship had limited cultural models on which to draw. In contrast to conventional representations of women in the 1940s and 50s as the source of emotional stability and security in the family, lesbians were frequently portrayed in medical and other literature as being unable to sustain lasting relationships. As discussed in Chapter 1, in Dr Albertine Winner's 1947 analysis of lesbianism, she contrasted the 'harmless' woman who simply experienced her primary emotional relationships with other women, but did not necessarily pursue a sexual expression of her attachment, with a second 'promiscuous Lesbian who, passing quickly and lightly from affair to affair, usually with physical relations, may cause great harm and unhappiness'.[53] Frank Caprio reflected that, 'many lesbians are 'insanely jealous' and possessive and consequently the relationship becomes a very trying one … Hostility is an emotion common to lesbians.' Eustace Chesser concurred, claiming that, 'There is another side to lesbianism. Some of its manifestations can be ugly. The dominant partner is frequently possessive and fiercely jealous if threatened by heterosexual rivalry'.[54]

Medico-scientific portrayals were reflected in wider cultural depictions of the subject. In Robert Aldrich's film, *The Killing of Sister George*, released in the UK in 1969, the central lesbian relationship between 'Sister George' and Childie is presented as inherently flawed. The inequality of their relationship, signified by the considerable age gap between the older George and simplistically infantile Childie, is evident in the brutality with which George treats the younger woman. In a caricature of the heterosexual marriage, George – whose masculine nickname is suggestive of her gendered role in the relationship – is portrayed as the career-focused breadwinner, while Childie merely plays at her more casual employment and is rarely shown outside of their shared flat. However, in a failure of the ideals of the marital relationship, Childie proves unable to support her partner after George is threatened with redundancy. George takes out her anger on the unfortunate Childie, before turning instead to a neighbouring prostitute for 'adult' emotional support. The relationship ultimately collapses under the pressure, when Childie betrays George by giving in to the advances of the television network executive who was responsible for George's work difficulties.[55] While *The Killing of Sister George* saw a lesbian relationship broken up by another woman, the 1968 film *The Fox* represented a lesbian partnership unable to withstand the attentions of a man. Jill and March had lived an isolated but contented existence running a farm together, before the grandson of the former owner returned from sea and proposed to March.[56] In accepting his offer, March reinforced a message that lesbian affairs were poor substitutes for the genuine satisfaction provided by heterosexual marriage.

These portrayals of lesbian relationships as short-lived and unsustainable resonated with lesbians' own perceptions of their relationships in this period. *Arena Three* published numerous letters from its readers in the late 1960s expressing the opinion that lesbians were unable to form lasting relationships. When 'Commutator's' article 'Myth – or unpalatable fact?' argued that most lesbians 'run from one partner to another in much the same way as adolescent heterosexuals', three readers wrote in to the following issue to agree, although qualifying their criticism with the argument that external social pressures acted against lesbian relationships.[57] Diana Chapman offered a similar picture of lesbian inconstancy in her account of the parties organised by the magazine. 'Of course, those New Year's Eve parties were terrible,' she claimed, 'because all the break-ups would happen, you see; a few weeks or months after a New Year's party, there'd be a great change round of partners.'[58] Lesbian portrayals of their relationships as short-term and vulnerable to pressure belied the evidence of their personal experience, however. Interview accounts demonstrate that most of the Hall Carpenter respondents had experienced long-term relationships of at least fifteen years. Some of those interviewed are identifiable as couples, including Julie Switsur and Cynthia Reid, who first met in 1963 and were still together at the time of their interviews in 1985.[59]

In the absence of affirmative models of lesbian relationships, women imagined and conducted relationships with other women in a variety of ways. Given the dominance of gendered models of relationships idealised in representations of marriage in the post-war period, it is not surprising that many lesbian relationships appear to have been imagined in gendered terms. Cynthia Reid described the thought processes she experienced when embarking on her first lesbian relationship:

> And it was only then that I really began to think in terms of homosexual relationships and to realise that it wasn't just me, an individual, being rather peculiar. And the alternatives that I had thought of, when I got involved with this girl at college were things like changing my sex. And I think the male-female married relationship was, to me, the only possibility, and if I fell in love with a woman, who was clearly a fairly feminine sort of woman, and I was clearly a tomboy, then I must be the one who was in some way wrong, and the way to put things right would be to have operations to change my sex and then we could get married and then perhaps we could have children.[60]

These comments demonstrate the influence of heterosexual models in setting the parameters of what might be conceivable in relationships. As a young woman in the late 1950s, it was apparently easier for Reid to comprehend physically changing her own sex than to imagine a relationship which was not based on polarised gender identities. Diana Chapman echoed these feelings in a description of her affair with a girl called Jean when she was nineteen. Completely besotted with Jean, Diana explained that she had wanted 'to be a man' in order to 'fulfil her proper function' and take Jean to dances. While both Cynthia and Diana subsequently found ways to build relationships with women without the need to change their own sex, others found the heterosexual marriage model the most compelling means of expressing same-sex desire. Incidences of women passing as men in order to marry other women had been documented during the eighteenth and nineteenth centuries, and in the inter-war period, tabloid readers had been shocked by the case of Colonel Barker, discovered to be a woman during a trial for theft. Passing as husband and wife continued to offer a means for two women to conduct a relationship in the post-war decades and, in 1966, the Sheffield *Morning*

Telegraph reported the case of Dorothy Jane Ward and Olive Annie Sykes, charged with 'making for the purpose of being inserted in the register of marriage for the City of Sheffield, a false statement as to the particulars required by law to be known and registered relating to the marriage'. Ward, who referred to herself as Peter, a bachelor, had been working as a labourer and living with Sykes before the couple married.[61] The following year the BBC2 documentary, Man Alive, exploring the topic of lesbianism, had featured what was described in Arena Three as 'a very long drawn out interview with Steve Rogers – a youthful "Colonel Barker" whose over-riding compulsion is to pass as a male, even to the point of "courting" and getting engaged to another girl and using an artificial penis'.[62]

Although few women modelled their relationships so closely upon heterosexual marriage, the most clearly defined lesbian relationship model of the post-war period, butch/femme, employed similarly gendered models of subjectivity. Pat Arrowsmith claimed that, in the 1950s and early 60s, 'the norm if you were a lesbian was to be one or the other, to be butch or femme and there wasn't a sort of mid-way position'.[63] Both Pat Arrowsmith and Rene Sawyer saw the source of butch/femme roles as the masculine/feminine binary which constructed heterosexual relations. Rene Sawyer, a butch lesbian in the 1950s, explained butch/femme in terms of gendered roles:

> It was actual role playing – most of my friends that were either butches or femme, they were couples, together – and their role playing was, one was like the man and the other was the woman … It was moulded on a hetero-sexual role.[64]

However, the deployment of butch/femme roles should not be inter-preted as an unthinking replication of heterosexual relationship patterns. For some lesbians, the similarities between butch/femme roles and those conventionally assigned to men and women in mainstream culture enabled them to structure their relationships along familiar cultural lines, providing a sense of security in the context of limited cultural and social options. This is apparent in Rene Sawyer's depiction of the practical application of a butch role in the domestic environment:

> The other point that one takes on in a relationship [is]: who is in charge of what. Well, one thing's for certain, you never had a butch really that ever did any cooking. I myself never knew really how to boil an egg until I was about 27/28 – did I ever have to do anything. I think my first time I ever scrambled eggs, well, they were literally scrambled. I mean it was just a mess: no one could have eaten them. My role as a butch was: I sat at the dinner table and my dinner was put down in front of me, as my father before me and my grandfather before that.[65]

For Rene Sawyer, the correlations between butch/femme and heterosexual marital relations enabled her to apply the notions of relationship norms learnt in wider culture to her lesbian relationships. She was thus able to use her father and grandfather as role models in making sense of her identity as a butch lesbian. In so doing, she ascribed to herself a marginal location within the domestic sphere. In keeping with contemporary masculine roles, she constructed herself as a secondary and passive figure in the home. The extent to which her understanding of butch/femme roles was based upon contemporary heterosexual models of marriage is apparent from her depiction of the femme role. She explained:

> the femme always took the role on as being the housewife and the mother. Of course, we didn't have any children: I don't know about any lesbians that I knew at the time that had children. So, consequently, it was usually a little dog or a cat that one had in the family and that was their little baby.[66]

Locating the femme at the heart of the domestic sphere, Rene Sawyer constructed an alternative model of domestic and family life.

However, although butch/femme roles offered a clear model for lesbian relationships in the post-war period, lesbian accounts suggest that many women were uncomfortable with this prescriptive gendering of roles. Pat Arrowsmith first encountered butch/femme models in prison in the early 1960s, and, although she did not fully understand exactly what butch/femme meant in respect of sexual roles, her experience of it unsettled her view of her own long-term relationship:

> And yes, this was a bit disquieting to me because it wasn't clear to me in my relationship with Wendy that we were one thing or the other really. If anything, we both looked slightly butch; we looked a bit alike and I can remember when I came out [of prison] on that occasion feeling rather troubled about this. It was all a bit queer for two kind of rather butch-like women to be getting together and I felt this was a bit abnormal you see.[67]

Pat Arrowsmith's initial response to butch/femme was a sense of discomfort that her own relationship did not appear to mirror its gendered roles. However, by the 1960s, attitudes to butch/femme began to shift in line with an emerging feminist critique of marriage. The post-war domestication of society came to be regarded in an increasingly negative light by an emerging women's movement, which represented the 1940s and 1950s as decades in which women were confined to the prison of the family home. The Housebound Wives Register and the National Housewives Register were formed after Maureen Nicol's letter to the *Manchester Guardian* in 1960, describing being at home as being 'in exile', struck a chord with other readers. These ideas were taken up in the writings of Hannah Gavron and Betty Friedan whose work, Wendy Webster has argued, developed a 'critique of home as over-private, isolated and oppressive'.[68] Judy Giles has claimed that 'feminist thought (quite rightly) has stressed the importance of "killing the Angel in the House"; liberating women from what has been perceived as a limiting "incarceration" in the home; and relegating scrubbing, polishing and washing to the margins of a woman's significant life'.[69]

Attitudes toward butch/femme echoed these criticisms of gendered divisions of domestic labour and Pat Arrowsmith, whose lesbian identity in this period was partially constructed in response to her sense of alienation from butch/femme roles, took great care, in her account, to explain that in her relationship there were no stratified roles. Rather, the roles adopted by herself and her partner in the performance of such domestic tasks as cooking, cleaning, shopping and the paying of bills, were those at which they excelled, or enjoyed undertaking.[70] Sharley McLean made a similar point in an account of her long-term relationship with her lover, Georgina:

> Georgina would say to me, 'What shall we do?' And I'd say, 'What do you want to do?' You know, in the beginning. And I said, we must take responsibility. I don't want to pressurise you into doing things and I don't want to be pressurised by you. I think we should be equal. Now she loved cooking, and I certainly didn't object to her cooking and she was more domesticated than I, but it didn't mean to say that she was into a domestic scene rather than I. She was certainly tidier. But it wasn't really role-play. I did not expect her to do things for me and she didn't expect me to do things for her. It was by mutual consent and it wasn't into a role-playing thing.[71]

These accounts suggest that some women regarded their relationships with other women as an opportunity to strive for greater equality in their relations than the perceived norm in heterosexual relationships of the era. Their insistence that they did not impose domestic tasks on their partners, but searched for alternative ways of distributing housework, echoes both feminist narratives of women's domestic burden as a form of male oppression and later lesbian feminist critiques of butch/femme as a replication of heteropatriarchal gender inequalities.[72]

In the absence of an explicit discourse of lesbian domesticity, many women in the post-war period were able to set up home together and express strong feelings of love and commitment without necessarily invoking concepts of lesbianism. Post-war journalist and television personality, Nancy Spain, lived with Joan (Jonnie) Werner Laurie and Jonnie's two children, Nicky and Tommy for thirteen years until her death alongside Jonnie in a plane crash in 1964. In her comic autobiography, *Why I'm Not a Millionaire* (1959), Nancy attempted to describe this relationship:

> What a difficult thing to write objectively of a relationship in which I have been happily bound up for five years, and which is still going on! Jonnie is, I think, one of the most remarkable people I have ever met: remarkable in her potential greatness and past achievement, but even more remarkable in being the only person I have ever met (except Lord Beaverbrook) who has never bored me. She is certainly the only person who has ever let me be myself … therefore the only person with whom I can cheerfully live in close disharmony.
>
> … It is easy enough to talk or write about casual acquaintances, friends even. But it is impossible for me to take a step without consulting Jonnie, it is inevitable that she will shape my behaviour, read everything I write, tell me what other people will think of it, and I cannot write lightly of her, for she saved my life.

Without explicitly labelling her relationship with Jonnie as lesbian, Nancy clearly demonstrates in this account the depth of her feelings for Jonnie and the central position Jonnie occupied in her life. Several years later, in a further autobiographical account, *A Funny Thing Happened on the Way* (1964), Nancy again referred to their relationship, explaining:

> Once, about ten years ago, my partner Jonnie and I decided to spend a weekend in a boat on the river.
>
> Jonnie, Joan Werner Laurie, the editor of *She* magazine, with whom I have lived for the best thirteen years of my life, is a character of great fascination. She is always perpetually, tirelessly, striving, expecting of others the near-impossible standards she sets on herself. She is, in my opinion, the greatest editor in London.[74]

Despite Nancy Spain's reference to Jonnie as her 'partner' and her description of their life together as the 'best thirteen years of my life', a review of the book in *Arena Three* complained that Nancy was not explicit about the nature of her relationship with Jonnie.[75] Such comments, and the terms in which Spain referred to her relationship, suggest that it was still possible in the 1950s and early 1960s for lesbian relationships in the public eye to be an open secret, recognisable as lesbian, but not explicitly named as such. Novelist and poets Sylvia Townsend Warner and Valentine Ackland, whose relationship spanned thirty-eight years from 1930 until 1968, apparently constructed their relationship along similar lines. The central importance of their relationship in both their lives is clear from Sylvia's final letter written to Valentine while the latter was in hospital just before her death. Sylvia wrote:

My Love,

Thirty-eight years ago I brought you a little bunch of herbs when you lay ill in a large bed with Sir Walter Raleigh and a tortoise. In all those years, my dearest, I have never doubted your love, nor my own. Much of what's to come is still unsure; but that glorious span of thirty-eight years of love and trust and happiness – care and courage too – will shine on us and protect us. I have always believed you. Even when you gave me scented shells, I believed in them. You are my faith, I will live and die in it. If I have to live on alone, I will live and die in it, and because you believe there is a life after death, I will believe in that too. Our love is the one thing I can never question.

Now in return you must believe that I will be sensible, take care of myself, use Palfrey and the Goring amenities for all they are worth, eat an orange a day, and take care of your possession, your Tib.

My love, my Love. And my heart's thanks for all you have given me, all your understanding, your support, your tenderness, your courage, your trust. And your Beauty, outside and in, and your delightfulness.

Never has any woman been so well and truly loved as I.[76]

In the preface to her edited collection of the couple's letters, Susanna Pinney commented:

I started to work for Sylvia in 1970. This collection of letters was the second piece of typing she gave me. I was touched that she should place such trust in me, because the letters revealed an intimate account of her relationship with Valentine, and Valentine was so newly dead. This perhaps was naïve, for Sylvia was proud of their relationship and wanted it known, though not while she was alive; she would have found it too painful, she told me. She also did not want others hurt.[77]

The relationship between Sylvia Townsend Warner and Valentine Ackland, just as that between Nancy Spain and Joan Werner Laurie, is characterised in terms of a primary emotional bond which is suggestive of earlier models of romantic friendship. The manner in which these couples both imagined and represented their relationships indicates that it was still possible in the post-war period for women to express strong feelings of love and commitment to each other without necessarily invoking the explicit language of lesbianism.

While these accounts demonstrate that some women were able to forge relationships with other women which provided the central focus to their lives, other women attempted to conduct same-sex affairs alongside other relationships. When the Minorities Research Group (MRG) first began to publish *Arena Three* in 1964, the magazine opened up new social possibilities for women who had previously married or committed to conventional family lives. In the September 1964 issue, the winning entry in a letter-writing competition reflected on the position of a hypothetical woman who meets and falls in love with another woman after seventeen years of married life. The writer speculated:

> I imagine the only course for most women would be to continue in their heterosexual life and suffer the torment of their homosexual feelings in silence. This causes great and deep suffering – to a woman married and with two children it would explain why her marriage is only 'fairly happy' – not very happy or even just happy, but only fairly. Possibly her homosexuality has troubled her many times during her married life but in such a quiet way that it has not been fully recognised. Now she is in a dilemma because she has found a woman who arouses within her such deep feelings that she 'can't live without her'.[78]

The writer's suggestion that the only appropriate course of action in this situation would be to remain married represented the dominant view expressed in the magazine in the 1960s. The editorial board were concerned not to appear to be encouraging married women to leave their husbands and had sought advice on this issue before setting up the organisation which published the magazine. As a result, MRG adopted a policy preventing married women from joining and subscribing to *Arena Three* without the signed permission of their husbands. A number of published letters explaining that such permission was impossible to obtain suggest that many married women were excluded by this rule. However, a significant number of married women were still able to join and some apparently did embark on affairs with women they met through the organisation. In September 1965, Mrs K. K. wrote into the magazine, requesting assistance for a woman she had met at an *Arena Three* social event:

> Dear Miss Langley
>   I am dreadfully worried about a Miss G. and wish you could do something to help her. You see, we met at the Bull's Head some while ago and started an affair but although it was only meant lightly she has now grown much too fond of me and wants me to leave my husband and children and go away with her. I hate to hurt her but this I cannot possibly do and I thought perhaps you could do something to help her as she is very lonely and unhappy. I never meant to upset her and believe me I have learnt my lesson now.
>   Mrs K. K. (London)[79]

Her concluding comment, 'I have learnt my lesson', indicates that, despite the limited options open to her as a married lesbian, she expected her actions to be viewed by the magazine community with disapproval.

Such anxieties concerning extra-marital lesbian affairs may have been linked to a desire on the part of the magazine community to distance themselves from characterisations of lesbians as sexually voracious. Cultural representations of lesbianism as socially marginal in the post-war period consistently framed the lesbian in sexual rather than affective terms. Post-war scientific and journalistic writings on lesbianism drew on the conventions of late-nineteenth and early-twentieth-century medico-scientific works, placing an active sexuality at the centre of their work. The popular psychiatrist, Dr Eustace Chesser, began the chapter on lesbianism in his 1949 study with an account of lesbian sexual practices. Again, in his 1959 work on male and female homosexuality, despite maintaining that the true test of the homosexual lay in whether there was a preference for an emotional rather than a physical relationship with a person of the same sex, he returned continually to the question of lesbian sexual behaviour.[80] Such assumptions were mirrored in the work of American psychologist, Frank Caprio. In a book-length study of female homosexuality in America and Europe, Caprio repeatedly emphasised the importance of sexual practices in lesbianism, commenting on its frequent manifestations in arenas – such as in prisons or amongst prostitutes – where heterosexual contact was impossible or undesirable.[81] Bryan Magee, in his journalistic work on lesbianism published in 1966, displayed a similar concern with the sexual. In an opening chapter, entitled, 'What Lesbians Do', he offered a detailed account of the range of lesbian sexual practices, clearly fundamental to his construction of the lesbian.[82]

Post-war medical accounts emphasising the importance of sexual behaviour to lesbian identities, characterised the 'true' sexual lesbian within a binary model of lesbian sexuality. The basis for such a distinction is apparent in early sexological definitions of lesbianism. Drawing upon active or 'masculine' and passive or 'feminine' models of sexuality, late-nineteenth and early-twentieth-century sexologists described a sexually active true lesbian identity in masculine terms, in contrast to a more passive, emotional and temporary feminine invert. By 1959, when Eustace Chesser wrote his account of male and female homosexuality, the influence of Freudian thinking on psychiatry had led to the reconstruction of notions of lesbian identity.[83] Chesser was inspired by Freud's theory of female sexual development to characterise the lesbian as an inferior male who, having failed to overcome the penis-envy phase of female sexual development, was trapped in an immature sexuality that set her up in competition with 'real' men. This was reflected in his 1971 account, in which he claimed that the '"butch" or masculine type may simulate ordinary intercourse and use an artificial penis or "dildo"'.[84] The progression from 'butch' as masculine to 'butch' as wearer of the dildo and thus artificial man is an obvious but highly significant one. However, Chesser drew upon earlier sexological notions of the passive feminine invert to explain the feminine lesbian. Such women were, again, only temporary lesbians, making do with an imitation male in the absence of the 'real thing'. Bryan Magee's account offered a noticeably different model of lesbian sexuality. Unlike the psychiatric sources, Magee's models of lesbian subjectivity were explicitly denoted 'butch' and 'fem'. Although Magee's construction of the two identities was at times confused, he was at pains to avoid setting up a binary opposition between the two. His chapter on the subject thus began:

> There are infinite gradations of both butch and fem, and the majority of lesbians are not clearly either but are somewhere in between – or, to put it differently, are one and the other by turns.[85]

For Magee, there was only one lesbian identity, but an identity that was manifested in degrees of masculinity or femininity. Nevertheless, in his subsequent discussion, he emphasised the butch identity as the 'true' lesbian identity, observing that fem lesbians frequently could not give any explanation for being attracted to butches, and that, to some, 'a butch is a "half-way house" to a heterosexual relationship'.[86]

Despite representations of lesbianism depicting women with a voracious and predatory sexual appetite, lesbian narratives frequently portrayed sexual experiences and relationships as uncertain and problematic. Myrtle Soloman, reflecting on a fifteen-year relationship with her partner, Jean, in the 1940s and 50s, commented that in retrospect she thought Jean had been 'a bit ashamed' of the 'sexual side' of the relationship. Mabel Hills described a similar reticence regarding the sexual aspect of her own relationship in the same period. While she and her lover did not think of their having sex 'as anything strange', they 'never discussed it' in twenty-one years of living together.[87] Negative representations of lesbian sexuality resurfaced in a number of other accounts of sexual relationships. Rosanna Hibbert, reflecting on a brief sexual affair she had had within another woman when she was in her late twenties, commented that she had never had a good sexual relationship and was afraid of her own body. Diana Chapman expressed a similar sense of frustration, describing how, despite having fallen in love with many women in her life, she was 'never able to reconcile sex and emotions'.[88]

Many identified butch/femme sexual codes as the source of difficult or unsettling sexual relationships in this period, and one mentioned it as a significant challenge. Rene Sawyer described her experience of butch sexuality in some detail, implying that sexual prowess was an integral part of her understanding of a butch lesbian's identity. She claimed that when she first realised she was capable of giving sexual pleasure to a woman, she decided that she would work extremely hard to be a 'great' and tender lover. This decision was motivated by a desire that no woman would ever wish to look at another while she was with her, because Rene would be the best lover she had ever had. In order to achieve this end, she practised 'until she knew a woman inside out', both mentally and physically, a process which was entirely about discovering the other woman's sexual needs and relegated Rene's desires as unimportant.[89] However, for other women, the codes of butch sexual behaviour posed difficulties. Margaret Cranch described the period when she lived in a butch/femme culture, in the late 1950s, as most sexually difficult of her life. She stated that although relationships in the early stages, with women who had not experienced butch/femme, were not problematic, difficulties arose when she began to date women with more experience. In those latter relationships, the pressure of conforming to and fulfilling expectations of butch sexual roles created problems in the sexual relations. Margaret became so confused that she developed a fear of all relationships, and remained intentionally single for several years.[90]

From the late 1960s onward, closer scrutiny of lesbians by journalists and sociologists prompted the emergence of a new attention to lesbians and their home environments.[91] Bryan Magee represented the home as a highly problematic arena for lesbians. Describing a visit to a lesbian household, he commented that he had found the emotional atmosphere stifling: a result of the occupants' 'obsessive concern with every detail of each other's lives'. Arguing that lesbians, like all women, are susceptible to cultural 'propaganda' in favour of women's role as home-makers, Magee claimed that lesbians were primarily domestically focused in their interests and leisure pursuits. Thus he painted a picture of a domestic idyll not dissimilar to that ascribed to heterosexual wives of the period:

> If you drop in on the home of a lesbian couple you are likely to find them on almost any evening sitting by the fire, or watching television, or darning socks, sewing, making something, reading, occasionally but not often having friends in. This way of spending their leisure contrasts with that of male homosexuals, who seem to seek their pleasure primarily outside the home.[92]

However, for Magee, this inward-looking way of life was not a healthy one. He represented the lesbian domestic scene as a pressure-cooker in which external pressures exacerbated uncontrolled and 'obsessive' emotional interaction between the two women. The inability of lesbian couples to express their feelings in public confined all emotional expression to the home, while the need to hide their relationship from social disapproval rendered the lesbian home a place of concealment and deceit. Magee observed:

> As one partner in a life-long lesbian partnership said to me: 'In normal circumstances if one has guests in the house one thinks nothing of taking the women into the bedroom, or asking guests to leave their coats on the bed; but I have to be always careful to keep guests out of the bedroom.'[93]

However, lesbian accounts of the domestic sphere suggest a different, more sociable understanding of the home. A number of Hall Carpenter interviewees referred to their own, and other people's, homes as important sites of social activities. Describing her lesbian social life in the 1960s, Rene Sawyer commented:

> But we used to do a lot of partying; a lot of social events went on in people's homes. Be it ever so humble – whether it was just a little single bedsitter or whether it was a flat. They used to do a lot of socialising in those days in your home, you know, where everyone used to bring a little bottle of wine or a couple of cans of beer, and you'd sit there and have a cigarette and a glass of wine and there'd be lots of laughter and fun and dancing.[94]

Rene Sawyer's account suggests that lesbians created sites of sociability in their homes, modelled on the types of entertainment provided by nightclubs in the same period. While the offer of the space was made by one individual, the creation of the party was a communal process, in which each guest would make a contribution to the collective drinks kitty. In December 1964, *Arena Three* contained a number of announcements under the heading 'Christmas Hospitality'. One item consisted of an invitation from some readers in Kew for up to six 'solitary' subscribers to join them for Christmas dinner. Another announced:

> As some London members have already heard, Miss Alison Laurie (ex New Zealand) plans to give a Christmas Party on Saturday 19th December, at a cost per head of 10 /- (MRG members) or 15/- (non members). Please write to her at 31 Pembridge Villas, Notting Hill Gate.[95]

Diana Chapman, describing house parties in the same period, suggested that individuals took turns to host parties, listing a number of people in her circle of friends who gave parties in the late 1960s. Such events were not confined to the same groups of people, however. Asked if they involved the same friendship networks, Chapman replied:

> Sort of, yes, but it would, I always think of the lesbian scene as, you know the Olympic Circles, that intertwine at points, well, it was a bit like that.

You'd sort of see people that you knew perhaps, and they knew people that you didn't know.[96]

Such parties were described as rowdy occasions in which 'everybody used to – there was a hell of a lot of drinking – everybody used to get quite plastered'. Sandy Martin, who often went to house parties at Maureen Duffy's house in the early 1960s, explained, 'And they had parties and I went and got drunk, and then I'd walk the dog the following day and I'd get put to bed at some, I don't know, one o'clock in the morning, drunk out of my head'. Diana Chapman gave a similar account, saying 'there'd be somebody being sick in the bathroom and a couple snogging in the bedroom and somebody crying in the hall'.[97]

Lesbian house parties in the 1960s demonstrated a different use of the home, not as the domain of private, family life, but rather as an arena of lesbian sociability. In providing this evidence of alternative meanings of the domestic sphere, lesbian narratives have complicated the picture of women's domestic experience in the 1950s and 1960s. The narrative of domestic aspiration which contemporary cultural media ascribed to women in the post-war period is also largely absent from lesbian accounts of their lives. Post-war representations of lesbians as urbane and sexually promiscuous, or isolated and unfulfilled, excluded lesbians from dominant notions of femininity as family-focused and domestically oriented. Literary and media portrayals painted a more destructive picture of lesbians as a threat to marital life. The absence of any contemporary narratives of lesbian domesticity was exacerbated by the practical difficulties of creating a home in the context of limited and poor-quality housing for single women or couples. Nevertheless, lesbians built domestic lives and imagined new relationship patterns in this period. While butch/femme codes of behaviour enabled some interviewees to construct an account of relationships and domesticity which was more compatible with contemporary cultural mores, others drew on feminist arguments in their representation of their relationships as a challenge to heterosexual models. In doing so, many women drew on new definitions of lesbian identity which were beginning to be forged by an emerging lesbian social scene in the post-war decades.

Notes

1 Commutator, 'Myth – or unpalatable fact', *Arena Three* 2:9 (September 1965), p. 6.

2 Alison Light, *Forever England: Femininity, Literature and Conservatism between the Wars* (London: Routledge, 1991), pp. 8–9.

3 Martin Pugh, 'Domesticity and the decline of feminism, 1930–1950', in Harold L. Smith (ed.), *British Feminism in the Twentieth Century* (Aldershot: Edward Elgar, 1990), p. 151.

4 Ferguson, *Forever Feminine*.

5 Pugh, 'Domesticity and the decline of feminism', p. 153.

6 Riley, *War in the Nursery*.

7 John Bowlby, *Child Care and the Growth of Love* (Harmondsworth: Penguin, 1953); Donald W. Winnicott, *The Child and the Family: First Relationships* (London: Tavistock, 1962). See Chapter 2 for a discussion of the impact of these arguments on women's employment.

8 Susan Pedersen, *Family, Dependence, and the Origins of the Welfare State: Britain and France 1914–1945* (Cambridge: Cambridge University Press, 1993).

9 Wilson, *Only Halfway to Paradise*, p. 22.

10 On the democratisation of housework, see Judy Giles, 'A home of one's own': Women and domesticity in England 1918–1950', *Women's Studies International Forum* 16:3 (1993); Webster, *Imagining Home*.

11 Angela Partington, 'The days of the New Look': Consumer culture and working-class affluence', in Jim Fyrth (ed.), *Labour's Promised Land? Culture and society in Labour Britain 1945–51* (London: Lawrence and Wishart, 1995); Carolyn Steedman, *Landscape for a Good Woman* (London: Virago, 1986).

12 For example, George Mitchell and Terence Lupton, *The Liverpool Estate* (Liverpool: The University Press of Liverpool, 1954); Michael Young and Peter Wilmott, *Family and Kinship in East London* (Harmondsworth: Penguin, 1962).

13 Giles, 'A home of one's own', p. 242.

14 NSA, HCC (C456), F2158–F2163, Sharley McLean; NSA, HCC F1607–F1612, Jackie Forster.

15 Bristol *Evening Post* (2 December 1965), p. 15.

16 *Arena Three* 2:1 (January 1965), p. 11.

17 *Arena Three* 2: 11 (November 1965), pp. 2–4.

18 Gale Wilhelm, *Torchlight to Valhalla* (London: Random House, 1938).

19 Ann Bannon, *Odd Girl Out* (San Francisco: Cleis Press, 2001 [1957]).

20 Liz Heron (ed.), *Streets of Desire: Women's Fictions of the Twentieth-Century City* (London: Virago, 1993), p. 2.

21 Ann Bannon, *Beebo Brinker* (San Francisco: Cleis Press, 2001 [1962]).

22 Sally Munt, 'The lesbian flaneur', in David Bell and Gill Valentine (eds), *Mapping Desire* (London: Routledge, 1995), p. 118.

23 Munt, 'The lesbian flaneur', p. 118.

24 Bell, *Just Take Your Frock Off*, p. 59.

25 NSA, HCC (C456) F2091–F2092, Elsa Beckett.

26 Doan, 'Acts of female indecency', p. 209.

27 Frank Caprio cites an example of a married woman seduced away from her husband by a lesbian in his *Female Homosexuality*, pp. 60–1. In literature, see, for example, Bannon, *Beebo Brinker*.

28 By May 1946, 48,500 divorce applications had been received through Command Legal Aid sections of the forces. Inability to meet this demand

prompted the government to set up the Denning Committee whose 1947 Report advocated making divorce more accessible. The 1949 Legal Aid and Advice Act made divorce more affordable to the less wealthy, resulting in a further surge of applications. See Murray, The Woman's Hour.

29 The Times (18 June 1954), p. 13.

30 'A girl lies dying in the shadow of the gallows', News of the World (24 February 1952).

31 Arena Three 1:1 (January 1964), p. 3.

32 Hemel Hempstead Evening Echo (4 November 1969), p. 8.

33 NSA, HCC (C456), F1622–F1624, Angela Chilton; NSA, HCC (C456), F1328–F1330, Rene Sawyer.

34 'The loneliness of the unmarried woman', Medical News (30 August 1963).

35 Bristol Evening Post (2 December 1965), p. 15; Sunday Times colour supplement (12 September 1965), p. 21.

36 Mass Observation, An Enquiry into People's Homes: A Report, prepared by Mass Observation for the Advertising Service Guild (London: John Murray for the ASG, 1943); Central Housing Advisory Committee, Dudley Report: Design of Dwellings (London: HMSO, 1944).

37 Alison Ravetz, 'Housing the people', in Fyrth (ed.), Labour's Promised Land?, p. 149.

38 Webster, Imagining Home, p. 168. Michael Young and Peter Willmott found over 50 per cent of unmarried women – and men – lived with parents, while over half of the remainder lived with other relatives. See Young and Willmott, Family and Kinship in East London.

39 NSA, HCC (C456), F2087, Mabel Hills; NSA, HCC (C456), F1325, Mary Wilkins.

40 NSA, HCC (C456), F1328–F1330, Rene Sawyer; NSA, HCC (C456), F2483–F2487, Sandy Martin.

41 Arena Three 2:3 (March 1965), p. 3. See, also, Radclyffe Hall's literary exploration of this subject in her novel The Unlit Lamp (London: Cassell and Co., 1924).

42 See, for example, Martha Vicinus, Independent Women: Work and Community for Single Women, 1850–1920 (London: Virago, 1985).

43 The Soroptomists were a charitable organisation founded by a group of professional women in 1938.

44 YWCA Accommodation and Advisory Service and London Council for the Welfare of Women and Girls, Staying in London: Hostels and Accommodation in London for Girls and Women (1976/77).

45 Francis Richard Banks, The Penguin Guide to London (London: Penguin, 1958).

46 Vicinus, Independent Women.

47 Arena Three 1:1 (January 1964); William Barnes, A Century of Camden Housing (London: London Borough of Camden, Housing Dept., 1972). It is also noteworthy that Antony Grey, Secretary of the Homosexual Law Reform Society, lived on the same road. See NSA, HCC (C456), F2088, Diana Chapman.

48 Alison Ravetz, The Place of the Home: English Domestic Environments, 1914–2000 (London: E and FN Spon, 1995), p. 43. Matt Houlbrook offers an interesting

discussion of gay men's housing patterns in London in the mid-twentieth century in his *Queer London*, pp. 109–38.

49 Ravetz, *The Place of the Home*, p. 44.

50 Banks, *The Penguin Guide to London*, p. 55.

51 I draw this tentative conclusion from the concentration of suitable accommodation in this area, and the extremely high numbers of Hall Carpenter interviewees and their friends who were resident in West London in the 1950s and 1960s. See NSA, HCC (C456), F1328–F1330, Rene Sawyer; NSA, HCC (C456), F2158–F2163, Sharley McLean; NSA, HCC (C456), F2088, Diana Chapman; NSA, HCC (C456), F1918–F1924, Olive Ager; NSA, HCC (C456), F1359–F1360, Margaret Cranch.

52 See NSA, HCC (C456), F2109, Cynthia Reid. This group later broke away to form the lesbian social organisation Kenric – see Chapter 5.

53 Winner, 'Homosexuality in women', p. 219.

54 Caprio, *Female Homosexuality*, pp. 60–1; Eustace Chesser, *The Human Aspects of Sexual Deviation* (London: Jarrolds Publishers, 1971), p. 174.

55 Robert Aldrich, *The Killing of Sister George* (UK, 1969).

56 Mark Rydell, *The Fox* (US, 1968).

57 Commutator, 'Myth – or unpalatable fact'; *Arena Three* 2:10 (October 1965), p. 6.

58 NSA, HCC (C456), F2088, Diana Chapman.

59 NSA, HCC (C456), F2108, Julie Switsur; NSA, HCC (C456), F2109, Cynthia Reid.

60 NSA, HCC (C456), F2109, Cynthia Reid.

61 'Two women fined after "marriage"', Sheffield *Morning Telegraph* (1966), p. 7.

62 Arena Three 4:7 (July 1967), p. 2.

63 NSA, HCC (C456), F1326–F1327, Pat Arrowsmith.

64 NSA, HCC (C456), F1328–F1330, Rene Sawyer.

65 NSA, HCC (C456), F1328–F1330, Rene Sawyer.

66 NSA, HCC (C456), F1328–F1330, Rene Sawyer.

67 NSA, HCC (C456), F1326–F1327, Pat Arrowsmith.

68 Webster, *Imagining Home*, p. xvi; Hannah Gavron, *The Captive Wife: Conflicts of Housebound Mothers* (London: Routledge & Kegan Paul, 1966); Betty Friedan, *The Feminine Mystique* (London: Gollancz, 1963); Betty Jerman, *The Lively-Minded Women: The First Twenty Years of the National Housewives Register* (London: Heinemann, 1981).

69 Giles, 'A Home of One's Own', p. 240.

70 NSA, HCC (C456), F1326–F1327, Pat Arrowsmith.

71 NSA, HCC (C456), F2158–F2163, Sharley McLean.

72 For lesbian feminist critiques of butch/femme see Sheila Jeffreys, 'Butch and femme: Now and then', in Lesbian History Group (ed.), *Not a Passing Phase*; Blanche Wiesen Cook, '"Women alone stir my imagination": Lesbianism and the cultural tradition', *Signs* 4:4 (1979); Rich, *Compulsory Heterosexuality*.

73 Spain, *Why I'm Not a Millionaire*, pp. 133–5.

74 Nancy Spain, *A Funny Thing Happened on the Way* (London: Hutchinson, 1964).

75 *Arena Three* 1:7 (July 1964), p. 6.

76 Susanna Pinney (ed.), *I'll Stand by You: The Letters of Sylvia Townsend Warner and Valentine Ackland* (London: Pimlico, 1998), p. 386.

77 Pinney (ed.), *I'll Stand by You*, p. vii.

78 *Arena Three* 1:9 (September 1964), p. 13.

79 *Arena Three* 2:9 (September 1965), p. 10.

80 Chesser, *Sexual Behaviour*; Chesser, *Odd Man Out*.

81 Caprio, *Female Homosexuality*.

82 Magee, *One in Twenty*, ch. 15.

83 Chesser, *Odd Man Out*.

84 Chesser, *The Human Aspects of Sexual Deviation*, p. 163.

85 Magee, *One in Twenty*, p. 150.

86 Magee, *One in Twenty*, p. 157.

87 NSA, HCC (C456), F2082–F2083, Myrtle Soloman; NSA, HCC (C456), F2087, Mabel Hills.

88 NSA, HCC (C456), F2095–F2096, Rosanna Hibbert; NSA, HCC (C456), F2088, Diana Chapman.

89 NSA, HCC (C456), F1328–F1330, Rene Sawyer. This is very much in keeping with US accounts of butch identities, on which see Davis and Kennedy, *Boots of Leather, Slippers of Gold* and Sheila Jeffrey's (albeit critical) review of personal butch accounts in 'Butch and Femme: Now and then'.

90 NSA, HCC (C456), F1359–F1360, Margaret Cranch.

91 This increased press coverage was prompted both by a wider interest in homosexuality linked with the debates about legal reform and the Sexual Offences Act (1967) and by the emergence of lesbian organisations such as the Minorities Research Group/*Arena Three* and Kenric which made lesbian communities more accessible to the media.

92 Magee, *One in Twenty*, p. 170.

93 Magee, *One in Twenty*, p. 171.

94 NSA, HCC (C456), F1328–F1330, Rene Sawyer.

95 *Arena Three* 1:12 (December 1964), p. 5.

96 NSA, HCC (C456), F2088, Diana Chapman.

97 NSA, HCC (C456), F2483–F2487, Sandy Martin; NSA, HCC (C456), F2088, Diana Chapman.

4

The Gateways club and the emergence of a post-war lesbian subculture

A vibrant lesbian bar culture emerged alongside gay male subcultures in London and other British towns and cities in the years before the Second World War and played an important role in the development of collective lesbian identities in the post-war period. However, while gay male subcultures have become the focus of considerable scholarly attention in recent years, no comparable work has examined the significance of commercial subcultures in histories of female homosexuality in the UK, despite a significant body of lesbian oral history collections, as well as Jill Gardiner's more recent oral history of the Gateways nightclub, having testified to their existence.[1] The reasons for this neglect can be traced to historical tensions within the lesbian bar community itself, centring on conflicting political agendas in the 1960s and early 1970s. Despite links with a broader culture of public leisure, the lesbian bar community of the immediate post-war decades remained largely enclosed and introspective, developing a network of lesbian sociability which could address the pressing issue of isolation faced by its members. This concern with enabling interpersonal connections reflected the contemporary preoccupations of homosexual politics in the era of the Wolfenden reforms.[2] However, by the late 1960s and early 1970s, it was coming into conflict with a feminist and lesbian and gay political agenda, which began to lay claim to broader rights of citizenship in the public sphere and came to regard the earlier bar subcultures not as early networks forging a lesbian community, but as apolitical and passive victims of oppression. The subsequent dominance of lesbian and gay history by political models rooted in the lesbian and gay politics of the 1970s has meant that this perspective has proved remarkably durable, and the significance of the post-war subculture in histories of lesbian socialising has not been recognised. If this omission is to be more clearly understood, the development of this arena of lesbian sociability must be explored and the origins of the conflicts which have shaped our understanding of the post-war bar culture considered.

The lesbian bar culture evolved over three broad stages of development, beginning with the presence of lesbians as part of a wider metropolitan social scene in the inter-war years. The second stage was marked by the gradual emergence, in the decade immediately after the Second World War, of a distinct lesbian subculture centring on a small number of bars and clubs. In his work on gay male subcultures in the eighteenth century, Rictor Norton has defined a subculture as:

> a body of social institutions and patterns of behaviour shared by a group of people who identify themselves as part of that group, who have several 'significant factors' in common, and who are viewed as 'deviant' by those in the mainstream of a larger, enclosing culture. Such subcultures usually have the following major characteristics: (1) social gatherings attended exclusively by members sharing the 'significant factor'; (2) a network of communication between members which is not generally recognised by the larger society; (3) specialised vocabulary or slang, used to reinforce a sense of membership in the group or to establish contact secretly; (4) self-identification with other members in the group, reinforced by common patterns of behaviour which distinguish the members from society at large, and (5) a self-protective community of shared sympathy caused by being ostracised by society for being 'different'.[3]

There is evidence that lesbian bar cultures were emerging in a number of urban areas across the UK in this period, with lesbians frequenting the Spotted Dog and Pigott's Bar, as well as the Variety Club and Queen of Clubs in Brighton and the New Union pub in Manchester.[4] However, this chapter will focus on the metropolitan lesbian scene in London and the Gateways nightclub in particular, where the collective identity of a lesbian subculture is more apparent and through which the intergenerational conflicts with the lesbian and gay political groups of the 1960s and 70s can be more clearly traced. These intergenerational conflicts arguably represented a third stage in the development of the lesbian bar culture, indicating a gradual opening up of the subculture to wider cultural influences and a consequent shift in the collective aims and identity of the group.

Contemporary accounts of London's nightlife in the first half of the twentieth century suggest that lesbians were integrated into the wider metropolitan social scene of the 1920s. Bohemian clubs such as Elsa Lanchester's Cave of Harmony club, the Orange Tree and the Ham Bone attracted a

variety of unconventional individuals, including artists, political radicals
and writers, as well as wealthy 'bohemian' lesbians such as Radclyffe Hall.[5]
The streets of Soho and the West End were the focus of this inter-war
culture, both for upper-class lesbians and the less well-off. Peter Ackroyd
has traced the area's 'reputation for heterogeneity and freedom' back to
the seventeenth century, when a large resident French population transformed the area into a locus for French and 'artistic' culture, dominated
by cheap cafes and restaurants. By the eighteenth century, it was notorious
for courtesans, establishing an association with transgressive sexuality
which continued into the twentieth century.[6] Frank Mort has claimed:

> In the years before 1914 Soho had become an established centre for
> sections of the cultural and artistic avant-garde … In the inter-war years
> Soho's population was augmented by the influx of new social actors,
> marked by sexual as well as cultural dissidence. Homosexual men began to
> patronise the Golden Lion pub on Dean Street in the 1920s, as the district
> became part of a network of homosexuality adjacent to the theatre world of
> Leicester Square.[7]

Contemporary travel guides reinforced this picture of Soho as both a
centre of entertainment and a locus of illicit pleasures.[8] By day, prostitutes,
homosexuals and lesbians mingled in the cafés and restaurants of this area.

Ellen, a West End dancer and lesbian, remembered the first-floor
restaurant of the Coventry Street Corner House at Piccadilly Circus as a
popular hangout before the Second World War. A central location on the
male homosexual scene in the 1920s and 30s, the restaurant was also
populated by lesbians:

> We used to go to the 'Lily Pond' – on the first floor of the Coventry Street
> Corner House at Piccadilly Circus, named because all the 'boys' used to go
> for afternoon tea on a Sunday, and the 'girls' started to get in – it was well
> known. It was a sight to come and see in London, the 'Lily Pond' on a
> Sunday afternoon. We'd all meet there in our Sunday best. The girls were
> very butch. The butch ones were butch. From there we'd go back to
> someone's flat.[9]

Pat James visited the Coffee Ann, a bohemian place in one of the back
streets around Tottenham Court Road, in the 1930s, and recalled the
lesbians mingling with a more diverse clientele: 'It was a very arty sort of
place. People went in, but they weren't homosexual or lesbian necessarily
– they were arty types mostly, or seemed to be'.[10] At night, lesbians
merged with the clientele of the nightclubs and bars which shaped
the night-time economy of the West End. Contemporary accounts portray
a constantly shifting landscape, made up of unregistered clubs and

unlicensed bars, 'clip' or strip joints and gambling dens. Robert Fabian takes his reader on an imaginary tour of these streets:

> Two or three more paces – and there is a glint of light from a cellar that tonight has thick curtains, and last night was bare. Another club that has sprung up, as a mushroom or a spotted purple toadstool might spring up suddenly in the middle of a woodland path where yesterday was a bare patch of moss. The West End is constantly changing – its faces and particularly its clubs, registered or unregistered, wink in and out like the lights of fireflies.[11]

The fantastical prose illustrates the magical, fairy-tale quality which many of its inhabitants and frequenters ascribed to this district.

Police files, however, offer a different picture, framing their accounts of attempts to control West End clubs within the language of moral outrage. One such club was the Caravan Club, at 81 Endell Street. An unregistered club run by a man known to the police as 'Iron Foot Jack', it first came to their attention in July 1934. In August, local residents complained to the Police Commissioner that, 'At the above address there is the "Caravan" Club: only frequented by sexual perverts, lesbians and sodomites. Its [sic] absolutely a sink of iniquity.' On the 25th of the same month, local police conducted an undercover raid on the premises, and found '[m]en … dancing with men and women with women'.[12] Contemporary accounts suggest that lesbians and homosexual men mingled with a wider population of prostitutes, drug dealers and criminals in this underworld. Zoe Progl, in her memoir of her life as a thief and gangster's moll in the West End, was drawn into this world during the war through Maxie's café in Gerrard Street:

> Maxie's café in Gerrard Street lured me. I was fascinated by the tough and obviously wealthy customers who were always lazing about there and who stared admiringly at me as they gave wolf whistles when I walked in. I was to discover later that this strange sleazy joint was the rendezvous of every type of villain and thug, including thieves, deserters, ponces, pimps, prostitutes, drug addicts, lesbians and homosexuals.[13]

Matt Houlbrook has argued that the 'craze for night-clubs and dance halls developed in response to the restrictions placed on public sociability by the DORA regulations of the First World War'.[14] The members-only club was thus initially a way of avoiding the constraints of licensing laws. While proprietors of public houses, restaurants and hotels were required, under the Licensing Act 1904, to apply to the local Magistrates' Court for an annually renewable licence, providing detailed information on the name and address of the owner and licensee and the address and plans of the

premises, club proprietors were not subject to such legislation. Due to a
legal loophole, a proprietor, regardless of character or criminal record,
was able to register a club, with the right to sell drink to its members, in
any premises. The registration process involved simply notifying the Clerk
to the Justices of the Petty Sessions of the clubs' existence, paying five
shillings, and supplying the title, address, rules and membership numbers
of the club. No license was required for the sale of alcoholic drinks, or for
any activity such as dancing or gambling carried out on the premises and
such clubs largely eluded regulation. Public-house proprietors could face
common-law charges of 'keeping a disorderly house' and the police
sought to regulate venues frequented by homosexuals by conducting
regular raids on premises, taking the names and addresses of patrons to
discourage them from returning and, from the late 1930s onwards, target-
ing proprietors rather than individual patrons in an attempt to encourage
self-policing. However, although it was possible for the Court of Summary
Justice to strike off a club for misconduct, such as selling liquor to non-
members in a registered club, evidence was difficult to compile, as the
police could only enter the premises with a search warrant obtained from
a magistrate, or as members.[15] As Houlbrook argues, police interest in
clubs appears to have been strictly limited; attempts at control focused
predominantly on 'the backstreet cafes and bars where queans mingled
with prostitutes, "criminals," and recent immigrants', while 'clubs were
relatively secure – almost invisible'.[16]

From the 1940s onward, police accounts provide further evidence of a
visible lesbian presence in the West End. Policewomen stationed at West
End Central Station regularly trawled the coffee bars and basement clubs
of the district searching for run-away girls and those who had absconded
from Approved Schools, as well as participating in night-time raids on
unregistered clubs suspected of serving alcohol without a license. Their
accounts suggest that lesbians occupied the same urban space as prostitutes and male homosexuals. Stella Condor, a policewoman in the West
End between 1951 and 1956, described her encounter with lesbians on
her patch:

> I had not been at West End Central Police Station long before I had pointed
> out to me certain notorious lesbians who were in the habit of frequenting
> snack-bars in the hope of finding a 'pick-up'. It was impossible to feel
> anything but disgust for these creatures. It is difficult for most of us to
> understand how anyone can fall in love with someone of the same sex; but
> we can, at least, sympathize with them. However, it was not love but
> depravity that caused these young women to congregate in Piccadilly
> Circus.[17]

WPC Condor suggests that the sphere of the lesbian and the prostitute often overlapped and merged in a more generalised world of sexual and moral depravity on the streets of the West End. The all-night ladies lavatory, she explains, was often the scene of early-morning quarrels between prostitutes over women, disagreements which often degenerated into profanities and blows. The coffee stalls near Tottenham Court Road revealed a further manifestation of this sexual deviance, where the girls '"went lesbian" as they called it, for the thrill, and at one time it was quite a cult among the teenagers who used to hang about the low-class cafés'.[8]

Such accounts point to a shift in the location of lesbians within the metropolitan leisure culture of the interwar years. Whereas the lesbian presence was most visibly located alongside male homosexuals and artists within the wealthy bohemian scene in the 1920s, by the 1930s and 1940s, a new lesbian culture was emerging in the West End. In the years leading up to and immediately after the Second World War, a recognisably lesbian presence can be detected in an array of locations across the metropolitan scene, from unregistered night-clubs and illegal drinking dens to coffee bars and the street. This proliferation of arenas saw lesbians sharing space on the social margins with prostitutes, immigrants and the criminal underworld, as well as male homosexuals.

In the aftermath of the Second World War, however, a more significant shift was beginning to take place, with the gradual emergence of a more coherent and physically discrete lesbian space distinct from the metropolitan social scene of the West End. The precise causes of this development are difficult to pinpoint, but the social upheavals of wartime may have been a contributory factor, forcing many women to leave their home town and migrate to London and elsewhere for directed work and precipitating a more fundamental change in attitudes toward women's access to public spaces and alcohol. Distance from the constraints of family and local community, and the disposable income which regular war work often provided, afforded young women greater freedom than they had enjoyed before the war. Williams and Blake argue that 'Whereas at one time drinking was principally an activity for men, during the war, while in the services or the factories, women acquired the habit'.[19] Rowntree and Lavers support this claim in their 1951 survey of leisure practices. While the prejudice against women's presence in some public houses remained, they suggest that a post-war wave of improvements in public-house amenities, offering greater comfort and more tasteful décor, encouraged 'respectable' women to enter them. Moreover, they identify the new style of bars which were appearing in urban areas as places that were frequented by groups of women in much the same way as men.[20] Such changes in circumstance coincided with an expansion in urban consumer culture centred on bars, nightclubs and dance halls and contributed to the specific development of the West End as a space of sexual licence, which had begun to take place from the 1930s onward.[21] It was this shift in wider public attitudes that enabled the emergence in the post-war years of a distinct lesbian subculture located in predominantly 'lesbian' bars and clubs.

While the lesbian presence in the broader leisure culture of the West End was still discernible after the Second World War, the most well-known lesbian venues of the post-war years were located farther out in the bedsitter lands and rooming districts of Kensington and Ladbroke Grove. In Notting Hill Gate, lesbians were regular customers at The Champion pub on the corner of Wellington Terrace and Bayswater Road. In the 1960s, Maureen Duffy and her friends used to meet at The Cricketers pub in Battersea, on the corner of Battersea Park Road and Albert Bridge Road. The two most popular lesbian clubs of the 1950s and 60s were also located in West London: the Robin Hood club on Inverness Terrace in Bayswater, and the Gateways on Bramerton Street, just off the Kings Road in Chelsea.[23] It was in these venues, and in the Gateways in particular, that a newly emerging lesbian subculture was located. Dominated by a coherent group of core members, this subculture possessed a network of communication; a unique collective style and codes of behaviour used to distinguish its members and regulate relations within the community; and a 'shared sympathy' caused by a sense of exclusion from mainstream ideals of heterosexual femininity.

The location of these popular lesbian haunts is clearly significant. Much of the literature on lesbian and gay bar communities has focused on their physical marginalization, arguing that gay bars tend to be found in the poorer, outlying areas of the city. Weightman has argued that 'gay bars tend to locate in what might be considered undesirable areas', an assessment supported by US histories of lesbian bar communities in the 1950s.[24] Certainly the social milieu of these areas may have facilitated the emergence of a lesbian bar subculture. The borough of Kensington and Chelsea, although affluent, possessed a well-established association with the artistic avant-garde, while the high proportion of private rental property, bedsits and hostels in neighbouring parts of West London produced a population characterised by transience and often low-paid employment. New immigrant communities, unwelcome in other residential districts of London, were similarly drawn to this area by housing needs, contributing to the locality's transient and socially marginal character.[25] However, Houlbrook has questioned this focus on marginality, maintaining that historical geographies of sexuality should, like recent work on queer subcultures, 'demonstrat[e] the ways in which gay men did not perceive themselves as anonymous, marginal, or immoral but as a recognizable, central, and positive presence in urban life'.[26] It is certainly helpful in this context to emphasise the significance of lesbian venues' location, not as distant from the mainstream entertainment environs of the West End, but as close to the lesbian-friendly residential districts of Kensington, Notting Hill Gate and Ladbroke Grove.[27]

The Gateways was undoubtedly the best-known and longest-running lesbian club in London in the 1950s and 60s, reflecting many of the characteristic trends in the post-war lesbian subculture, and as such is worth more detailed consideration. Having first opened in the 1930s, it was owned until 1943 by a retired Colonel who served tea and coffee in the afternoon and drinks in the evening, accompanied by dancing to a three-piece orchestra. Clientele described the Gateways as a predominantly bohemian club before the war, welcoming lesbians as part of this wider culture as in the artistic metropolitan scene in Soho in the same period. In the late 1930s, the clientele was relatively quiet, with 'all the pairs sitting sedately about'.[28] Maureen Duffy, writing in 1966 about Gateways before the war, claimed: 'The older members regret it, remembering the panache of white flannels and blazers, with nostalgia for the days when to be different was to be doubly different.'[29] The bohemian atmosphere of the club continued into the late 1940s, by which time the Colonel had sold it to a new owner, Ted Ware.[30] Throughout the 1940s and 50s, the club hosted a mixed and rowdier clientele, including artists, prostitutes and male and female homosexuals, for whom black jazz pianists provided entertainment at the grand piano. By the 1960s, although the Gateways continued to attract Chelsea fashion designers and celebrities such as Diana Dors, it had emerged as an almost exclusively lesbian club.[31] The Gateways was increasingly managed by Gina, Ted Ware's wife since 1953, in partnership with an American ex-air-force woman, Smithy, and many regulars pointed to the presumed lesbian relationship between Gina and Smithy as an explanation for the club's increasingly lesbian identity. However, it seems more probable that the character of the club simply evolved, facilitated by the tolerance of both Ted and Gina Ware and given a final impetus with the retirement of Ted Ware, when his absence caused many of his male acquaintances to stop visiting the club.

The club itself was located in a basement and patrons entered through the famous green door in the side of the building, walking down a flight of stairs to enter the club proper. Visitors had to pass the searching glance of Gina Ware, the 'madam of the Gateways': regulars maintain that it was

Gina's practice to seat herself at the foot of the stairs in order to appraise those who entered the club. Margaret Cranch claimed that 'Gina would look you up and down when you walked in, to see if you were a respectable enough person for the Gateways, and to see if she liked the look of you', an attempt at self-policing which may have been prompted by the threat of police raids on unruly premises.[32] The club was dark, smoky and relatively small – with a capacity of only two hundred, it was regularly packed on Friday and Saturday nights. Sandy Martin described the interior of the club as it looked when she went in the mid-1960s:

> It was a fairly largish room, basement room, or cellar really, which had been converted and the walls were completely covered with murals, paintings of, there were peoples' faces, it was like a painted collage, if you like of peoples' faces and different scenes, in the Gateways. Different people who'd been to the Gateways, and the members. All the members, they would all be portrayed all around the walls, friends of Gina and Smithy's, and – Gina was married as well, and she was married to this guy called Ted … and his portrait was up there. There was a big portrait of Ted, that's right, on the wall, but I just loved it. It was very dark. The paint, all the paint in this mural was very very dark: dark browns and reds. Very very dark. And it was dimly lit.[33]

Cubicles with pews to sit on lined the left-hand wall of the club, so that friends could withdraw there to have private conversations, while large chairs, made out of barrels, were arranged around an open fire for more general socialising. In the centre was a small dance floor, which drew the fascinated attention of journalist Bryan Magee when he visited the club in the mid-1960s. The dancing he observed was: 'overtly sexual, though no more so than is normal in public places between heterosexual couples. Some clung to each other, kissed each other, fondled each other, stroked each other as they danced. Others throbbed erotically in twists and shakes.'[34]

The increasing dominance of the lesbian clientele in the 1950s and 60s was reinforced by a number of restrictions on access to the club. The Gateways was a members-only club throughout the 1950s and 60s and prospective patrons had to apply for membership, in writing, forty-eight hours in advance of their visit. The annual cost of membership was low, being only ten shillings in 1966, but members had to show their cards in order to enter the club and non-members were only admitted if a member signed them in.[35] Although the capacity of the club was only two hundred, Gateways had thousands of members in 1966.[36] Oral testimonies demonstrate that women who lived in the rural and suburban counties surrounding London – notably Essex and the Home Counties – were in the habit of travelling into the metropolis in order to participate in this subculture, swelling the numbers at the weekends. Others came from further afield. Journalist Clare Marc Wallace visited a lesbian night-club recognisable as the Gateways in 1966 with a friend. Asking a young femme called Greta if she had travelled far to get to the club, she was told:

> 'Well quite a way,' Greta said. 'We came up for this weekend in London from Devon. Do you see that group over there?' … 'They come up from Southampton. Jill is the girl in drag; she works on a farm during the week. And those two over there – they come down from Durham every Friday.'[37]

An interdependent relationship similarly existed between lesbian bars and clubs in the capital and seaside resorts such as Brighton. One lesbian inter-viewee who lived in London in the mid-1960s described outings she went on to Brighton with a group of friends from the Gateways, while, accord-ing to one regular at the Robin Hood, the club management there organ-ised occasional coach trips out of London:

> Every now and again the people who ran the Robin Hood in London would have a coach party and they'd take us, the favourite place of course was Brighton because that was the gay Mecca, and we'd do a tour of all the clubs, get absolutely paralytic. They'd pick you up at a certain point in London, in this coach with crates of God knows what went on.[38]

Word-of-mouth recommendations were important in communicating the existence of clubs such as the Gateways and the Robin Hood, and in attracting clientele. Barbara Weightman commented in 1980 that 'Gay bars incorporate and reflect certain characteristics of the gay community: secrecy and stigmatization. They do not accommodate the eyes of outsiders, they have low imageability, and they can be truly known only from within.'[39] This lack of visibility was matched by an equal physical obscurity. Many of the bars were located in inaccessible and poorly iden-tified places, rendering them difficult to find either by outsiders or by lesbians. The Robin Hood club, on Inverness Terrace in Bayswater, was located on what seems to have been a quiet side street, sandwiched between small hotels and residential housing.[40] The Gateways was simi-larly situated in a smaller street away from the activity of the Kings Road in Chelsea. Diana Chapman's story of her attempts to find the club after the war is not untypical:

> I was living in Chelsea, and I knew that the Gateways existed but I didn't know where it was, and I couldn't find out where it was. Part of me was attracted by the idea, and the other half was repelled. But I used to walk up

and down the King's Road looking for tall, handsome women with cropped hair …

So I used to trot up and down the King's Road, looking. What I was hoping to see was a whole stream of Dora Biggs [a masculine woman she had known as a child] look-alikes going down into what I assumed would be the entrance of the Gateways. I didn't know where it was, it wasn't in the 'phone book and I had nobody to ask.[41]

The development of lesbian social networks was thus vital in helping to spread the news of this emerging subculture, and, for many women, the only means of locating lesbian clubs was to be told of them and their whereabouts by another lesbian. Venues were not listed in any public forum until the late 1960s, partly through a fear of drawing hostile attention to themselves, but also due to the reluctance of most major newspapers to carry advertisements which alluded to homosexual women.[42] Most women, therefore, learnt of the lesbian subculture through friends or acquaintances. Rene Sawyer found out about the existence of lesbian clubs when she was working at Marks and Spencer in the early 1960s. A woman who used to come in regularly invited her to the Robin Hood:

And she said, 'Here, why don't you come down to Robin Hood one night'. And I said, 'Oh, what's that?' in all my ignorance. So she said, 'Oh, you know, all us girls, we're all down there together. You know, it'll be nice, you know, music, and we can have a drink' and all this … I thought, 'oh, yes, take a chance, do this'. So I get on the back of her Lambretta – you didn't have to wear a crash helmet in those days – and off we tore down to this club one evening.[43]

For Pat Arrowsmith, it was during a term in prison that she was first introduced to the emerging subculture. Several of the lesbians in prison told her of the existence of clubs such as the Robin Hood, and when she was released she visited the club to see what it was like: she found 'a slightly wicked atmosphere, all a bit underground'.[44] For Pat, this atmosphere was summed up in a story she had been told by a prison warden at Holloway of how, arriving at the Gateways one night, she had found a row of her ex-charges lined up in front of the bar.

From the late 1950s, psychiatrists and counsellors also apparently performed an important role in providing individual women with information about the subculture. Cynthia Reid, who visited a number of psychiatrists after the break-up of her first lesbian relationship in the mid-1950s, received a range of information about the lesbian subculture. The first psychiatrist she consulted advised her: 'I've heard that people like that meet down at the Pier Hotel in Chelsea. You could try standing out there one night.' Dispirited by this, Reid asked to swap psychiatrists.

This second doctor introduced Reid to another lesbian patient who took her to Gateways and a number of other lesbian clubs.[45] Jean White recalled a similar experience when she consulted a counsellor recommended by the editor of the lesbian magazine, *Arena Three*. The counsellor introduced her to some other women, who took her to the Rehearsal club on Archer Street.[46] Such accounts suggest that medical professionals were not only in a position to acquire information about the lesbian subculture from their patients, but that they were frequently willing to pass it on to other women patients. However, this was clearly not always the case. Julie Switsur, whose psychiatrist also informed her of the existence of lesbian bars, refused to give her more precise information, observing that they were 'quite rough', and that he 'didn't want to upset her'.[47]

Despite Gina Ware's attempts to regulate admission to, as well as behaviour within, the club, the Gateways clearly remained part of a broader metropolitan subculture. Zoe Progl, gangster's moll and habituée of the Soho club scene, was surprised to find herself at the Gateways one night:

> In this mood I was delighted to get a phone call from my ex-WRAC friend, Hazel. The coloured man she was living with had gone to Paris to buy some weed … and she was on the loose. Some kind of rave was planned that night for a few specially chosen people and Hazel invited me to go along. I jumped at the opportunity.
>
> Feeling ultra-glamorous in the most expensive dress Gerry had bought for me, I headed with Hazel for a club in Chelsea, the place where the crowd were to meet and have a few drinks before going on to the party. At first glance, it seemed to be a normal club, with couples either sitting at tables, standing around or dancing, but Hazel, who came in late, put me in the picture. 'We're normal compared with this lot', she whispered. 'When they get stoked up you'll see what I mean'.
>
> After going to the ladies' and seeing three men's jackets hanging up, it dawned on me that the club was no ordinary den and I found myself trying to distinguish males from females.[48]

Progl's account suggests a reluctant intermingling of the lesbian subculture with a wider criminal and drug-oriented underworld. The dominance of the lesbian crowd within Gateways by the 1960s is also clear, however. Progl and her friend may not have found the manifestations of lesbianism to their liking, but they shared their views discreetly, in whispers.

Throughout the 1950s and 60s, the core of the Gateways clientele was a tight-knit community of a few hundred regulars. Maureen Duffy claimed in 1966 that:

The hard core live in London but all have their favourite nights. Friday and Sunday are usually full house with Saturday an unbelievable crush. Thursday and Wednesday have their following and a few people drop in at lunchtime for a quiet drink and talk.[49]

Many frequented the club on an almost nightly basis, to the extent that the Gateways became the centre of information sharing and communication in the lesbian community. Angela Chilton, who frequented the club in the late 1960s and early 1970s, claimed:

But it was the thing that everybody would appear one of those three nights [Fridays, Saturdays and Wednesdays] in the Gateways, so if you really wanted to see somebody and they weren't on the phone ... you sent somebody down the club to pounce on them and say 'phone us' or 'meet us at such and such a time'.[50]

The type of lesbian identity expressed in these early post-war lesbian clubs was constrained by the desire for a distinct, collective identity and the need to structure this small, closed community. Butch/femme identities strictly defined codes of behaviour and dress and, in the immediate postwar decades, when the Gateways dominated the London lesbian scene, a butch or femme identity was the only option available to women wishing to be accepted in the bar subculture.[51] Pat James claimed that: 'There was role-playing and that was the way it was. If you weren't one way or the other, if you didn't conform, they derided you for it and said you didn't know what you were.'[52] Dick Hebdige has identified the appropriation of a distinctive style to signify deviance as a fundamental component of postwar subcultures and physical image was undoubtedly central to the presentation of butch/femme culture.[53] While butch lesbians were expected to dress in suits with ties, femme lesbians wore dresses or skirts and carried handbags. Rene Sawyer, a butch lesbian in the 1950s, explained the dress code:

Now if you were a butch – one butch always knew another butch because it was the mirror image of yourself. It would be shirts or casual sweaters; trousers; and jackets. That would be the butch. And the femme always but always wore skirts, blouses, high-heeled shoes. Always carried a black patent leather handbag – or it needn't be black patent, but it was definitely a handbag – earrings, make-up. Butches never wore make-up. Femmes always wore make-up. So you never had any problem in those days because you always knew who to ask for a dance.[54]

Some butch lesbian interviewees had experienced oppression as a result of their style, describing hostile encounters with strangers when out in public. Margaret Cranch described being stared at when travelling to the

Gateways on the London Underground and 'having to shout back'. Cranch interpreted these incidents politically, commenting that she saw her presentation of a butch identity as 'doing [her] bit for the lesbian cause'.[55] However, Rene Sawyer interpreted similar situations very differently:

> If you went anywhere, if you were going to a gay club, and they were always up in the Bayswater area, you always went incognito: the collar turned up, dark glasses on, so that people wouldn't know who you were when you were travelling on the underground. It was all very secretive: nothing open about it at all.[56]

For Sawyer, her butch identity played a crucial role in her interaction with the lesbian community of which she was a member: it was not an attempt explicitly to declare a lesbian identity to a hostile wider culture. As Sawyer's initial description suggests, the need to identify individual lesbians as either butch or femme, rather than the desire to make a statement of resistance to mainstream culture, was the primary function of these dress codes. The rules governing personal presentation were fundamentally important so that, in a group environment, 'one butch always knew another butch because it was the mirror image of [her]self'. Sandy Martin, a regular at the Gateways and the Robin Hood in the 1960s, supports this interpretation in her account:

> The extremes in dress were fascinating, I mean some of the more butch women. I mean, navy blue suits, immaculate white shirts, you know, ties with a Windsor knot. Short cropped haircuts. I mean some of the women could really pass as men ... And I can remember, at the Robin Hood, sometimes, you know I can remember a particular couple – I can't remember their names now: the butch was Stella, I can't remember the femme's name – and Stella had an evening suit on, and her girlfriend had some sort of really, almost evening dress number on. I mean real, total opposite.[57]

Her emphasis on the dress codes as 'extremes' and 'total opposites' indicates the importance of visual recognition in distinguishing between the two identities.

Historiographical debates regarding the significance and role of butch/femme identities in lesbian culture have tended to focus on this visual aspect of butch/femme identity.[58] The often heated discussions have been broadly split along feminist and anti- or non-feminist lines. Thus lesbian feminist historians such as Sheila Jeffreys have defined butch/femme identities as 'role-playing': an imitation of heteropatriarchal gender divisions which constitute the 'male' as superior to, and more powerful than, the 'female'. Passionate defenders of butch/femme culture, including the US historian and writer Joan Nestle, have represented butch/femme identities as uniquely lesbian identities, located within a naturalised sense of the 'essence' of lesbianism. Alternatively, recent theorists, Sherrie Inness and Michele E. Lloyd, drawing on Judith Butler's notion of gender as performative, argue that 'it is apparent, after discussing the butch's masculine clothing, image, and attitude, that the butch must repeatedly present/create herself as butch in order to be butch'.[59] Many lesbian oral history narrators construct their narratives of butch-ness in these terms as a performance. Margaret Cranch claimed that: 'In those days you either had to be butch or femme – I mean I'm glad it's not like that these days – but it was decided, probably by myself and others as well, that I was definitely butch.'[60] For Cranch, adopting a butch persona was a conscious decision, made in collaboration with lesbian friends. She goes on to describe the creation of her butch identity, a process involving the purchase of shirts and a tie from Marks and Spencer and a suit from the Littlewoods catalogue. Cranch drew on a number of models in the construction of her butch identity, which included the lesbian central character, Stephen, in Radclyffe Hall's novel *The Well of Loneliness*, combined with her understanding of the behaviour of men. She locates her engagement in fights and the exhibition of aggression within this narrative of performing masculinity. Sandy Martin echoes this construction of butch identity as a performance of masculinity in her account. For her the performance is a collective process, in which audience expectation plays a crucial role:

> Yes, [being butch] also meant you had to portray a bit of a tough image as well. You know, other lesbians – especially the more butch ones – actually expected you to be quite tough. They didn't like it if you were a bit soft, they didn't like it.[61]

While it is possible to explore the construction of butch identities in the post-war bar culture through a variety of historical sources, the meanings ascribed to femme lesbian identity are much less accessible. The historical devaluation of the feminine has frequently been noted by feminist historians and the elision of the 'femme' within the 'butch' in butch/femme can in part be recognised as an aspect of this wider historical phenomenon. However, the prioritisation of essentialist models of sexual identity by the lesbian and gay political movements of the 1970s would also appear to have favoured the historical recuperation of a butch identity at the expense of the femme. While women who assumed a butch lesbian identity in the post-war bar culture tended to regard their lesbianism as a 'natural' or essential identity, femme lesbians may have been disposed toward presenting a range of sexual identities in different locations and at different stages in the life-cycle, often combining a

femme lesbian identity with that of a heterosexual married woman or a
non-sexual single woman. This fluid approach to sexual identity has posed
difficulties of identification for oral historians, with the result that femme
lesbians are rarely present in a sample of interviewees. It is, however,
possible to gain some understanding of femme identity by exploring the
butch/femme behavioural codes, which shaped interaction between individual lesbians in the club environment, and it is perhaps this aspect of
butch/femme which provides the key to its function in the subculture.

Dancing to music, provided either by a three-piece orchestra or band
in the 1940s and 50s, or by a juke box in the 1960s, was the primary form
of entertainment in most lesbian clubs. However, strict codes of behaviour
structured who might dance with whom, so that it was not considered
acceptable for two femme or two butch lesbians to dance together. Rene
Sawyer, a butch, explained that 'you never danced with another butch. You
might bump into 'em on the floor when you were dancing, but you never
actually danced with them because, I mean, that would be like two sexes
together. It would be like homosexuals and heterosexuals all in one go.'[62]
Sawyer's inability to articulate specifically why it would be inappropriate
for two butch lesbians to dance with each other suggests that she had
rarely had cause to question the reasoning behind this convention.
However, her use of examples such as 'like two sexes' and 'like homosexual and heterosexual', as comparisons, suggests that she felt such
behaviour would breach an important distinction between friendship and
sexual attraction. In a small community constructed around same-sex
desire, butch/femme established boundaries defining who was sexually
available to whom, performing a similar organisational function to that
provided by notions of gender in mainstream society. Thus, in a subculture where sexual relationships between a butch and a femme were
regarded as the norm, a butch dancing with another butch would indicate
'queer' sexual attraction. Further conventions governed interaction
between butch and femme lesbians on the dance floor. Angela Chilton
explained that, 'if one of the other butches wanted to dance with somebody else's femme, they had to ask the butch, and it was up to the butch
whether her femme danced or not'.[63] Many butch lesbian narrators
recalled being involved in fights with other butches when this code
governing butch/femme relations had been perceived to be breached,
suggesting that it was an important means of regulating relationships
within the community.[64]

While butch/femme codes performed an important function in defining appropriate behaviour within the community, lesbian accounts
suggest that they were equally significant in reinforcing the sense of the

subculture as a tight-knit community. Familiarity with butch/femme culture offered a means of demonstrating inclusion within the group, while outsiders were excluded by their lack of knowledge of the subcultural norms. Sandy Martin, a regular at the Gateways in the 1960s, thus described the club as 'just wonderful', representing the subculture as a supportive, homogeneous environment.[65] Rene Sawyer also described her first visit to the Robin Hood club in this way:

> Well, it was an eye-opener for me, I can tell you. It was all these women all like me. All wearing trousers and shirts and oh, this was wonderful. It just opened up a whole new thing.[66]

Sawyer represents the moment of entering the club as a positive experience, in which the encounter with other lesbians helped to affirm her identity. For Margaret Cranch, this sense of a lesbian subculture as a community was dependent upon the specific environment: while she felt at home in the Robin Hood club, she was less comfortable in the Gateways:

> We went to the Robin Hood Club, which was an easier type club I always felt than the Gateways. It was more relaxed and people weren't such posers down there. It was quite a nice club. People were more friendly. If you were a new person going into the Robin Hood Club, people behind the bar would actually talk to you a lot more and introduce you to other people, and that didn't seem to happen at the Gateways. It was very cut and dry down there and it was very cliquey. I was never really in with the clique of the Gateways.[67]

Margaret Cranch's comment that she 'was never really in with the clique of the Gateways', suggests that each club possessed a distinct community of regulars, with its own sense of collective identity. While behavioural codes such as butch/femme were apparently widespread throughout the subculture, membership of one club and its community did not necessarily imply familiarity with all.

Although regulars on the London scene described the lesbian bar communities as affirmative and familiar, other women emphasised a sense of alienation from the subculture. Historiographical accounts of the US lesbian bar culture in this period have focused on class as the important distinguishing feature of different lesbian communities, constructing the bar community as working class, in contrast to a more discreet middle-class lesbian community. In her analysis of middle-class lesbians' narratives of bar life in Colorado Springs, Katie Gilmartin argued that the identities projected within the bar communities posed a challenge to middle-class lesbian identity. For middle-class women, fear of bar raids

and exposure as a lesbian, as well as the presentation of publicly identifiable lesbian images such as butch/femme identities, rendered encounters
with the bar culture uncomfortable experiences. However, Gilmartin
found that, while such practical considerations shaped middle-class
lesbians' response to bar culture, their accounts of bar communities were
expressed less pragmatically:

> This accounting of the costs and benefits of discretion is misleading,
> however; P. J. was never so dryly analytical about decisions as whether to be
> out of the closet and where to socialize. While cognizant of the risks to her
> class status, she lived her life not according to an evaluation of these risks,
> but according to the attitudes, expectations, and mores of that class. When
> P. J. spoke about how she lived her life, she spoke about what 'type of
> people' she and her friends were, and what 'type of people' they were not.[68]

This narrative of 'not belonging' was occasionally employed as a middle-
class reaction to the lesbian bars and clubs in the UK. In 1965, New
Statesman reader, Elizabeth Ormsby, claimed in the letters page that:

> The working-class lesbian is, anyway, not badly catered for in the way of
> clubs. Only her better-off sister lacks the sort of club of which there were
> several in London before the war – reasonably sophisticated places where
> homosexual men and women could meet, dance, drink and be gay.[69]

However, Ormsby's suggestion that post-war lesbian clubs had more
appeal to the working-class lesbian than those from a middle-class background is not reflected in other accounts, and it seems more probable that
the lesbian clubs of this period catered to a cross-class clientele.

In the Hall Carpenter accounts, narratives of 'not belonging' identified
a sense of alienation from a specific culture and identity rather than a
broader class distinction. Sharley McLean gave this account of her first visit
to Gateways:

> And I went in and I could see all the eyes turning and women were into
> suits in those days ... I was wearing a frock still. I wasn't even wearing
> slacks. You know, I was just wearing sort of a frock and a cardigan some-
> thing like that, very ordinary, very straight. And I could feel them looking
> at me and I suppose they thought 'What has the cat brought in?' and I could
> feel myself blushing and looking around and I thought 'I can't go in any
> further' and I turned tail ... I left. I couldn't. I went back and I said to [my
> friend], 'Oh God, I'm not one of those'.[70]

Sharley's account focuses on differences in clothing and her failure to
conform to butch/femme roles as the cause of her sense of alienation
from the club and its patrons. Her account suggests that she regarded the
members of the Gateways community as presenting a unique style,

distinct from the 'ordinary' dress which she was wearing. Cynthia Reid, who was taken to the Gateways by an acquaintance, similarly defined her sense of incongruity in terms of cultural exclusion:

> It was just that it was a totally alien environment. There were all these very masculine-looking women, dancing with their partners who, to me, were very feminine looking women. It was all very butch femme in those days and not at all what I had envisaged. There didn't seem to be any people like me – sort of ordinary quiet shy middle-class girls. And everybody seemed to be so frightfully self-confident, knowing all the latest dances and the latest pop tunes. Knowing each other obviously so very well, totally in their environment, whereas I felt like a fish out of water. And as I say, very, very shy and very, very frightened.[71]

Although Cynthia Reid suggested that there seemed to be no middle-class girls like her, she presented her sense of difference, not in class terms, but in the language of inadequacy. Both Sharley McLean and Cynthia Reid felt that they were inappropriately dressed and Reid described herself as being prevented from participating by her ignorance of the wider cultural languages of music and dance. The extent to which knowledge of the cultural codes of the bar community, and awareness of the lesbian identity performed by its members, shaped reactions to the subculture is apparent in Reid's further comments:

> I was absolutely horrified by the place. Looking back, I can't quite think why, because in later months, you know within a few months, I was going there quite regularly, enjoying their log fire and saving my heating bills. But my first visit was so horrific to me because it was such an emotional shock that after I got home I was physically sick and yet nothing disastrous happened.

Her extreme initial sense of alienation was apparently a reaction to her unfamiliarity with the culture, but she was able to overcome this and become a regular member.

As a distinctly lesbian space, with limited connections to a male homosexual subculture, the Gateways appears to have been largely unaffected by the legal reforms constituted in the Sexual Offences Act 1967. However, the debates surrounding legal reform which had been ongoing throughout the 1960s had a broader impact, prompting greater media and public discussion of homosexuality. As a result, the lesbian subculture was gradually exposed to public view in ways which would impact significantly on its collective identity and community. The first significant intervention occurred with the 1968 release of the film *The Killing of Sister*

George, which featured a scene in the Gateways. The film described the lesbian relationship between Beryl Reid's character 'Sister George' and her young lover, played by Susannah York, and showed the characters meeting friends in the club. The scene was filmed in the Gateways, using club regulars as extras and starring Gina and Smithy behind the bar. The level of involvement of the club's community in this decision is difficult to assess, but Veronica Groocock claims that the decision to allow filming and to encourage the appearance of regulars in the film was Gina Ware's.[72] Given the bar community's previously introspective character, the decision to admit film crews appears difficult to explain. However, the club itself had an established reputation on the local social scene, as well as long-standing connections with the artistic avant-garde and it is possible that Ware sought to enhance the club's reputation by building on these connections. Jill Gardiner suggests that a personal desire to return to the spotlight may have motivated Gina, a former actress, to agree to the filming, while the payment of a 'realistic fee' may have confirmed her decision.[73]

The admittance of film crews into the Gateways imprinted itself into the collective history of the club, as is evident in clients' accounts. Descriptions of the club in the earlier period of the 1940s, 50s and early 60s, and those of the later years, are commonly distinguished by the phrase 'that was before *Sister George*', or, 'They'd already filmed *The Killing of Sister George* before I went', suggesting that the film was indeed instrumental in attracting new lesbian clientele to the club and in exposing the community to wider public scrutiny. However, while the Gateways scene was widely viewed as lending authenticity to the film, Aldrich's representation of the central lesbian relationship as unequal, predatory and constrained by gender stereotypes shaped the film and thus the public's understanding of the lesbian community and bar culture. The film constructed the lesbian bar community as pathological and bizarre and Beryl Reid, who had starred in an earlier theatre production of the play, subsequently claimed to have been taken aback when she visited the club:

> Yet when I did the film and Robert Aldrich took me to the Gateways, the club in Bramerton Street, Chelsea, I nearly had a fit. I said, 'If I'd been here before I did the play, I'd never have done it.' I didn't realize they held each other's bums and went to the gents' loo. What did they do in the gents' loo? And Archie, the chucker-out with all the tattoos on her arms! But she was lovely.[74]

In a *Gay News* review in the 1970s, Jack Babuscio said the film 'presents the lesbian world as a grotesque collection of the sick and the predatory' and subsequent interpretations of the Gateways community were undoubtedly influenced by this representation.

Nevertheless, the immediate impact of the film was to raise the public profile of the club, locating it within an expanding metropolitan youth counter-culture and attracting a new and younger clientele. By the end of the 1960s a range of lesbian and mixed nightclubs were beginning to open up across London, part of the 'growth of discotheque-type clubs with pop music and dancing' which Jeffrey Weeks identifies in the male homosexual subculture at this time.[76] This trend constituted a third stage in the development of the lesbian bar culture, marked by the growing significance, once again, of the West End as a locus for lesbian socialising and, in particular, an increasing overlap of the social spaces occupied by lesbians and gay men. Lesbians frequented the Kandy Lounge in Gerard Street, Soho, and the White Raven club in the late 1960s and, in the 1970s, lesbian members of the Gay Liberation Front (GLF) and Campaign for Homosexual Equality were socialising with their male friends at the Rehearsal. These mixed social arenas were characterised by new ways of understanding lesbian and gay identity, influenced by the emerging gay political movement of the 1970s. From 1971 onwards, the Gay Liberation movement set out a new political agenda, which focused on visibility and the public statement of one's gay identity as essential to the achievement of social equality for lesbians and gay men. Believing that lesbians and gay men shared a common experience of oppression, gay liberation politics regarded a fundamental challenge to social attitudes as the only means of combating social marginalisation and was therefore concerned with the relationship between lesbians and mainstream society in a way which the previous generation had not been.

The arrival at the Gateways of this younger generation of women produced tensions within the lesbian bar subculture between the older members and these newcomers. Women who frequented the Gateways in the late 1960s recall these intergenerational conflicts taking on an almost territorial aspect. Many of the younger women, committed to a notion of lesbian community as the basis for political activism and social challenge had little sympathy with the codes of behaviour and style which had shaped the previously introspective subculture. For these women, finding no need to adopt the extremes of masculine and feminine which were central to butch/femme clothing, their ability to wear trousers and to follow their personal preferences in dress went unquestioned, while many were uncomfortable with the notion of asking a butch's permission to dance with a femme and refused to comply with accepted conventions. Angela Chilton described her experience of this tension in the Gateways when she started to visit the club in 1970:

There was still quite a bit of the butch and femme thing. A lot of that was

to do with age groups as well. We seemed to be the new lot, appearing on
the scene and we always seemed to have the same attitude – we were gonna
wear what we want and not what you say we should wear ...Well, some of
the butches, their attitude was that their femme didn't dance with anybody
else except them and my attitude was I'd dance with who I like – who I
went home with was something entirely different ... Well, we didn't like
that attitude so we changed all that. There was a sort of friction for a few
months ... Yes, because we would dance with who we wanted to, regardless ... but the other side – the butch and femmes – used to sit and glare at
us because the butches didn't think we should be doing it and the femmes
were dead jealous that we were all getting away with it, you know, they
didn't dare.[77]

She suggests that, while the Gateways continued to host evenings which
were exclusively 'butch/femme', the club became increasingly mixed on
other nights.

The political dimension to this tension within the lesbian subculture is
apparent from an incident that occurred in February 1971, which Jeffrey
Weeks has described in his discussion of the GLF. As part of their campaign
of revolutionary acts, a number of members of the GLF carried out a 'zap'
at the Gateways. The leaflet distributed apparently stated:

The Gateways has made thousands of pounds out of women who come to
the club (precisely how much money and publicity was gained from The
Killing of Sister George?) ... We are not sick and don't like people who
condescendingly treat us as such – especially when they are making a living
off us.[78]

The incongruity of delivering such a leaflet to a long-established lesbian
club apparently struck those involved at the time. Angela Chilton, a
member of the GLF, was asked about the incident in her interview for the
Hall Carpenter Collection. She recalled that, although her group had deliv-
ered leaflets at the Rehearsal, a mixed club frequented by gay men and
women, on a previous occasion, 'everybody was too scared to stand
outside Gateways and hand out leaflets – Gina and Smithy would have
killed them'.[79] However, the wording of the leaflet demonstrates the level
of anger at the portrayal of lesbians in The Killing of Sister George. While the
GLF may have assigned blame for the portrayal inappropriately, the leaflet
clearly revealed their perception of the members of the bar community as
passive and misguided victims of oppression.

Chilton's assessment of Gina and Smithy's attitudes was confirmed by
their reaction: the leaflets were confiscated by Smithy and one of the GLF

girls was banned from the club for life. In an account of the incident in
the GLF newsletter, *Come Together*, Elizabeth Wilson, one of the leaflet
distributors, described how she and her friends had been accosted by
Smithy. In a lengthy conversation, Smithy explained to Wilson that she did
not agree with GLF aims and did not welcome their leaflets in the club,
apparently saying:

> When you come down to it, we are abnormal. We're a minority ... I think
> everything is beautiful the way it is – we have a lot of freedom – two girls
> can walk down the street hand in hand if they want to ... I'm opposed to
> your aims because I don't think changing the law can alter attitudes ... You
> think you're going to change the world, love, but let me tell you all you're
> going to do is bring people down on us and we'll all end up worse off.
> That's all you're going to do.[80]

Smithy's reported words indicate that the issue of visibility was at the
heart of this conflict. While Smithy, and the subculture she was a part of,
equated 'freedom' with invisibility and thus impunity from social disapproval, Wilson was committed to a political ideology which foregrounded
a visible sexual identity as the route to, and evidence of, 'freedom' through
social challenge.

Commenting on Smithy's words in *Come Together*, Wilson maintained
that, despite a long argument, Smithy 'could not listen [to] or take in' the
GLF's ideas. For Wilson, the root of these attitudes lay in Smithy's negative
attitude toward her own lesbianism and specifically her adherence to
butch/femme models of identity. 'I would include as part of her negative
attitude and distorted self-image the rigidly sex-defined roles she and her
girlfriend [Gina Ware – widely assumed to be Smithy's lover] feel
compelled to play – 'butch' and 'femme', as among the most tradition-
alist heterosexual couples.'[81] Rejecting Smithy's ideas, Wilson denied
Smithy's ability to speak for herself. In language reminiscent of the original accusation that *The Killing of Sister George* – and the Gateways proprietors
– had portrayed lesbians as 'sick', Wilson cast Smithy's lesbian identity as
'distorted' and 'compelled'. In a second encounter, later in the month, GLF
activists returned to the Gateways to protest against the banning of their
member.[82] On this occasion, Gina Ware summoned the police and arrests
ensued. The opinions expressed, both by the Gateways proprietors and the
GLF activists, illustrate the shape and ferocity of this conflict. To the
members of the lesbian subculture for which the Gateways provided a
focus, GLF politics represented a threat to a way of life based on largely
introspective social networks. For those involved in the emerging Gay
Liberation movement, the Gateways occupied an ambiguous position as
both an important public symbol of lesbian community and as an

example of a culture and identity they wished to reject. The views established in this period of conflict shaped the structure of subsequent debates about the lesbian bar culture and the ways in which lesbians would interpret their involvement in it.

Since the 1970s, lesbian and gay history has been dominated by interpretive models which have their roots in the lesbian and gay politics of this era. Research has prioritised visible models of lesbian identity, focusing on those aspects of lesbian experience in the past which might be presented as posing a challenge to an oppressive social order. Within this perspective, the introspective lesbian subculture of the post-war decades has been cast as, at best apolitical and, at worst the knowing and submissive victim of oppression and as such has been neglected as a subject of historical research. However, examined in historical context, a much more complex picture of the post-war bar culture emerges. Oral histories and contemporary accounts point to the presence of lesbians on the metropolitan scene throughout the twentieth century. In the inter-war wars, lesbians occupied liminal spaces alongside prostitutes, criminals and male homosexuals in the entertainment culture of the West End. In the post-war decades, however, a distinct lesbian subculture emerged in the outlying areas of West London. Characterised by a network of communication and collective codes of style and behaviour, the subculture represented a unique space and collective identity forged in response to the pressing difficulties of isolation faced by its members. Perhaps the clearest indication of its significance is suggested by its position as a key site of intergenerational conflict in the late 1960s and early 1970s. Having dominated the post-war lesbian scene for decades, the Gateways club and the subculture which it represented inevitably became an arena for the negotiation of new models of lesbian identity, influenced by the lesbian and gay politics of the 1960s and 1970s. However, the lesbian bar scene was not the only forum in which lesbians contested their identities in this period: the launch of the lesbian magazine *Arena Three* in 1964, provided a further forum for the negotiation of collective lesbian identities.

Notes

1 See, for example, Mort, 'Mapping sexual London'; Higgs (ed.), *Queer Sites*; Inwood, 'Policing London's morals'; Houlbrook, *Queer London*; Neild and Pearson, *Women Like Us*; Brighton Ourstory Project (eds), *Daring Hearts*; NSA, Hall Carpenter Collection; Gardiner, *From the Closet to the Screen*.
2 The Wolfenden Committee was established in 1954 to examine the case for reform of the laws relating to prostitution and male homosexuality. Its

conclusions, proposing that male homosexual acts in private be decrimi-
nalised, were published in the Wolfenden Report 1957. See Mort, 'Mapping
sexual London'.

3 Rictor Norton, *Mother Clap's Molly House: The Gay Subculture in England 1700–1830*
(London: Gay Men's Press, 1992), pp. 9–10.

4 Brighton Ourstory Project (eds), *Daring Hearts*.

5 Hamer, *Britannia's Glory*, p. 81; Jeffrey Weeks, *Coming Out: Homosexual Politics in
Britain from the Nineteenth Century to the Present* (London: Quartet Books, 1977),
p. 87; Terry Castle, *Noel Coward and Radclyffe Hall: Kindred Spirits* (New York: Columbia University Press, 1996); Kevin Porter and Jeffrey Weeks (eds), *Between the
Acts: Lives of Homosexual Men 1885–1967* (London: Routledge, 1980).

6 Peter Ackroyd, *London: The Biography* (London: Vintage, 2001), pp. 531–5.

7 Frank Mort, *Cultures of Consumption: Masculinities and Social Space in Late Twentieth-
Century Britain* (London: Routledge, 1996), p. 153.

8 Arthur Tietjen, *Soho: London's Vicious Circle* (London: Allan Wingate, 1956), p. 11.
For other contemporary accounts, see Stanley Jackson, *An Indiscreet Guide to Soho*
(London: Muse Arts, 1969); Daniel Farson, *Soho in the Fifties* (London: Joseph,
1987).

9 Ellen, in Neild and Pearson, *Women Like Us*, p. 47.

10 Pat James, in Neild and Pearson, *Women Like Us*, p. 59.

11 Robert Fabian, *London After Dark* (London: The Naldrett Press, 1954), p. 12.

12 TNA, MEPO 3/758, The Caravan Club, 81 Endell Street WC1: Disorderly
House, Evidence of Clarence Campion, Div. Det. Inspector. E, Minutes to Bow
St Station, 10 August 1934 and Letter 11 August 1934.

13 Zoe Progl, *Woman of the Underworld* (London: Arthur Baker, 1964), pp. 23–4.

14 Matt Houlbrook, '"A Sun Among Cities": Space, identities and queer male
practices, London 1918–57' (PhD dissertation, University of Essex, 2002),
p. 93, n. 15.

15 John Parry Lewis, *Freedom to Drink: A Critical Review of the Development of the Licensing
Laws and Proposals for Reform* (London: Institute of Economic Affairs, 1985).

16 Houlbrook, *Queer London*, p. 78. This is confirmed by my own research. I have
been unable to locate any evidence of police surveillance or raids on the
lesbian nightclub, the Gateways, despite being located on the same site for
over fifty years.

17 Stella Condor, *Woman on the Beat: The True Story of a Policewoman* (London: Robert
Hale, 1960), p. 149.

18 Condor, *Woman on the Beat*, p. 150.

19 Gwylmor Prys Williams and George Thompson Blake, *Drink in Great Britain
1900–1979* (London: Edsall, 1980), p. 202.

20 Benjamin Seebohm Rowntree and George Russell Lavers, *English Life and Leisure:
A Social Study* (London: Longmans, Green and Co., 1951).

21 See Mort, *Cultures of Consumption*.

22 NSA, HCC (C456), F2483–F2487, Sandy Martin; London Metropolitan
Archive (hereafter LMA), PS/ KEN/ F/ 10, Register of Licences for the licensing district of Kensington and Chelsea.

23 NSA, HCC (C456), F2483–F2487, Sandy Martin. LMA, PC/ENT/2/12, List

    of applications for licenses from 1 January 1936: London County Council Entertainments Committee.

24 Barbara A. Weightman, 'Commentary: Towards a geography of the gay community', *Journal of Cultural Geography* 1 (1981), p. 11; H. P. M. Winchester and P. E. White, 'The location of marginal groups in the inner city', *Environment and Planning D: Society and Space* 6:1 (1988). On post-war lesbian bars in the U.S., see Davis and Kennedy, *Boots of Leather, Slippers of Gold*.

25 Webster, *Imagining Home*.

26 Matt Houlbrook, 'Toward a historical geography of sexuality', *Journal of Urban History* 27:4 (2001), p. 501.

27 Hunter Davies (ed.), *The New 'London Spy': A Discreet Guide to the City's Pleasures* (London: Corgi, 1966); Magee, *One in Twenty*. The availability of housing for single people in this area attracted a high proportion of single women.

28 Ceri Ager, in Neild and Pearson (eds), *Women Like Us*, p. 39.

29 Davies (ed.), *The New 'London Spy'*, p. 231.

30 Jill Gardiner claims this transaction took place in 1943. Gardiner, *From the Closet to the Screen*, p. 9.

31 Gardiner, *From the Closet to the Screen*; Veronica Groocock, 'Gina Ware: Obituary', *Guardian* (1 September 2001), p. 23; Lucy O'Brien, *Dusty: A Biography of Dusty Springfield* (London: Sidgwick and Jackson, 1999).

32 NSA, HCC (C456), F1359–F1360, Margaret Cranch.

33 NSA, HCC (C456), F2483–F2487, Sandy Martin.

34 Magee, *One in Twenty*, p. 180.

35 NSA, HCC (C456), F2483–F2487, Sandy Martin; Davies (ed.), *The New 'London Spy'*, p. 235. The average weekly earnings of a full-time woman worker in 1963 were 163s. 9d.: *Britain: An Official Handbook*, prepared by the Central Office of Information (London: HMSO, 1964), p. 459.

36 Davies (ed.), *The New 'London Spy'*, p. 235.

37 Clare Marc Wallace, 'All Girls Together', *She* (July 1966), p. 35.

38 Janice and Vicky, Brighton Ourstory Project (eds), *Daring Hearts*, p. 59.

39 Barbara A. Weightman, 'Gay bars as private places', *Landscape* 24 (1980), p. 9.

40 Westminster City Archives, WBA 804/56, Register of licence transfers.

41 Diana Chapman, in Neild and Pearson (eds), *Women Like Us*, pp. 98–9.

42 NSA, HCC (C456), F2108, Julie Switsur; NSA, HCC (C456), F1622-F1624, Angela Chilton.

43 NSA, HCC (C456), F1328–F1330, Rene Sawyer.

44 NSA, HCC (C456), F1326–F1327, Pat Arrowsmith. See also NSA, HCC (C456), F1359–F1360 Margaret Cranch, who was first taken to Gateways by friends from the Women's Royal Army Corps.

45 NSA, HCC (C456), F2109, Cynthia Reid.

46 NSA, HCC (C456), F2086, Jean White.

47 NSA, HCC (C456), F2108, Julie Switsur.

48 Progl, *Woman of the Underworld*, pp. 129–30.

49 Davies (ed.), *The New 'London Spy'*, p. 236.

50 NSA, HCC (C456), F1622–F1624, Angela Chilton.

51 Lillian Faderman, *Odd Girls and Twilight Lovers: A History of Lesbian Life in Twentieth-Century America* (London: Penguin, 1992) has discussed the term 'kiki' as

applied to lesbians in the US bar culture who failed to conform to butch/femme roles. While it is clear that some British lesbians also resisted pressure to conform to these categories, they were apparently marginalised by the butch/femme community and there is no evidence that a specific term was applied to these women.

52 Pat James, in Neild and Pearson (eds), *Women Like Us*, pp. 59–60.

53 Dick Hebdige, *Subculture: The Meaning of Style* (London: Routledge, 1979).

54 NSA, HCC (C456), F1328–F1330, Rene Sawyer.

55 NSA, HCC (C456), F1359–F1360, Margaret Cranch.

56 NSA, HCC (C456), F1328–F1330, Rene Sawyer.

57 NSA, HCC (C456), F2483–F2487, Sandy Martin.

58 Jeffreys, 'Butch and femme'; Joan Nestle, (ed.), *The Persistent Desire: A Femme-Butch Reader* (Boston: Alyson Publications, 1992); Joan Nestle, *A Restricted Country: Documents of Desire and Resistance* (London: Pandora, 1996).

59 Butler, *Gender Trouble*; Sherrie Inness and Michele E. Lloyd, 'G. I. Joes in Barbie Land: Recontextualising butch in twentieth-century lesbian culture', in Brett Beemyn and Mickey Eliason (eds), *Queer Studies: A Lesbian, Gay, Bisexual and Transgender Anthology* (London: New York University Press, 1996), p. 16.

60 NSA, HCC (C456), F1359–F1360, Margaret Cranch.

61 NSA, HCC (C456), F2483–F2487, Sandy Martin.

62 NSA, HCC (C456), F1328–F1330, Rene Sawyer.

63 NSA, HCC (C456), F1622–F1624, Angela Chilton.

64 NSA, HCC (C456), F2483–F2487, Sandy Martin.

65 NSA, HCC (C456), F2483–F2487, Sandy Martin.

66 NSA, HCC (C456), F1328–F1330, Rene Sawyer.

67 NSA, HCC (C456), F1359–F1360, Margaret Cranch.

68 Katie Gilmartin, 'We weren't bar people: Middle-class lesbian identities and cultural spaces', *GLQ* 3:1 (1996), p. 23.

69 Elizabeth Ormsby, 'Letters to the editor', *New Statesman* (2 April 1965), p. 530.

70 NSA, HCC (C456), F2158–F2163, Sharley McLean.

71 NSA, HCC (C456), F2109, Cynthia Reid.

72 Groocock, 'Gina Ware', p. 23.

73 Gardiner, *From the Closet to the Screen*, p. 133.

74 Bourne, *Brief Encounters*, p. 210.

75 Bourne, *Brief Encounters*, p. 213.

76 Weeks, *Coming Out*, p. 180.

77 NSA, HCC (C456), F1622–F1624, Angela Chilton.

78 Weeks, *Coming Out*, p. 193.

79 NSA, HCC (C456), F1622–F1624, Angela Chilton.

80 Aubrey Walter (ed.), *Come Together* (London: Gay Men's Press, 1980), p. 51.

81 Walter (ed.), *Come Together*, p. 52.

82 Walter (ed.), *Come Together*, p. 81.

5

Arena Three and the articulation of a collective lesbian identity

In the spring of 1964, the first British lesbian magazine, *Arena Three*, was produced and circulated to a small number of subscribers.[1] A landmark event in itself, the story of *Arena Three* provides a valuable case history of British lesbian cultures and identities in the 1960s. The project represented a first attempt to speak as a lesbian community and as such the history of the magazine's production, as well as the attitudes voiced within its covers, is a history of lesbian collectivism. The differing aims and interests of the women involved in *Arena Three*'s production – many of whose accounts were recorded in interviews for the Hall Carpenter Oral History Archive – reflect the concerns of individuals forging a group identity for the first time. These tensions were played out in the relationships between the constant and dominating figure of the editor, a succession of transient editorial boards and a geographically dispersed readership. Alliances and conflicts between the groups can be clearly traced in the editorial and letters' pages of the magazine and delineate a group of individuals struggling to adjust to the differing lesbian identities projected by others. The attitudes expressed within the magazine itself, both by the editorial board and contributors, illustrate the debates and issues with which this group of lesbians was eager to engage. The magazine initiated dialogues with both the medical and psychiatric professions and with the media, indicating the perceived importance of these professions in constructing a discourse of lesbianism prior to and during the 1960s.[2] Additionally, often highly charged debates within the community over dress, social behaviour and sexuality reflected a deep concern with the image represented by the lesbian community to itself and the wider society. Such concerns focused on a politics of privacy, representing lesbians as 'ordinary' people with a right to personal expression in the private sphere, which was similar to that espoused by the bar subculture and homosexual law reform societies.

Initially formed by a group of four or five lesbians, the magazine was dominated by its editor, Esme Langley, a published author and experienced journalist. The only one of the four key founder members not to have recorded a Hall Carpenter life-history interview, Langley remains an indistinct figure. A strong personality, it was Langley's appearance that seems to have struck her acquaintances the most forcefully. Diana Chapman commented that when she first met her she was 'quite appalled by her appearance', describing it as 'very peculiar; very peculiar', while a mutual friend, Rachel Pinney, allegedly once ordered her away from her doorstep, telling her to go and dress properly.[3] Highly possessive of the magazine, Esme Langley retained tight control and, with the exception of a few months, remained its Managing Editor throughout the period of publication. When the magazine ceased publication in 1971, it was because she had resigned editorial control, allegedly departing for Malawi with the magazine's entire capital.[4]

Accounts of the process by which the founder members of Arena Three came together offer an interesting illustration of the contact networks open to lesbians in the early 1960s. Although Langley had apparently been considering the possibility of a magazine for some time, the catalyst for the venture was provided by the publication, in late 1962, of an article on the subject of lesbianism in the current affairs quarterly, Twentieth Century.[5] Dilys Rowe's article, 'A quick look at lesbians', angered Esme Langley, who was subsequently to respond: 'What did Miss Rowe's "quick look" amount to? In my view, a skiddy, slide-eyed glance along a row of oddballs – as representative of the chosen terrain as a quick look at Penzance, or Detroit, might be if confined to the city's prisons, psychiatric clinics, night clubs and delinquent café society.'[6] However, she was pleasantly surprised to read an 'eminently sensible, self-reflecting retort by "A Lesbian"' in the following issue and decided to contact its author and request her assistance in the production of the magazine.[7] Diana Chapman – 'A Lesbian' – was in hospital recovering from a hysterectomy when she read and replied to the Twentieth Century article, and was convalescing in Australia when she received Langley's letter:

> She wrote me this letter which reached me in Australia and she said that she'd been thinking of – she made it sound, actually, as though she was halfway through preparing – this magazine for lesbians and would I like to go and lick a few envelopes. And of course she hadn't got anywhere, she was just thinking about it. And she met me at the airport when I came back.[8]

Langley was, in fact, simultaneously making a number of tentative enquiries, contacting Antony Grey of the Albany Trust for advice and to enquire whether he knew of anyone else who might be interested in collaborating in the venture. At a time when lesbians' visibility in the UK was close to non-existent, the small network of contacts provided by homosexual law reform organisations such as the Homosexual Law Reform Society (HLRS) and the Albany Trust were clearly a focal point for some women as well as men.[9]

Cynthia Reid, another London lesbian, had also contacted Antony Grey in the hope that other women like her would regard the HLRS as a means of meeting each other.[10] Although she was disappointed in her initial aim – the fear of legal sanctions against homosexual men meant that the HLRS did not organise social events, and the few women who attended the policy and fundraising meetings appeared to be those with a philan-thropic interest in homosexual law reform, not lesbians – Antony Grey was nevertheless sympathetic to her interest in a social club and was able to provide her with a number of introductions. The first was to a clergy-man counsellor named 'Eric'.[11] Having been involved in counselling a number of lesbians, 'Eric' had reached the conclusion that most of the emotional difficulties experienced by the women he encountered were caused by the problem of isolation, and he had been considering the possibility of establishing a lesbian social club in the crypt of his London church. While this project did not come about, 'Eric' introduced Cynthia Reid to one of the women he was counselling, Julie Switsur, and the two became lovers. When Esme Langley contacted Antony Grey regarding her magazine, he introduced her to Cynthia Reid and Julie Switsur, suggesting that the magazine idea and proposed social club might be combined. With this notion in mind, Esme Langley, Diana Chapman, Cynthia Reid, Julie Switsur and a fifth woman, 'Paddy' Dunkley, who apparently dropped out of the project soon afterwards, met and agreed to form a group which would make the publication of the magazine its first priority. The organi-sation formed was given the ambiguous title of the 'Minorities Research Group' (MRG). Cynthia Reid explained the title as a compromise: 'The idea was this was not specific enough to offend anyone who, er, you know, it didn't reveal itself as a homosexual organisation or as a specifi-cally female homosexual organisation and the term "research" lent a certain air of respectability.'[12]

The magazine was entitled '*Arena Three*', signifying its intention of providing subscribers 'with a special forum, platform, or "arena" in which to meet a dozen times a year'.[13] Esme Langley had initially conceived of the magazine as a small circulation newsletter, which she planned to produce in her spare time. This proved impracticable, however. Although it remained a duplicated broadsheet until 1970, it was a full-time job from the start, and Esme Langley co-ordinated it from her house in Broad-hurst Gardens, Hampstead, London, while Diana Chapman – now her partner – continued to work to support them both financially.[14] Early subscribers were drawn largely from the personal contacts of the founders and from the US, where the ten-year-old lesbian magazine, The Ladder, had given Arena Three extensive pre-publication publicity.[15] With small announcements of the first issue of the magazine in the British press, the circle of subscribers began to grow. Subscribers were predominantly, but not exclusively, lesbian, and were asked to sign a statement supporting the aims of the Minorities Research Group before taking out a subscription. Married women were additionally obliged to seek their husband's signed permission before subscribing, in an attempt to avoid accusations of alien-ation of affection being levelled against the magazine.[16] Of the remainder, a significant body of subscribers appears to have comprised individuals and organisations with a 'professional' interest, including psychiatrists and other medico-scientific researchers, journalists and social reformers.[17] The absence of any magazine for homosexual men at this time meant that a small number of homosexual men subscribed to Arena Three, although the embargo on men placing personal advertisements in the contact section of the magazine, and their exclusion from social activities, meant that these subscribers had a relatively low profile.[18] In the early years of production, Arena Three reflected a largely middle-class perspective. The founding members were all drawn from middle-class professional backgrounds and the magazine was initially advertised in middle-class publications such as the New Statesman. However, a conscious attempt to broaden the scope of advertising meant that the magazine increasingly reflected a more cross-class outlook. The circulation of the magazine was never large, totalling between 400 and 450 in mid-1965. The readership was apparently constantly changing, with subscribers frequently failing to renew their membership, but being replaced by new readers. Thus, in April 1971, despite considerably increased press coverage, the number of subscribers had only increased to six hundred, although with a further 1400 copies being produced for sale in newsagents and booksellers.[19] How far these figures reflect the actual readership of the magazine is difficult to assess. The editorial team clearly believed that subscribers were sharing copies with partners and friends, an assumption which was supported by admis-sions in the letters pages. It is unlikely, however, that the 'conservative estimate' of ten thousand readers, suggested by the editor in April 1971, is realistic.[20]

The first issue of Arena Three proclaimed the aims of MRG to be:

[T]o conduct and to collaborate in research into the homosexual condition, especially as it concerns women; and to disseminate information and items of interest to universities, institutes, social and education workers, writers, poets, editors, employers and, in short, all those genuinely in quest of enlightenment about what has been called 'the misty, unmapped world of feminine homosexuality'.[21]

The initial objectives of the organisation and its magazine were primarily externally focused and the founders regarded the magazine as a forum in which it would be possible to contribute to existing debates concerning homosexuality. The women involved in this venture claimed for themselves a unique knowledge regarding lesbianism and the ability to 'enlighten' others on the subject, identifying as their target audience those conventionally defined as knowledge-givers: educationalists, researchers, social workers and the media. Articles in the early issues, which were contributed almost exclusively by the four founder members, and two other women involved in the initial stages, Jackie Sheady and Doreen Holly, reflected this focus. The first issue included articles exploring the public image of lesbians, a response to Dilys Rowe's *Twentieth Century* article, and a consideration of whether homosexuality was acquired or innate. However, as the number of subscribers grew, the magazine was increasingly filled with contributions from readers and, as a result, the content and style of the magazine varied considerably over the seven years of its publication. Reviews of books, plays and films with lesbian content, and biographical accounts of historical figures associated with same-sex desire, were a relatively regular feature of the magazine, as were short stories and poems.

Changes in format gave the magazine a degree of unpredictability which must have disconcerted regular readers. Attempts to introduce more sophisticated printing methods frequently resulted in unexpected delays in the production of issues, so that issues arrived late, or merged two months in one issue. However, stability and an increasing sense of community were provided both by the opening editorial notes and the readers' letters pages which were constant features throughout the magazine's existence. These forums provided a space in which the editorial team and readers could explore ideas of lesbian identity and develop a sense of their community, and their increasing popularity defined the nature of the magazine as more introspective in later years.

Despite variations in content and focus in the latter years of the magazine's history, the emphasis on assisting research and providing information to universities, identified within the initial statement of aims, remained a constant theme throughout. The intention, 'to conduct and to collaborate in research into the homosexual condition, especially as it concerns women', was the first stated aim of MRG, indicating a belief that the medico-scientific profession played a central role in shaping understandings of lesbianism and reflecting the concerns of earlier sex reform groups such as the inter-war British Society for the Study of Sex Psychology.[22] This belief in the influence of medical and, in particular, psychiatric, conceptualisations of lesbianism recurs in *Arena Three* in the repeated use of medical theories as a point of reference in defining aspects of lesbian identity. In the first issue, an article entitled 'Scouting for – the public image' sought to explore the public image of the woman homosexual. It is significant that psychiatry was one of only four arenas on which the author focused in her exploration.[23] Identifying medical science as a key forum in which the aetiology and characteristics of lesbianism were debated, the MRG sought to open up a dialogue between the profession and themselves. This goal was pursued by collaborating in research projects, reviewing new contributions to the field, and debating many of the fundamental questions raised by psychiatrists.

Amongst the most heated debates enacted in *Arena Three* throughout its eight years were those which touched upon issues identified in sexological and other medical and scientific writings on lesbianism. In an article entitled 'Bent or straight mates?' in the first issue of the magazine, Diana Chapman posed the question, 'Why are some girls bent (i.e. Lesbian) and some straight mates?' The question went to the heart of psychiatric approaches to sexual identity, exploring the cause and development of lesbianism. Chapman outlined two possible approaches to the question, which defined homosexuality either as an 'acquired neurosis' or as an 'inborn characteristic predisposition'. Emphasising its compatibility with curative attempts, she identified the first approach as that 'commonly held by psychiatrists and members of the medical profession'.[24] Chapman clearly found this interpretation problematic, drawing upon the writings of Simone de Beauvoir as well as individual 'case histories' such as that of Radclyffe Hall, to point up the weaknesses in this explanatory model. Of the theory of 'inborn characteristic predisposition', which Chapman fails to attribute to any specific source, she comments:

> If the second theory is true, however, no amount of 'mental hygiene' and 'clean thinking' is going to remove the homosexual from society, in this or any future generation; and no amount of 'psychotherapy' is going to 'cure' them. The proper approach then would be to recognise homosexuality as a legitimate and natural part of the human condition, instead of insisting

that homosexuals should live like heterosexuals, which they obviously cannot do.[25]

Whilst Chapman's preference for the latter model is unremarkable given its historic associations with homosexual law reform, her conceptual framework is significant. Both her identification of the question regarding the origins of lesbianism, and her binary opposition of an 'acquired neurosis' versus 'inborn predisposition' explanatory model, are closely reflective of medical discourses of sexual identity.

The response to an article in the following issue on psychiatric methods of 'curing' homosexuality indicates the extent to which this subject touched upon the experience of many *Arena Three* readers. The article, 'Scouting for ... THE CURE', by 'Hilary Benno' offered a satirical review of possible 'cures' ranging from 'getting between the sheets with James Bond' (following in the footsteps of Pussy Galore) to aversion therapy or simple self-control.[26] While the article sought to view the issue in a humorous light, the response from readers was considerably more serious. In one of a number of letters published in the subsequent issue, one reader commented:

All my life I have been trying to resolve this problem, and am now convinced, after 18 sessions under lysergic acid, that it is practically congenital, but may easily be united to a strong maternal instinct.[27]

Another wrote:

I had a period of several years of homosexual relationships, which produced considerable emotional distress ... As this was just a part of my more general emotional disturbance I underwent a course of intensive psychotherapy ... I am now heterosexual.[28]

These letters imply a very personal engagement with medico-scientific thought and psychiatric methods for at least a section of *Arena Three* readers. The letter writers demonstrate a long-term, personal investment in debates concerning the aetiology of lesbian identity and a willingness to seek assistance from the medical profession in resolving this issue, which supports other positive lesbian accounts of psychiatric intervention. However, their accounts also suggest that women critically evaluated medical thinking in the light of their personal experience.

MRG established a more direct dialogue with medico-scientific discourse through collaboration in research projects. This formed an ongoing part of the organisation's work throughout its existence. While there is no evidence to suggest that MRG or *Arena Three* actively solicited any of the research projects in which they became involved, the easy access to lesbian research subjects, which the organisation and its magazine represented, certainly prompted a renewed academic interest in lesbian sexuality in the late 1960s and early 1970s.[29] The group represented a community of research subjects who were drawn, for the first time, not from the ranks of psychiatric patients, but from the wider lesbian population and thus provided opportunities for statistical research which had previously not been available. Cynthia Reid later commented:

> One of the consequences of the early publicity was, of course, that people in hospitals, academic institutes, who had an interest in sexuality as their own subject, saw this as a possible means of getting subjects for research purposes which is frequently very difficult in that sort of area … The idea of being able at last to get a selected sample of admitted homosexuals was something new and so there were research projects right from the start.[30]

Interest was considerable, with nine researchers, from the UK and US, undertaking research with MRG and *Arena Three* subscribers.[31] Renewed media and legal interest in male homosexuality in the late 1950s and 1960s, sparked by debates about the Wolfenden Report's proposals for homosexual law reform, reached a height in the late 1960s with the enactment of the Sexual Offences Act 1967 and such debates inevitably raised the profile of homosexuality, and encouraged further medico-scientific research in this area.[32] Alison Oram has argued that MRG sought to exploit medico-scientific interest in lesbianism, believing that collaborating in research would offer an opportunity to push MRG's own agenda. Oram states:

> It is clear that the MRG expected 'unbiased' research to reflect their own views. They believed that the 'truth' of their own minds and bodies could reshape the scientific agenda, away from pathologising lesbianism and towards their concept of lesbian normality. Its largely middle-class and educated readers were possibly more inclined to believe in the ultimate neutrality of science, whose authority could be used to make their case to the general public.[33]

The scale of the studies varied from individual PhDs to larger, university-funded projects, as did the level of MRG's participation. While some studies were conducted by postal questionnaire, others required a greater commitment from volunteers. Diana Chapman described one project which sought to discover whether there were any measurable anatomical and physiological differences between lesbians and heterosexual women:

> And we all assembled at some hall, some medical centre in Bloomsbury and we were asked to strip off. I think maybe we were allowed to keep our

knickers, I'm not sure. And it was all extremely embarrassing. And somebody remarked that it was the most uninhibited party they'd ever been to.
And we also had to bring along a 24 hour specimen of urine and we, they
took photographs of us, and they measured us and they measured the
sub-cutaneous fat and, oh and they took buckle smears – which is, buckle
being the inside of the cheek – apparently that shows hormone levels or
shows something. I don't know, it all took about an hour and a half, and
also, I think that, as far as I remember, we all took a psychological test,
answering some psychological questionnaire. And then we all dressed and
went home.[34]

Her account points to a renewed scientific interest in endocrinological
explanations for lesbianism. While hormone levels had provided the focus
for much of the research into male homosexuality in the 1930s and 40s,
these ideas had been overtaken by psychoanalytic approaches after the
Second World War. However, lesbians were rarely the subject of such
research in the 1930s and 40s, and Chapman's account suggests that the
availability of a group of lesbian research subjects had prompted
researchers to explore this avenue.

Many of the research projects, however, were primarily influenced by
psychoanalytical approaches, regarding the existence of MRG as an opportunity to test earlier hypotheses. Eva Bene, the first researcher to approach
the MRG, compared the questionnaire responses of a group of lesbians
(from the Minorities Research Group) with a control group of married
women.[35] The stated purpose of Bene's research was to test the claims
made in psychiatric and, particularly, psychoanalytic literature concerning
the role of parent-child relations in the genesis of female homosexuality.
In a paper entitled 'On the genesis of female homosexuality', Bene was
concerned entirely with familial – indeed parent-child – relationships,
and concluded that a link existed between a dislike or fear of the father,
and a tendency for the father to be weak and incompetent, and the genesis
of lesbianism in the daughter. The second research project, conducted by
June Hopkins in 1965, similarly sought to test established theories of
lesbianism. An American psychologist based at Cambridge University,
Hopkins had apparently met lesbians during her service in the women's
forces in America and 'couldn't understand what the difference was
[between homosexual and heterosexual women] – what all the fuss was
about'.[36] Her survey was therefore conceived as an attempt to dispel the
notion of lesbians as 'neurotic' and her analysis of personality variables
amongst lesbian and heterosexual women was based on a 'Personality
Factor' questionnaire. She concluded that lesbians were not 'neurotic', but
were more independent, resilient, reserved, dominant, bohemian, self-
sufficient and composed than their heterosexual counterparts.[37] However,

in positing differences between the lesbian and heterosexual female personality, Hopkins reproduced the idea of a fundamental physiological distinction between the two. The predominance of active, 'masculine' traits in those Hopkins ascribed to lesbians, reaffirmed long-standing notions of adult lesbians as potentially predatory.[38]

Both Eva Bene and June Hopkins enjoyed close cordial relations with MRG during and after the completion of their research. Eva Bene appears to have stayed with Esme Langley in the early stages of her research project and continued to participate in debates and other social activities organised by the group as late as December 1966.[39] June Hopkins, while seemingly less involved in the group's activities, wrote regular progress reports on her research and sent occasional donations throughout the magazine's existence. However, while *Arena Three* and the MRG clearly welcomed the interest of such researchers as an important aspect of their work, they were careful to adopt a stance of critical distance both toward individual projects and medico-scientific discourse more generally. In the first instance, the editorial board of *Arena Three* positioned themselves as gate-keepers to their lesbian community, verifying the integrity of each researcher before affording them access to the wider body of members. In a 1965 article, 'Psychology and the homosexual', Cynthia Reid reassured *Arena Three* readers:

> However, you can rest assured that all applications for research material are closely examined by the executive officers of the Group. They must be satisfied with regard to sincerity, qualifications, method, and respect of confidence, among other things; and applications have more than once been turned down which seem to fail on one or more of these points.[40]

Commitment to the wider project of promoting scientific research into lesbianism did not mean implicit trust in the medico-scientific establishment and Reid's comments suggest that the editorial board regarded each researcher as a potential threat to its members.

The decision to participate in a specific research project was clearly not regarded by the MRG as an automatic endorsement of its aims or conclusions. Researchers were expected to inform the MRG of the research results, which were subjected to critical review in the magazine. Dr Kenyon, who contacted the MRG in August 1965 to request assistance with his research on the social status, family background and sexual experience of lesbians, received a mixed response to his work, published in two parts in November 1968 and April 1969.[41] Commenting on a summary of his second study in 1969, Esme Langley endorsed his conclusions on age at first homosexual experience, using his findings to support her own argument of the need to reach teenage lesbians with *Arena*

Three. Julie Switsur, however, recalled his questioning technique as 'closed ended' and his turn of phrase as 'irritating', commenting in her Hall Carpenter interview that: 'He did a dreadful bit of research which we all hated him for ... I felt he was seeing it all from a very masculine traditional point of view and I didn't like it.'[42] Her objections seem to have been directed at Dr Kenyon's manner and attitudes rather than at the research conclusions themselves. However, it was not unusual for questions to be raised regarding researchers' findings. In June 1966, the author of an article on 'MRG and research' noted that Eva Bene's discovery of a link between lesbianism and a poor father-daughter relationship had been contradicted by a US study. The Reiss/Grundlach Study, which had been based on research with MRG's US counterpart, the Daughters of Bilitis, apparently found 'no more sign of a pathological background in lesbians than in the heterosexual control'.[43] While this author relied upon a second scientific study to challenge Eva Bene's findings, a more direct criticism of a later research project illustrates the complex relationship between the lesbian research subject and the finished study.

In May 1968, *Arena Three* published a research request from Dr Charlotte Wolff, a Fellow of the British Psychological Society, who required a 'complete emotional autobiography, together with [the subject's] own appreciation of the origin of [her] own homosexual feelings'. The author of the article urged readers to 'Please write', emphasising that Dr Wolff was 'seeking information not from patients but from people' and that she was interested in the subjects' own interpretation of their lesbian experiences.[44] On its publication, in 1971, Charlotte Wolff's *Love Between Women* attempted to set out a new theory of lesbianism, which represented lesbianism as the result of a mixture of biological and psychological factors. Wolff claimed to have been influenced by pre-war endocrinological studies, as well as more recent psychoanalytic approaches and the existentialist views of Simone de Beauvoir. After a detailed discussion of her research methodology, Wolff outlined the key features of what she termed 'The Characteristic Lesbian'. Lesbians, she suggested, were commonly aggressive, both in the positive sense of being focused and dynamic, and, more often, in a negative sense as destructive and jealous. They demonstrated high levels of inhibition, indicated through nervous tension, defensive attitudes and shyness, and as a result were prone to bursts of bad temper, abusive behaviour and alcohol-fuelled violence, in an attempt to release the pressure. They were more insecure, and less able to adapt to social situations than the heterosexual women she compared them with, and had a lower tolerance of stressful situations. Wolff concluded her study with a reproduction of three of the 'emotional autobiographies' she had undertaken with lesbians. The book received a glowing review in *Arena Three*:

> Somehow Dr Wolff has merged a medical text book, with a human document, which will absorb the general reader as much as the specialist. She, herself, is very much part of the book, which gives a warm authenticity to what she writes, instead of the usual clinical pronouncements to which Lesbians have been martyrs.[45]

However, a few months later, a letter offering a very different perspective was sent in to 'Free Speech', the readers' letters section of *Arena Three*:

> When Dr. Wolff was doing her research for Love Between Women, we went to be interviewed, glad to think some attempt was being made to dispel popular 'myth' about lesbians. Having just read her book we now wonder how far our image has been helped by the writing of it.
>
> The 'characteristic lesbian' of Dr. Wolff's book seems to be unhappy, aggressive, often neurotic or at best sublimated … (Indeed, the book painted a picture so alien to us that we suspect ours were the two questionnaires which Dr. Wolff admits got lost!).[46]

In disagreeing with the official *Arena Three* interpretation of Charlotte Wolff's study, the co-authors of the letter drew on their personal role as contributors to the study as authority for their criticism. Their ironic suggestion that their personal contributions may have been mislaid underscores their assumption of a direct connection between an individual source and the final study. *Arena Three* had for some time now been claiming the authority to evaluate research as lesbians in possession of a unique understanding of the aetiology and characteristics of lesbianism; the authors of this letter sought to stake a further claim as individuals who had contributed to this specific study. It is undoubtedly significant that such an objection arose in a research project which invited lesbians to take an active role in the research process, evaluating, rather than simply recounting, their own experiences.

A second forum for critical engagement with medico-scientific research was provided through book reviews. Reviews of fiction and non-fiction works with a lesbian interest were a regular feature of *Arena Three*, and scientific studies appeared relatively frequently. Reviews inevitably focused on contemporary works rather than 'classics' in the field, although there was often a considerable time lapse between the date of publication and the appearance of a review in *Arena Three*. Reviews were almost entirely critical, suggesting that anger at an author's conclusions was a primary motivation in the writing of these reviews. In this sense, the magazine was apparently regarded as a supportive 'space' in which lesbians could express and share their emotional reactions to negative stereotyping by the medical profession. Thus, a review of American psychologist Daniel Cappon's *Toward an Understanding of Homosexuality* claimed: 'The book is an epitome of all the most grotesque clichés about homosexuality.'[47] Adopting a different style, a review of Anthony Storr's *Sexual Deviation* by 'a woman psychotherapist' offered a comprehensive critical summary of Storr's argument, highlighting any inconsistencies or inaccuracies point by point.[48] Nevertheless, despite the academic rubric employed by the reviewer, and her obvious personal investment in medico-scientific approaches to sexuality, the reviewer's conclusions were typically negative:

> On the whole I think it is fair to say that Mr. Storr's analysis of female homosexuality is disappointingly stereotyped and facile. He seems to have nothing original or creative to offer on this subject; which is surprising in view of his background as a psychiatrist and a predominantly Jungian analyst.[49]

In contrast to the hostility levelled at psychiatric approaches to lesbianism, those studies that adopted a more sociological or statistical angle tended to receive positively encouraging reviews. A review of Kinsey's *Sexual Behaviour in the Human Female*, published in July 1967, praised Kinsey for dismissing Freud's explanations of the aetiology of sexual identity, although Kinsey's own theory that sexual identity is determined by the 'accident' of the gender of an individual's first sexual partner was oddly dismissed as 'just as unlikely to stand up to the acid test of statistical research'. The notion of statistical research as an 'acid test' was at the heart of much of *Arena Three*'s approach to medico-scientific research.[50] Regarding much of the existing literature as stereotyped, derivative and inaccurate, the contributors to *Arena Three* apparently hoped that large-scale empirical studies would afford the necessary ammunition to discredit earlier works. This thinking is set out in a review of the American sociologists, John Gagnon and William Simon's study, *Sexual Deviance*:

> The last part of this uniquely thoughtful book consists of a single long article by the editors themselves on female homosexuality. The decision to write it, we are told, arose from a basic dissatisfaction with 'the literature'. It was out of this same dissatisfaction that the decision to publish 'A3' [*Arena Three*] arose; and it is pleasing to find that John Gagnon and William Simon have also set out to deal with their subject within the context of sociology – a most refreshing change from the small twilit area of the amateur sexologists who have set themselves up in the past as experts in the field.[51]

Such comments are evidence of an increasingly hostile and dismissive attitude, which developed in the later issues of the magazine, toward the medico-scientific project as a whole.

While researchers such as Eva Bene and June Hopkins, who contacted *Arena Three* in the first two or three years of its production, apparently received an encouraging response from the editorial team, by 1966, references to the profession as a whole were less positive. An editorial in June 1966 blamed the 'muddled thinking' of psychiatrists for the harassment of MRG by heterosexual men 'under the erroneous impression that lesbians are looking to set up home with a man'.[52] In October of the same year, an article on the future of MRG by Esme Langley, commented on the 'acute shortage' of qualified people in the 'medico-social' world who really understood what homosexuality was about. Such comments suggest a growing disillusionment, both with the claims to expert knowledge made by these professionals, and with their interest in furthering such 'knowledge'. Langley claimed:

> As to research, people sometimes ask what research MRG actually does, as distinct from projects we have assisted in over the past three years. One simple answer to this is that until ample material has been collected, no serious research can be done anyway. However, we have amassed a considerable body of data during our three years of life which is already quite sufficient to provide drastic refutation of previous 'authoritative' works (few as they are) in the field of female homosexuality. One need only read Dr. Caprio's opus on the subject to perceive that it is high time to put the whole subject in a more realistic light ... Given time and opportunity, then, we hope in 1967 to produce some of MRG's own findings.[53]

Langley's comments suggest a significant shift in MRG's objectives in this area. While still claiming a specialised knowledge on the subject of lesbianism – one increased by three years' amassed data – the intended method of disseminating this information had apparently changed. Having initially planned to 'disseminate information and items of interest to universities, institutes, social and education workers' and others, MRG was now considering bypassing the medico-social world and publishing their findings directly into the public domain. The proposed book never materialised, but the suggestion was an indication of a growing disaffection with the medical professions.

A disjuncture between the objectives of the founder-members and the priorities of subscribers may be partly responsible for this shift in attitudes. It is clear, both from Hall Carpenter interviews and from the statement of aims itself, that at least three of the founder members – Diana Chapman, Cynthia Reid and Julie Switsur – were strongly committed to this aspect of the MRG's work.[54] However, this was a view which may not have been shared by the majority of subscribers. An article by Cynthia Reid in the April 1965 issue of *Arena Three* indicates that she considered many subscribers to be reluctant to support this aspect of the MRG's commitments:

> This article is prompted by the attitudes I have met towards the subject of psychology among homosexuals in general, and among MRG members in particular. This was illustrated by reactions last year to Dr. Eva Bene's research on family relationships during childhood, the first project in which our co-operation was sought. While most of those we approached offered their services willingly, many others expressed uneasiness, and some, outright horror, at the idea of being involved in psychological research.[55]

Reid's comments indicate that, despite having signed a statement committing them to the ideal of collaborating in research, many subscribers were, in practice, much more reluctant. She attributes this reluctance to a widespread fear either that researchers would attempt to 'cure' volunteers of their homosexuality, or that participation carried with it the implication that volunteers were mentally ill. She hoped that, by setting out the distinction between psychologists, who sought to observe and explain behavioural phenomena such as homosexuality, and psychiatrists, who aimed to '[adjust] the individual to society and to himself', she would persuade subscribers to participate in psychological research projects. The extent to which she was successful is difficult to assess, but it was after her departure from MRG and *Arena Three* in the autumn of 1965 that the magazine became more explicitly hostile to medico-scientific projects.[56]

However, the change in attitudes could also be interpreted as an indication that, as the community centring on *Arena Three* became more established, a more confident sense of lesbian identity was fostered. As readers developed a stronger sense of themselves as members of a recognisable and assured community, they became increasingly indignant in their response to perceived external hostility. An exchange in the 'Mailbag' section of the magazine in May 1967 illustrates this. A reader with three sisters and a brother, all of whom were heterosexual, wrote:

> I do want emphatically to say how much I dislike the outlook of the so-called 'experts' who say we are not 'born this way' but made like it by one parent or the other whether the mother or the father. It mostly seems to be 'Mother' who gets the blame ...
>
> My mother is the sweetest, gentlest woman in the world, and I very deeply resent any suggestion that it might be her fault I am what I am, that she singled me out for some kind of 'special' mismanagement and not my sisters.[57]

The language used in the letter, referring to the medical professions in terms of derision, is suggestive of a new-found confidence emerging in anger. The writer's sentiments of frustration at being misinterpreted, and her anger at being made the object of the medical gaze, are echoed in an editorial later the same year:

> On our own side of the field we have had a helpful suggestion, too. Why do we not set up a homosexual study group to do some serious research into the mentality of heterosexuals (including researchers into homosexuality)?[58]

The ironic comment is indicative of an increasingly self-confident collective lesbian identity: one which sought actively to define itself and its relation to medical science. As such it anticipates the anger expressed by Gay Liberation Movement activists in the early 1970s at aversion therapy and other medical attempts to define and 'cure' homosexuality.[59]

Equally important to *Arena Three* in defining its relationship with mainstream society was the magazine's interaction with the printed and broadcasting media. Media representations of homosexuality remained the primary source of the wider public's understanding of lesbianism and were thus regarded by *Arena Three* as highly influential in shaping popular attitudes. For many isolated lesbians, such representations also provided one of very few indications of a broader context to their personal experience. In the absence of contact with a wider lesbian community, media representations of lesbianism played a key role in shaping individuals' understanding of their self-identity and society's attitudes toward that identity. *Arena Three*'s attitude toward the media was thus ambivalent, criticising the media for its hostile or ill-informed articles on lesbianism while simultaneously depending on the media to positively influence public opinion and to reach other lesbians with news of *Arena Three*'s existence.

Articles on female homosexuality rarely appeared in the British press in the 1950s and early 1960s.[60] Infrequent references – largely confined to the tabloid and popular press – overwhelmingly represented lesbianism in a negative light, as an adjunct to a sensational account of divorce or violent crime.[61] *Arena Three* performed an important function for its readers from the outset, in providing a supportive forum in which they could share their reactions to such hostile media representations of lesbianism. For the founders, this appears to have been a primary aim of the magazine. As we have seen, Dilys Rowe's *Twentieth Century* article, 'A quick look at the lesbians', had constituted the catalyst that prompted Esme Langley actively to pursue her ambition of editing a lesbian magazine.[62] In her letter to Antony Grey, requesting his advice for the enterprise, Langley cited the article, commenting:

> I expect you will have read the recent contributions to 'Twentieth Century'
> (Winter and Spring issues) on the topic of lesbianism ... editorially
> described as a 'misty and unmapped territory'. It is high time it was prop-
> erly charted, surely. Also I think it would do many people a power of good
> to be able to contribute to their own magazine, even if anonymously, and
> say what they have always wanted to say without let or hindrance.[63]

Langley conceived of the magazine as having a dual purpose: that of
providing information about lesbianism and that of facilitating lesbian
expression. *Arena Three* was to give lesbians the opportunity to speak for
themselves. For Langley herself, the first act of speech was to respond to
Dilys Rowe's article, describing with disgust the women Rowe referred to:

> The professional woman eager to be thought 'repulsive', the toughie up in
> court for robbery with violence, the married woman who drifted into it for
> kicks; the lady 'always ready to have a bash ... Sometimes I don't even know
> who it was'; the woman with a passion for cuddling little girls ... Recog-
> nise them? I don't. And I've been around for several decades – including
> nearly seven years in the women's services in wartime.[64]

Her accusation that Dilys Rowe's representation of lesbians was limited
and inaccurate was indicative of the approach *Arena Three* took toward many
media accounts and in February 1965, a BBC radio programme in which
a panel discussed homosexuality was criticised for its solely male focus
and for its limitation of the debate to the possibilities of eradication or
cure. Two years' later, tabloid coverage of a case in which six WRAC
women were discharged was criticised as too vague. 'So what precisely
these girls had been up to is anybody's guess,' the *Arena Three* editorial
complained. 'If the press must report such items, it should be more
explicit; this kind of mumbling about "vice" etc. can only mislead its
readers.'[65] The frustration implicit in these complaints demonstrates the
extent to which lesbians were dependent on the media for information
about each other. Repeated editorials both advised readers of any recent
media coverage of lesbianism and requested that readers supply such
information to the editors. From 1970 onward, this need was reflected in
an increasing tendency to reprint, in their entirety, articles from the press
which related to lesbianism. Readers' questionnaires indicate a continued
interest in this material from *Arena Three* subscribers. Readers both
contributed items from their local press and used the letters page to
express their own reactions to media portrayals of lesbianism.[66]

While the magazine offered lesbians a forum to vent their frustration
at negative publicity, *Arena Three* was also keenly aware of the media's influence on wider social attitudes toward lesbianism. Reviews frequently
expressed concern at the image of lesbianism which a certain article or

programme projected to the wider public. In a write-up of the Man Alive television programme on lesbianism, in which a number of lesbians associated with Arena Three participated, the author bemoaned 'a very long drawn out interview with Steve Rogers – a youthful "Colonel Barker"':

> [W]e still feel that to devote so much programme time, in a Lesbian sequence, to this rare and way-out case of transvestism (if not indeed of trans-sexuality) was unfortunate, and could only add to the confusion of the public that the programme was meant to enlighten.[67]

MRG's aim, 'to promote intelligent and properly informed press and radio comment', was indicative of a desire to emphasise those aspects of lesbianism which might be seen as more compatible with wider social mores.[68] Press interest in the subject was, however, roused only sporadically, often prompted by related events. The formation of MRG and publication of Arena Three prompted a small flurry of press interest, which was revived in the mid-1960s by debates about male homosexual law reform, and again in 1969 by the release of the lesbian films, The Killing of Sister George and Les Biches. Encouraging journalists to interview either herself or other subscribers, Langley sought to exploit these sparks of interest and reconfigure media portrayals of lesbians in a manner more reflective of her own experience.

In July 1964, Arena Three embarked on a collaboration with the television company Associated Rediffusion to produce a television programme on lesbianism. Bryan Magee, the journalist responsible for the project, had already aired a programme on male homosexuality as part of the This Week current affairs programme and hoped to make a lesbian counterpart. As part of his research, Magee was invited to attend one of MRG's monthly meetings, normally barred to men, suggesting that Arena Three was committed to assisting him in offering a detailed and accurate picture of the magazine and group.[69] The final programme, aired early in 1965, was taped and played back to members at an MRG meeting, and public reactions to the programme were closely reviewed in Arena Three.[70]

Despite the level of Arena Three's involvement in the project and a positive reaction to the television programme, the relationship deteriorated when Bryan Magee published an article on the subject in the New Statesman in late March 1965.[71] In a relatively detailed article, Magee outlined the debates regarding the cause and potential treatment of lesbianism and explored the relationship between lesbianism and marriage, lesbians' isolation, their sexual behaviour and the culture of butch/femme. While the television programme had allowed individual lesbians' descriptions of their experience to exemplify general points, in the article Magee assumed a personal authority to pronounce opinions on the subject. This prompted a number of criticisms from members of the homophile community, who questioned the accuracy of his 'ex cathedra' pronouncements, reflecting, 'one simply wonders how on earth he could know such esoteric facts'.[72] Magee drew further criticism with his comments on the Minorities Research Group and *Arena Three*. In a single paragraph on the group, Magee claimed:

> MRG has some serious faults – it is too middle class in its membership and assumptions, its monthly publication *Arena Three* is written at school-maga-zine level, many of its members are people with severe personality prob-lems who just also happen to be homosexuals – but it has changed life for the better for a number of very unhappy people, and this alone is enough to justify its existence.[73]

His comments are an indication of the growing hostility in the contest over authority to describe homosexuality. The MRG reacted to Magee's criticisms with anger, both in a letter by its Press Officer, Tony Geraghty, to the *New Statesman*, and within the pages of *Arena Three* itself.[74] Expressing surprise that Magee should be so 'bitchy' about MRG just three months after it assisted him in the production of his television programme, Geraghty responded:

> Mr. Magee suggests also that MRG is 'too middle class'. One can only guess at what the phrase is meant to imply. The founder members were, respec-tively, engineer, sociologist, journalist, librarian and shop assistant. Subse-quently, since only such 'middle class' publications as the New Statesman were willing to accept its advertisements, membership reflected the reader-ship of such journals – until last December, that is. Since then, by virtue of the News of the World and television, the pattern of membership has changed radically.[75]

The accusation was refuted with equal strength in *Arena Three*, where it was insisted that recent publicity had 'created a much wider social spread'.[76]

Despite its ambivalent attitude toward the media, the *Arena Three* edito-rial board was largely dependent on the national and local press to adver-tise its existence to potential subscribers. *Arena Three* was circulated by post to a database of members, and did not go on open sale in lesbian venues and in newsagents until 1969, making it particularly important in the early years to attract postal subscriptions. The magazine's initial readership was attracted by pre-publication notices in the American lesbian maga-zine, *The Ladder*, with the result that many of the first subscribers were American. However, in the early months of its release, the magazine attracted some press interest in the UK, resulting in short profiles and announcements in the *Sunday Times* and *Observer*.[77] This last, Langley claimed, 'produced a flood of letters and telephone calls which has still not abated'.[78] Building on this publicity, the editorial board sought to broaden the readership base through commercial advertising. This decision reflected both a financial need to acquire sufficient subscribers to make the magazine's production economically viable, and a more altruistic desire to welcome further isolated lesbians into the community. Thus, in August 1964, *Arena Three* took out advertisements in the *Spectator* and *Private Eye*, 'inviting "lonely lesbians" to read *Arena Three*' and, in the following November, embarked on a national advertising campaign.[79]

However, the campaign 'met some reluctance from some newspapers' to print adverts, a difficulty which became increasingly problematic as *Arena Three* became more established and acquired a larger advertising budget. A segment in the October 1967 issue of *Arena Three* reprinted a letter of refusal from the *Sunday Telegraph* advertising section, commenting that the wording of the advert was 'rather bald' and liable to cause offence to some readers, and inviting *Arena Three* to alter it and resubmit. Esme Langley's reaction followed:

> It is the kind of twisted thinking that we must tackle collectively, unless the views and wishes of sane and responsible people are to go on being smoth-ered in favour of twilight fantasy and embattled ignorance. Write now, and get your friends to write, to the Editor of the 'Sunday Telegraph', in no uncertain terms.[80]

Two months later, copies of further letters sent by Esme Langley to the editors of the *Observer* and *Sunday Times*, protesting at their refusal to publish adverts for *Arena Three*, were reprinted in the magazine. The decision to take direct action and complain to the respective editors is indicative of the militancy which characterised *Arena Three's* response to this issue and Langley's reporting of the dispute indicates her belief that collective action could be effective. Contributions to the *Arena Three* letters page, stating that their writers had done as she had asked, indicate that some readers agreed.

The situation did not, however, improve and in August 1970, an entire issue of *Arena Three* was dedicated to the problem.[81] The magazine contained reprints of letters from advertising executives refusing *Arena Three's* adver-tisements, juxtaposed by a letter of acceptance from the *Sunday Telegraph* and a letter from a probation officer thanking Esme Langley for *Arena Three's* assistance in a recent case.[82] An editorial claimed:

> Fifty different 'magazines for women' are published regularly in Britain. All of them cater EXCLUSIVELY for heterosexual interests.
>
> *Arena Three* is the only publication in Britain representing the interests of homosexual women and presenting their OWN viewpoint to the general public... Our own viewpoint is to be smothered. The weird and wildly

distorted 'views of homosexuality' presented by so many writers, film makers, playwrights and others must on no account (say the Fleet Street bosses) be challenged by a publication such as '*Arena Three*' which sets out simply to present the TRUTH to the general public.

Where is the 'freedom of speech' of which Fleet Street loves to boast?

… The GAY LIBERATION movement is going great guns in the States. It is high time we had a little more positive action over here.[83]

This appeal demonstrates the growing sophistication of Esme Langley and *Arena Three*'s political thinking. The 1967 article, while indicating a desire for direct and collective action, drew on traditional British models of political protest in writing 'Letters to the Editor'. By 1970, the influence of current political ideologies had rendered *Arena Three*'s press campaign more politically radical. The riots which followed a police raid on the Stonewall gay bar in New York in 1970 had been reported in the English press. *Arena Three* followed developments closely, recording the subsequent establishment of the US Gay Liberation movement and its commitment to a political struggle for full citizenship. The Gay Liberation Front (GLF) drew on the ideas of other contemporary civil uprisings such as the civil rights movement and women's movement, in its emphasis on political acts of resistance to oppression.[84] This language of discrimination permeates the *Arena Three* editorial, contrasted with the established ideal of 'freedom of speech' which the British press has failed to fulfil. Explicitly claiming the US Gay Liberation movement as an inspiration, the editorial seeks to ally itself with a campaign for homosexual equality rather than with a feminist one. 'Heterosexual interests' are amply catered for in other magazines, and it is *Arena Three*'s status as a magazine for homosexual women which renders it vulnerable to discrimination. In referring to Gay Liberation, the editorial also signified a change in campaigning tactics to one of 'positive action'. A 'Freedom of the Press Meeting' was called at a London pub which was attended by eighteen people. The Press Freedom Group was formed and participants agreed to each send an advertisement, stating '*Arena Three*, the same-sex magazine for women …' to their local paper and to report back to a second meeting, a fortnight later. Little progress was made and Jackie Forster, *Arena Three*'s newly appointed Advertising Manager, lodged a complaint with the Press Council which was rejected in April 1971, on the grounds that editors must be allowed to reserve the right to refuse advertisements.[85] Three months later, the issue was rendered irrelevant when internal divisions within the community prompted *Arena Three* to cease publication.

Despite the external focus of the magazine's initial declared aims, *Arena Three* performed an equally important function for its readers in providing the basis of a discursive community of lesbians. Early issues carried numerous letters from subscribers expressing their joy at having made contact with other lesbians and their gratitude to the editorial board for making this possible. Such letters stressed the commonality of lesbians, claiming to have finally found 'others like me'. However, once the initial flush of excitement at the company of fellow lesbians had passed, members became slowly aware of the differences between others and themselves. The attitudes expressed in *Arena Three* and the debates and conflicts which emerged, give testimony to the processes at work in the formation of a lesbian community. As the magazine became increasingly confident in its attempt to undermine and assume the authority of medico-scientific and other 'experts' to define lesbianism, the community could set about identifying certain values as of importance to the group, and others as alien to it. Thus, *Arena Three* readers began to forge a sense of collective identity and common ideology.

When a London member placed the following request in the classified advertisements section in September 1964, she was apparently voicing the feelings of many of MRG's members:

> Is there someone civilised, with mature mind, not too neurotic, who wants constructive relationship? Any replies treated in strict confidence.[86]

For many readers, *Arena Three* afforded their first contact with other lesbians so that the social function it served answered a primary need. In defining the type of woman whom she wished to meet, this reader revealed both her own notions of a potential lesbian ideal and her fears of what other lesbians might be. Although her ideas of a positive lesbian identity were vague, her emphasis on the word 'civilised' – the only positive word she used to define the woman she wished to meet – was not untypical of contributions to *Arena Three*. Reminiscent of British imperialism, the word implied the core middle-class values of 'respectability' and 'decency', while her promise of 'strict confidence' assumed a shared desire for discretion. Her remaining description offered a much clearer picture of the type of person she did not wish to answer her advert: someone who was uncivilised, immature, neurotic and emotionally destructive. This lesbian 'type' – strongly reminiscent of medical and literary characterisations of the lesbian in the half-century before – haunted the imaginations of *Arena Three* subscribers, helping define their notions of lesbian identity.[87]

A proposal to establish a social club, suggested in the first issue of *Arena Three*, enabled many readers to crystallise their early notions of lesbian identity and to define the boundaries of their community. The club, inspired by the Dutch COC club, was to comprise a clubhouse, at which members could socialise, attend lectures and conduct other group activities.[88] In her article, 'A club for human beings', Helena Drew explained:

> There are two needs, and the club would serve two purposes. First, it would offer a place where Lesbians could meet one another. A decent, open and above-board place – no different, in fact, from hundreds of social clubs in England, except for the people it existed to serve. Second, it would provide a venue for talks, to which men could be invited without falling foul of the existing laws.[89]

The emphasis on respectability is again apparent in her description of the club as 'decent, open and above-board', while her aside, 'no different, in fact, from hundreds of social clubs in England', carries with it an assumption of 'normality' and commitment to the values of the wider community. In a second article on the proposed club, Drew tackled the issue of the club's membership. She established the basic principle of inclusivity in her opening comment: 'As a minority which has been socially ostracised for so long it would do us little credit to be too exclusive in our turn.' However, there were to be some exceptions and, in defining the boundaries of membership, the values of respectability and decency were again called upon. Membership should be open to anyone willing to pay a subscription and 'behave in a reasonable and civilised manner'. 'As the formation of this club would undoubtedly receive a certain amount of publicity, press and otherwise, it is essential that the "image" of the club member should be that of a responsible member of society', Drew stressed.[90] Her comments reflected the dual concerns of the *Arena Three* membership: the desire to promote a specific 'public image' to wider society and the desire to form a community in which the members shared certain common values. The ensuing debate about the club and its membership enabled readers to define the boundaries of their own community and identify who was to be included and who excluded from it.

Overseas clubs, such as the COC club in Holland referred to by Helena Drew, were a clear source of inspiration for a number of readers. One reader wrote in to describe a club she had visited in Berlin where members of the management committee took it in turns to host meetings, which began with a talk or debate and ended with socialising. She wrote: 'The atmosphere was relaxed, easy and friendly, and there was also a certain dignity, as the members felt it a privilege to belong to the club. I felt myself to be among women who had asked for something better than a smoozy [sic] den.'[91] Others stressed the importance of an international membership. While European and other overseas clubs provided a model of ease and sincerity to be emulated, readers were quick to emphasise that their club should be a social club but not a nightclub. One reader wrote that she supported the club idea but wanted it to be more than 'the kind of meeting-places which are familiar in Paris', where lesbians 'only want to dance, chat, smoke'.[92] Another said: 'I have heard there are clubs in London, but have been hesitant to go, and I would warmly welcome a "decent club" for the decent people which of course we are.'[93]

It is clear that few members were aware of the existence of lesbian clubs in London – and elsewhere in the UK – at this time, and fewer still had actually visited one. Impressions of these venues were thus derived from the broader literature on lesbianism and from stereotypes of the Soho and London nightlife.[94] Some attempt was made in *Arena Three* to offer a clearer picture of lesbian clubs with the series 'Meeting places of today'. In what were billed as the 'first two reports', descriptions were given of two London venues frequented by homosexuals.[95] The first depicted a 'sophisticated' supper club, peopled by male homosexuals and entertained by a woman soloist; the second recounted a night at the Gateways club. Neither venue was identified by name or location, thus preventing readers from making use of the information to visit them. The magazine's reluctance to provide such practical information was matched by a similar reticence on the part of readers. No letters were published requesting this information and, when the series was quietly dropped after its first instalment, there do not appear to have been any complaints. However, for several years the lesbian nightclubs of London and other cities remained a symbol of a culture that the *Arena Three* community did not wish to be associated with.

The notional attempts to define the boundaries and identities of this community were rendered more concrete through the experiences of the group meetings. Requests from subscribers for social gatherings had resulted in the establishment of monthly group meetings early in 1964, initially developing from the co-founders' administrative meetings conducted in their own homes. However, by March 1964, the meetings had proved so popular that this was no longer practicable and other possible venues had to be sought. Organisers explored the possibility of a restaurant or public hall, before ultimately hiring a pub function room, and the first such meeting was held at the Shakespeare's Head on Carnaby Street on Thursday 28 May.[96] An admission fee of 2/6d was charged to cover the cost of the venue and it was proposed that the evening begin with some form of talk or discussion.[97] This social aspect of the MRG's activities was clearly popular with many members, for whom this was a first opportunity to interact with other lesbians. However, the transition from a discursive to a material community was problematic, forcing members to confront their assumptions regarding their own and their fellow members' lesbian identities. Almost immediately, the issue of members' physical appearance became a source of contention, and, in the June 1964 issue of *Arena Three*, an editorial note commented:

> We must also regretfully voice a complaint. A good many members who have attended the first two MRG meetings have been somewhat piqued by the exhibitionist tendency of one or two others, and want to know if it is really absolutely necessary to turn up to these meetings dressed in what is popularly known as 'full drag'. As the majority of women homosexuals are not 'transvestites' … we shall be glad if at future meetings there will be no further cause for wounded sensibilities.[98]

A satirical article in the same issue entitled 'I haven't a thing to wear', made a further attack on 'masculine' dress, commenting:

> For my money the Lesbian who errs a trifle on the conservative side looks a whole lot better than the one who goes about looking like a send-up of a male impersonator (if you get the idea). Better look female than funny, as one of the wiser ones once remarked.[99]

Readers' letters appeared overwhelmingly to support these views, stating clearly that such styles of dress were not an acceptable symbol of lesbian identity to many *Arena Three* subscribers. A heated discussion within the pages of *Arena Three* ensued, and it was decided that the matter should be debated at the August meeting. The subsequent issue reported a record attendance of seventy members and guests, to hear the motion: 'That this house considers the wearing of male attire at MRG meetings is inappropriate.' At the final count, a small majority rejected the motion, but the more vocal proponents seem to have won the larger argument, and the *Arena Three* write-up noted: 'As an interesting footnote, we observed that only one of the 70 was wearing all-male attire; and indeed many of the stoutest opponents of the motion were wearing cool summer-dresses. Perhaps a case of 'Never mind what I say; just watch what I do' -?'[100] The point had been made that 'butch' lesbians were not welcome in the *Arena Three* community. The editorial response to a solitary letter of defence from a member who had attended meetings in trousers and tie, gives some indication of the motivations for the attack. 'One of the original objects of MRG, as set out in the application form which all who join are asked to read, understand and sign, is "to seek ways of improving the public image of the Lesbian"', she was told.[101] No clear explanation was offered as to how masculine dress was the cause of worsening the public image of lesbianism, but such an identity was presumably considered incompatible with the aim of emphasising the commitment of lesbians to wider social norms. In breaching the conventions on masculine and feminine dress, so-called 'transvestite' lesbians subverted this message.

A second objection to such 'transvestism' centred on the visibility of this expression of identity. Described as 'one of the most obvious outward symbols of the homosexual', it was the public association of cross-dressing with homosexuality which was a source of concern to many *Arena Three* readers. In a letter to the readers' letters section of the magazine, Diana Chapman expanded upon this theme, claiming:

> A lot of our members have led rather isolated lives, disguising their predilections from those around them. It probably takes a lot of mental effort for them to come along and freely admit they are lesbian, even amongst their fellows. If they think that by coming to our meetings they are going to get themselves labelled or identified, they'll just stop coming, which would be a great shame, and we will be left with the exhibitionists.[102]

Chapman's letter suggests that fear of exposure as a lesbian was a real concern to many MRG members. For some, who had never acknowledged their lesbianism to others, attendance at MRG meetings was a first step in identifying themselves as such. It is these women whom MRG apparently regarded as its core membership and Chapman clearly states her commitment to the sensitivities of this group of members over those with a more explicit lesbian identity. Emily Hamer has identified a class dimension to this emphasis on discretion, suggesting that the 'butch' lesbian was perceived by middle-class readers to be presenting an explicitly sexualised lesbian identity to the public. She argues that, from the perspective of many *Arena Three* readers:

> 'Butch' working-class lesbians were blatantly sexual and dangerously stupid because they did not care what straight society thought of them. Straight-acting middle-class lesbians were 'decent people', i.e. not 'butch', not working-class and not dangerous. They could not afford to be recognised as lesbians and did not wish to be seen as sharing a common identity with 'butch dykes'.[103]

In addition to pointing up the differences between its members, the establishment of organised MRG social activities was itself a source of fundamental tensions within the community. The monthly meetings became increasingly popular and, in November 1964, had to be moved to larger premises at the Bull's Head in Clapham.[104] Numbers had become so high that smaller London area groups began to form in North London and Kew, while members' different requirements were reflected in the establishment of interest groups such as outdoor sports, indoor games, musicians, metaphysics and a literary circle. However, their location in London meant that they were accessible only to those who lived in the capital or surrounding area and this became a source of resentment to members from elsewhere in the UK. In June 1964, the editorial notes commented:

> A good many provincial and overseas members have asked whether it would be possible for MRG to start a 'Correspondence Club', pointing out that London members have an unfair advantage: they are able to get to our monthly meetings, whereas isolated members in further-flung towns and villages have no such enviable opportunities of meeting others to swap notes, discuss problems or just enjoy pleasant social occasions.[105]

By September, volunteers had been identified to organise social meetings in Brighton, East Anglia, Devon, Nottinghamshire, Cheshire, Salisbury and Bournemouth. While this lessened the sense of regional favouritism, a fundamental conflict between the role of MRG in promoting social contact and in magazine production remained. Although the magazine's initial publication had offered a vital point of contact for lesbians, the formation of a physical community was, for many, the ideal. Once local social groups had been established, membership of the discursive community of *Arena Three* became less important to these women, and some allowed their subscriptions to lapse.[106] For those whose sense of their lesbian identity was less socially oriented, or who were prevented from attending meetings by familial commitments or geographical remoteness, the magazine remained a lifeline.

In addition to the fundamental conflict that existed between the material and discursive communities of MRG and *Arena Three*, the organisation of social meetings, particularly in London, exacerbated existing financial and administrative tensions. The magazine faced financial difficulties from the outset, which continued throughout its existence. The initial MRG annual membership fee of thirty shillings was designed 'merely to cover the cost of advertising, publishing and circulating our newsletter'. However, as MRG and *Arena Three* became more established and widely known, the number of enquiries and referrals increased to the extent where a full-time staffed office seemed essential and funds were required for salaries and office rental. In its first year, the running costs of the magazine and group were apparently partially subsidised by a loan from Esme Langley and in December 1964, the membership fee was increased to three guineas.[107] At the same time, production of the magazine moved from Esme Langley and Diana Chapman's home address to an office at 41 Great Russell Street, WC1. The office was shared with a publishing company who rented it to Esme Langley personally for her freelance secretarial and press agency work.

The overlap between the magazine's finances and the private finances of Esme Langley was a considerable source of friction throughout this period as any expenditure had to be requested directly from Esme Langley who paid it out of her personal account. The extent to which the cost of organising these meetings was paid for out of magazine finances is unclear. An admission charge was made to the monthly meetings and Esme Langley claimed, in August 1965, that, 'the London social activities are not subsidised out of subscriptions paid by all-region and overseas members. If any social activities are to be subsidised at all, obviously all must be.'[108] However, an editorial in November of the same year proposed the introduction of a new category of simple subscription to *Arena Three*, which would exclude contributions to social activities, while Cynthia Reid, who had become the London social organiser in January 1965, recalled that any money required for booking social venues for MRG had to be paid by Langley.[109] In May 1965, underlying tensions were brought to a head when Diana Chapman left both Esme Langley and the magazine.[110] London members, including Cynthia Reid and Julie Switsur, who had long had concerns over the autocratic manner in which Esme Langley controlled *Arena Three* and MRG, as well as Langley's prioritising of the magazine at the expense of social activities, and prompted by concern that Langley could not bear the administrative or financial burden alone, proposed the formation of a democratically elected committee who would be responsible for policy decisions and financial control.[111] While Cynthia Reid organised a debate of the issue at a London meeting and distributed a postal petition to subscribers, Esme Langley used the magazine itself to portray this debate as an attempted coup.[112] Editorial notes and articles were published emphasising the extent to which she personally produced the magazine, while the letters pages were filled with letters describing the petition as a 'dirty trick' and proclaiming: 'I am with you all the way over this take over bid!'[113]

Many of the basic values by, and against which, the *Arena Three* community defined itself resurfaced in readers' reactions to this dispute. Many readers, prompted by Langley's representation of the situation, understood the dispute simply as a power struggle in which a group of London members were seeking to take over control of the magazine from its founder and editor. All announced their loyalty to Langley, and in so doing provided an indication of readers' views of their editor. One reader's comment – 'it's your baby as far as I'm concerned, and you've taken all the knocks for people like me who stay nameless' – was typical of many.[114]

Such comments suggest that readers had regarded the figure of the editor as a solution to the conflict between MRG's aim of promoting a positive lesbian image, and its members' reluctance to be identified as lesbians. Esme Langley constituted the public face of both *Arena Three* and its lesbian community, thus facilitating the discretion which many members valued. This understanding was acknowledged in a subsequent discussion regarding membership badges. A proposal to adopt a badge as a means for members to identify each other was dismissed on the grounds that the wider public would soon become aware of its symbolism, exposing the wearer to public recognition. Langley shared this view, arguing: 'Main drawback is that the general public would soon catch on, this could lead to the kind of "pestering" and "pruriosity" [sic] which I have been personally exposed to for more than two years – and would much prefer to spare our other members!'[115] In her own and some readers' eyes, Esme Langley was the representative of the community, to whom loyalty was owed in return for her courage in publicly identifying herself as a lesbian.

Other letters indicate that hostility toward the London club culture, and the 'transvestite' lesbians who were thought to inhabit it, remained strong. T. D. from Hampstead wrote in:

> I went to the Clapham meeting last Thursday and have resolved not to go there again. You once said that the 'Undesirable' types usually weeded themselves out; well, the reverse has happened as far as those meetings are concerned. There is now only about 10 per cent of the original 'Shakespeare's Head' group there, and the rest are a collection of morons, dyed blond hard-faced 'Tarts' and betrousered fat tough guys. All the atmosphere of the early days has completely departed and in its place is a loud-voiced, grasping big-headed element … Let them talk, and talk, and if they like, break away – MRG would be better without them.[116]

The hatred and contempt expressed in this letter toward lesbians who adopted butch/femme identities dramatically illustrated the force with which T. D. sought to distance them from her own community. The language was extreme and prompted one reader to object that 'although I am personally not attracted by that type of person, male or female, I find distressing the tone of criticism of this type'.[117] However, the sentiment was one which other readers clearly shared. M. S. from Gloucester commented, in the following issue, that:

> The 'public image' of the lesbian is so often a warped, unbalanced woman whose only interest, outside the minimal hours spent earning a living, is in gratifying an immoderate and irregular sexual lust. The thousands of other lesbians, who are probably no more highly sexed than their heterosexual

counterparts, are just too normal and unremarkable in their habits and activities to be picked out by any chance acquaintances or colleagues, and are doing perfectly normal and useful jobs for the community. It is the image of these lesbians which needs to be put over. I don't believe that the lesbians who gravitate to London's square mile or two of vice are typical of the breed – they certainly aren't in need of being rescued from loneliness. It seems to me that they are already very well catered for compared with the rest of us who are scattered throughout the country.[118]

M. S. here constructs, for herself and her fellow *Arena Three* readers, a persona of the 'normal', 'useful' member of society to whom their lesbianism is just one facet of a broader being, in opposition to a 'warped, unbalanced' lesbian obsessed with her own lesbian identity. Such an identity was, for M. S., a predominantly sexual one and was enacted on the stage of the London club scene.

In rejecting the importance of sexuality to her model of lesbian identity, M. S. reflected a view commonly expressed in *Arena Three*. Esme Langley occasionally reported having been contacted by heterosexual men requesting sample subscriptions of *Arena Three* for the purposes of 'erotic titillation' or offering marriage or hospitality to lesbian subscribers. Langley and others attributed such approaches to representations of lesbians in medical and popular literature as promiscuous and 'skilled in bizarre sexual practices'. MRG members regarded these requests as a hindrance to their central aims and, commenting on the issue in September 1964, Diana Chapman reflected:

> The most unfortunate aspect of this unholy mesalliance between lesbianism and pornography is that it diverts attention from the really important problems, which are social, to the comparatively minor ones of sexuality. It also means that respectable journals often put an embargo on the whole subject – thus helping only to perpetuate the unsavoury images.[119]

The desire to distance themselves from such characterisations of lesbianism, and the aim of promoting a 'respectable' public image, apparently prompted *Arena Three* to downplay sexuality. Fears of the legal consequences of publishing any material that might be regarded as sexually explicit may have been a further motivating factor. In her 1963 letter to Antony Grey proposing the publication of a lesbian magazine, Langley asked: 'Before I start advertising for editorial and other assistance … what legal snags am I likely to run into? It will naturally be a perfectly reputable publication …'[120] Drawing on his experience of the legal threats to male homosexual ventures, Antony Grey advised caution. Diana Chapman commented on the issue in her Hall Carpenter interview, claiming:

> We were very concerned. We hadn't realised that there was this interest in lesbianism as pornography. And that we found quite shocking. We'd sort of have men, knocking at the door or ringing up. We were very concerned that it should be a proper, decent magazine and that there should be no overt sort of sex, or nothing that could be remotely described as titillating because, when we set it up, funnily enough, just up the road in Broadhurst Gardens, lived Antony Grey. You know Antony Grey? And so he used to appear, stooping vulture-like uttering terrible warnings that we might be prosecuted for uttering an obscene libel and we didn't know, in the climate of the time, you see, so we had to be very careful that it was fearfully respectable.[121]

The practical reluctance to discuss issues of sexuality in *Arena Three* was reinforced by occasional editorial assertions that the subject of sexuality was of greater interest to men than to women.[112]

However, by the late 1960s, *Arena Three* demonstrated an increasing tendency toward mutual tolerance. As the community grew in confidence and a sense of security, its members became more open and the group as a whole became more inclusive and less hostile to other lesbian identities and cultures. While early issues had stressed the genuine dangers of acknowledging one's lesbianism in the workplace and elsewhere, views gradually shifted. When two readers wrote in, in June 1965, to complain that 'too much publicity about your club's activities in the popular press is making it very difficult for two women to live together unnoticed, without being viewed with suspicion' other readers accused them of talking 'a lot of rot' and wishing 'to perpetuate ignorance and prejudice as opposed to truth and enlightenment'.[123] An article, 'Healthy homosexuality', in June 1967, questioned whether lesbians were right to be so anxious about exposure of their identity and argued in favour of greater openness. A year later, a letter from Jane Marshall in Edinburgh demanded:

> What age are your contributors? – or readers for that matter? At 18 I am a Lesbian and proud to feel different. Why all this mealy-mouthed talk of being secretive ..., when we should surely be rejoicing in our freedom in this country?[124]

The editorial policy reflected and, to some extent, encouraged this trend. The magazine's reports on the Stonewall riots and the birth of the Gay Liberation Front in New York, followed its evolution through to the first British GLF meeting at the London School of Economics in 1971. Letters from GLF members canvassing female supporters were published and, in March 1971, readers were encouraged to contribute to a proposed GLF book on homosexuality.[125] *Arena Three*'s attitudes toward other issues also changed. In February 1970, a reader wrote in advocating the publication of a lesbian sex manual and a series of articles on the subject in *Arena Three*. The following month, a letter was published endorsing this idea and suggesting a number of heterosexual manuals which could be adapted by the lesbian reader. When Miss J. B. from Buckinghamshire wrote in, in December 1970, to complain that, 'nothing on this earth would attract me to a butch lesbian. I find them as revolting as men', not only was a response from a butch lesbian published, but several others endorsed it.[126] Commenting on the butch lesbian's letter, the editor wrote: 'Never you mind, love. If our Editorial Board went in for high heels, frills and lipstick, we'd never get A3 out at all', while another reader exclaimed: 'Take heart, RMC Gloucester, because there are plenty of feminine ladies, who prefer their butch partners to be as masculine as possible'.[127] Moreover, in July 1966, less than a year after the London club culture was referred to as a 'square mile or two of vice', members were issued with a 'Social Activities' membership card which 'serve[d] as an introduction to a famous and old-established club called "The Gateways"'. The next and subsequent MRG meetings were held there.[128]

This rapprochement came too late, however, for Cynthia Reid and the 'London Volunteer Committee' who had proposed change in 1965. The Volunteer Committee's suggestion, in the summer of 1965, that financial and administrative control be given to a committee elected by postal vote, was rejected by Langley, despite attempts at mediation by the MP and member of the MRG Board of Directors, Dr David Kerr. Esme Langley failed to attend the arbitration meetings and instead registered the magazine as a public limited company in her own name.[129] Exasperated by the situation, one of the London area social groups, the Kensington and Richmond group, decided to break away from MRG and *Arena Three* and establish their own group. The group was named Kenric, after the first three letters of Kensington and Richmond, respectively, and the secretary, treasurer and chairman of the old local group formed the first committee of the new group. Cynthia Reid, Julie Switsur, and those MRG members who had become frustrated with MRG joined the new group. Reid commented:

> We just felt that we'd had enough, we couldn't continue in the pattern that things had been going, that a democratically elected committee was really the way forward and the social organisation was really what most people seemed to want. The magazine was good for people who felt isolated, but it didn't meet the needs of people who actually wanted to meet face-to-face, have a drink, have a chat, go out for a meal, have a party, this sort of thing. And that was the prime need, I think, of something like 80 to 90% of the people who actually joined. What they got was a magazine, but what they wanted was to meet other people.[130]

Kenric members attempted to organise the new group in a more democratic manner, based on the constitution, which had been drafted by
Cynthia Reid and others for MRG. The group was primarily a social organisation, with meetings held in members' homes, and described itself as
non-political. A low-profile, but permanent fixture on the post-war
lesbian scene, Kenric sought to establish a lesbian community based on
different values from those of *Arena Three*. Looking to the immediate needs
of its members, Kenric aimed to alleviate isolation and forge a material
community through the organisation of social meetings and parties.

However, for Esme Langley and the *Arena Three* community, the primary
focus of the lesbian organisation should be external. In March 1967,
Langley cited, with approval, a speech by Antony Grey on the role of
homosexual organisations:

> Lots of us want to do something inward-looking – get the 'group' together,
> make it cosy and comfortable in a nice little clubhouse with a chromium-
> plated bar and a dance floor upstairs. But this is something that must follow,
> and not precede, a good deal of much more outward-directed work.
> Because even this desire, for innocent social gatherings, can appear to the
> over-anxious, non-homosexual person as a 'drive for recruits', the passport
> to the 'nameless orgies' which so inflame some people's rather lurid imag-
> inations.[131]

The magazine's aims were therefore those of changing public attitudes to
lesbianism through the promotion of scientific research and the education
of the media. *Arena Three* represented a forum through which the 'truth'
about lesbianism, as its editors and readers understood it, could be
projected to wider society. In this respect, *Arena Three* can be regarded as
anticipating the concerns of subsequent Gay Liberation politics. Alison
Oram has argued:

> When we consider what Jeffrey Weeks identifies to be three novel princi-
> ples of the Gay Liberation Front – the importance of collective action and
> self-help, asserting the validity of homosexuality ('Gay is Good') and open-
> ness about one's sexuality ('Coming Out') – it can be seen that the MRG
> and *Arena Three* played a pioneering role in every respect. In terms of collec-
> tive action, it was the first organisation in Britain to be led by self-declared
> lesbians representing their own interests. Its leaders were neither ashamed
> of nor convert about their sexuality in the hostile environment of the mid
> 1960s. And, as its readership grew over the remainder of the decade, *Arena
> Three* came to see itself as the main voice of British lesbians, with a key
> position in the spectrum of gay groups and organisations and in public
> debates.[132]

Through its intervention in medico-scientific debates and media coverage of lesbianism, *Arena Three* had been instrumental in promoting alternative representations of the lesbian in the mid to late 1960s. However, despite this emphasis on external work, *Arena Three* was equally influential in forging a collective lesbian identity and establishing a lesbian community.

Notes

1 The magazine, *Urania*, produced between 1915 and 1940, had touched upon lesbian themes and advocated same-sex relationships for women. Its primary concern, however, Alison Oram has argued, was in building 'a feminist theory of radical transgender'. See Alison Oram, '"Sex is an accident": Feminism, science and the radical sexual theory of Urania, 1915–1940', in Lucy Bland and Laura Doan (eds), *Sexology in Culture: Labelling Bodies and Desires* (Cambridge: Polity Press, 1998).

2 See Waters, 'Havelock Ellis, Sigmund Freud and the state', on the influence of medical models on homosexual writings in the post-war period.

3 NSA, HCC (C456), F2088, Diana Chapman.

4 NSA, HCC (C456), F2088, Diana Chapman; NSA, HCC (C456), F1607–F1612, Jackie Forster.

5 Dilys Rowe, 'A quick look at lesbians', *Twentieth Century* (Winter 1962/63), pp. 67–72.

6 *Arena Three* 1:1 (January 1964), p. 6.

7 *Arena Three* 1:1 (January 1964), p. 6.

8 NSA, HCC (C456), F2088, Diana Chapman.

9 The HLRS was an organisation founded in 1958 to lobby for homosexual law reform. The Albany Trust was established as its fund-raising body. See Weeks, *Coming Out*. NSA, HCC (C456), F1336–1338, Antony Grey.

10 NSA, HCC (C456), F2109, Cynthia Reid.

11 Both Cynthia Reid and Julie Switsur are careful not to identify this individual.

12 NSA, HCC (C456), F2109, Cynthia Reid.

13 *Arena Three* 4:7 (July 1967), p. 13. Esme Langley went on to explain that the 'Three' had no 'esoteric meaning'. 'When I christened the new publication, back in 1963, I found there were already two other magazines titled "Arena", so I added the word "Three" to avoid confusion.'

14 The magazine's initial format of a number of A4 duplicated sheets stapled together in one corner, eventually gave way to A5 pamphlet-style booklets and finally, in 1970, to glossy printed issues to enable the public sale of the magazine.

15 See Faderman, *Odd Girls and Twilight Lovers* for a brief discussion of *The Ladder*.

16 NSA, HCC (C456), F2088, Diana Chapman.

17 Records of subscribers were destroyed for reasons of confidentiality when the magazine ceased publication in 1971, but it is possible to deduce from editorial comment that Iris Murdoch and Mary McIntosh were among the magazine's subscribers.

18 The HLRS did produce two publications – *Spectrum*, a newsletter keeping supporters in touch with campaigns etc. and *Man and Society*, a journal in which the society's theoretical views were set out. Neither, however, served as a social 'magazine' for homosexual men.

19 In 1970 and 1971, the back cover of each issue listed those newsagents and bookshops at which *Arena Three* could be bought, although Angela Chilton recounted buying her copy of *Arena Three* at a 'porn shop': NSA, HCC (C456), F1622–F1624, Angela Chilton.

20 *Arena Three* 8:4 (April 1971), pp. 6–7.

21 *Arena Three* 1:1 (January 1964).

22 Lesley Hall, '"Disinterested enthusiasm for sexual misconduct": The British Society for the Study of Sex Psychology, 1913–47', *Journal of Contemporary History* 30 (1995).

23 Hilary Benno, 'Scouting for – the public image', *Arena Three* 1:1 (January 1964), p. 3. The remaining three were the media, the law, and the 'man on the street'.

24 Diana Chapman, 'Bent or straight mates?', *Arena Three* 1:1 (January 1964), p. 8.

25 Diana Chapman, 'Bent or straight mates?', *Arena Three* 1:1 (January 1964), p. 8.

26 'Hilary Benno', 'Scouting for … THE CURE', *Arena Three* 1:2 (February 1964), p. 3. 'Hilary Benno' was one of Esme Langley's pseudonyms.

27 'Comment on "The cure"', *Arena Three* 1:3 (March 1964), p. 12.

28 'Comment on "The cure"', *Arena Three* 1:3 (March 1964), p. 12.

29 For example, June Hopkins, 'The lesbian personality', *British Journal of Psychiatry* 115 (1969); F. E. Kenyon, 'Studies in female homosexuality', *British Journal of Psychiatry* 114 (1968); Eva Bene, 'On the genesis of female homosexuality', *British Journal of Psychiatry* (1965).

30 NSA, HCC (C456), F2109, Cynthia Reid.

31 Bene, 'On the genesis of female homosexuality'; an unnamed psychiatric social worker and member of MRG who proposed collaborating with MRG on research in the field of 'mental health'; Hopkins, 'The lesbian personality'; Kenyon, 'Studies in female homosexuality'; D. Stanley-Jones, whose proposed research was into 'The unmarried lesbian and maternal instinct'; Wolff, *Love Between Women*; Mrs Morwenna Jones, conducting research into the erotic imagination of lesbians on behalf of an unnamed American psychologist; Mary Cecil, conducting a handwriting study; Marvin Siegelman, Associate Professor in Psychology at the City University of New York comparing the personality, attitude and parental background of homosexuals and heterosexuals.

32 On the Sexual Offences Act 1967, see Weeks, *Sex, Politics and Society* and Weeks, *Coming Out*.

33 Alison Oram, 'Little by little? *Arena Three* and lesbian politics in the 1960s', in Marcus Collins (ed.), *The Permissive Society and its Enemies: Sixties British Culture* (London: Rivers Oram Press, forthcoming). I am grateful to Alison Oram for allowing me to see a copy of this article.

34 NSA, HCC (C456), F2088, Diana Chapman.

35 Bene, 'On the genesis of female homosexuality'.

36 NSA, HCC (C456), F2108, Julie Switsur.

37 Hopkins, 'The lesbian personality'.
38 Established in Forel, *The Sexual Question*, p. 252; Moll, *Perversions of the Sex Instinct*, pp. 231, 233. See Doan, 'Acts of female indecency'.
39 'MRG and the "Public Image"', *Arena Three* 3:11 (December 1966).
40 Cynthia Reid, 'Psychology and the homosexual', *Arena Three* 2:4 (April 1965), p. 10.
41 Kenyon, 'Studies in female homosexuality'.
42 NSA, HCC (C456), F2108, Julie Switsur.
43 'MRG and research', *Arena Three* 3:5 (June 1966), pp. 15–17.
44 'People – please write', *Arena Three* 5:5 (May 1968), p. 9.
45 *Arena Three* 8:4 (April 1971), p. 16.
46 *Arena Three* 8:7–12, p. 7. The letter was published in the final issue of *Arena Three* so that it would not have been possible for any other readers to respond to this letter, either endorsing or disagreeing with the authors.
47 *Arena Three* 2:3 (March 1965), p. 6.
48 Anthony Storr, *Sexual Deviation* (Harmondsworth: Penguin, 1964). Other books in the series examined alcoholism, depression and suicide, the violent criminal, and 'the meaning of madness'.
49 *Arena Three* 1:5 (May 1964), p. 9.
50 This reflected a contemporary trend toward statistical surveys.
51 *Arena Three* 4:8 (August 1967), p. 7.
52 *Arena Three* 3:5 (June 1966), p. 2.
53 Esme Langley, 'MRG, yesterday and tomorrow', *Arena Three* 3:9 (October 1966), p. 9. Caprio's *Female Homosexuality* received particularly negative coverage in *Arena Three*.
54 NSA, HCC (C456), F2109, Cynthia Reid; NSA, HCC (C456), F2108, Julie Switsur; NSA, HCC (C456), F2088, Diana Chapman.
55 Cynthia Reid, 'Psychology and the Homosexual', *Arena Three* 2:4 (April 1965), p. 10.
56 Julie Switsur and Diana Chapman, the other advocates of medical research, also left *Arena Three* in 1965.
57 *Arena Three* 4:5 (May 1967), p. 16.
58 'Us and the social scene', *Arena Three* 4:10 (October 1967), p. 2.
59 Weeks, *Coming Out*.
60 The media portrayal of lesbians in 1964 was summed up in an *Arena Three* article thus: 'A BBC friend told me he'd wanted to do a documentary programme on Lesbianism some time back now. But it had been strangled at birth. High-level shush-shush policy, he said sadly': Hilary Benno, 'Scouting for – the public image', *Arena Three* 1:1 (January 1964), p. 3. The first indexed reference to lesbianism in *The Times* in the post-war period was *The Times* (2 November 1970), p. 8.
61 'A girl lies dying in the shadow of the gallows', *News of the World* (24 February 1952); 'Her woman friend cleared in "initials only" suit', *News of the World* (16 March 1952); 'In my experience', *Observer* (6 November 1966); 'If you want her have her', *Titbits* (20 April 1968); 'An affair', *Brighton Evening Argus* (9 September 1969).

62 Dilys Rowe, 'A quick look at lesbians', *Twentieth Century* (Winter 1962/63), pp. 67–72.

63 London School of Economics (hereafter LSE), Hall Carpenter Archive / Albany Trust / 14 / 80, Letter from Esme Langley to 'The Secretary, Homosexual Law Reform Society', 10 May 1963.

64 Esme Langley, 'Quick look – dead loss', *Arena Three* 1:1 (January 1964), p. 6.

65 *Arena Three* 4:10 (October 1967), p. 3.

66 For example, reports from the *Sheffield Morning Telegraph* (9 December 1966) and the *Kilburn Times* (30 December 1966), which were referred to in 'What goes on', *Arena Three* 4:1 (January 1967), pp. 3–6.

67 *Man Alive*, BBC 2 (14 June 1967); *Arena Three* 4:7 (July 1967), pp. 2–3. On Colonel Barker, see James Vernon, '"For some queer reason"'.

68 'Relations with the press', *Arena Three* 1:11 (November 1964), p. 14.

69 *Arena Three* 1:12 (December 1964).

70 *This Week*, ITV (Thursday 7 January 1965); *Arena Three* 2:1 (January 1965); *Arena Three* 2:2 (February 1965).

71 Bryan Magee, 'The facts about lesbianism', *New Statesman* (26 March 1965), pp. 491–2.

72 Antony Grey, 'Letters to the editor', *New Statesman* (2 April 1965), p. 530.

73 Magee, 'The facts about lesbianism', *New Statesman* (26 March 1965), pp. 492.

74 *Arena Three* 2:4 (April 1965), p. 8.

75 Tony Geraghty, 'Letters to the Editor', *New Statesman* (2 April 1965), p. 530.

76 There is not sufficient evidence to make an assessment of the class background of *Arena Three*'s membership, but a questionnaire survey completed by fifty readers as late as 1971 indicated that a small majority were engaged in predominantly middle-class occupations. Of the fifty readers who responded, 20 classed themselves as 'professional', 2 as 'executive', 8 as 'clerical', 7 as 'housewife', 4 as 'other', 1 was a student, 3 were in the forces and 5 in nursing.

77 *Observer* (9 March 1964); *Sunday Times* (16 March 1964).

78 *Arena Three* 1:3 (March 1964).

79 *Arena Three* 1:8 (August 1964). A second advert was also placed in the *New Statesman*, stating 'Women with homosexual problems read *Arena Three*'; 'Relations with the Press', *Arena Three* 1:11 (November 1964), p. 14.

80 *Arena Three* 4:10 (October 1967), p. 7.

81 *Arena Three* 7:7 (August 1970), p. 1.

82 The *Sunday Telegraph* had apparently changed its policy since 1967 and decided to accept advertisements for *Arena Three*.

83 *Arena Three* 7:7 (August 1970), p. 6.

84 See Martin Duberman, *Stonewall* (Harmondsworth: Penguin, 1993).

85 *Arena Three* 8:4 (April 1971), pp. 10–11; *The Times* (29 May 1971), p. 3.

86 *Arena Three* 1:9 (September 1964), p. 14.

87 Katie Gilmartin has discussed this tendency in relation to middle-class lesbian communities in 1950s Colorado Springs: Gilmartin, '"We weren't bar people"'.

88 The Cultuur-en OntspanningsCentrum (Culture and Recreation Centre) was founded by homophile advocates in 1946.

89 Helena Drew, 'A club for human beings', *Arena Three* 1:1 (January 1964), p. 11.
90 Helena Drew, 'A club for human beings – 2', *Arena Three* 1:2 (February 1964), p. 10.
91 *Arena Three* 1:5 (May 1964), p. 12.
92 *Arena Three* 1:3 (March 1964), p. 11.
93 *Arena Three* 1:5 (May 1964), p. 12.
94 For example, Tietjen, *Soho*; Progl, *Woman of the Underworld*, pp. 23–4; Fabian, *London After Dark*, p. 12. Radclyffe Hall's negative portrayal of the Parisian lesbian bar culture in her novel *The Well of Loneliness* was, however, likely to have reached a wider lesbian readership.
95 *Arena Three* 1:5 (May 1964), p. 13.
96 *Arena Three* 1:5 (May 1964).
97 The structure of the meetings changed over the years, including debates on lesbian motherhood, speakers such as Bryan Magee and Eva Bene, and showings of television documentaries on lesbianism.
98 *Arena Three* 1:6 (June 1964), p. 14.
99 'I haven't a thing to wear', *Arena Three* 1:6 (June 1964), p. 3.
100 *Arena Three* 1:9 (September 1964), p. 12. A Readers' survey conducted in 1965 found that 61 per cent of readers thought drag should be allowed at meetings, as opposed to 36 per cent against. Opposition apparently increased with age. *Arena Three* 2:2 (February 1965).
101 *Arena Three* 1:7 (July 1964), p. 12.
102 *Arena Three* 1:7 (July 1964), p. 13.
103 Hamer, *Britannia's Glory*, p. 174.
104 *Arena Three* 1:11 (November 1964).
105 *Arena Three* 1:6 (June 1964), p.2.
106 This was a continuing problem, forcing Barbara Todd, a member of the editorial team, to complain in 1971 that she had written to twenty area co-ordinators requesting reports on their groups' activities and had only received three replies: *Arena Three* 8:4 (April 1971).
107 *Arena Three* 1:12 (December 1964).
108 *Arena Three* 2:8 (August 1965), p. 12.
109 *Arena Three* 2:11 (November 1965), p. 2; NSA, HCC (C456), F2109, Cynthia Reid.
110 NSA, HCC (C456), F2088, Diana Chapman; Diana Chapman, 'Mummy of them all', *Out* (February/March 1977).
111 NSA, HCC (C456), F2108, Julie Switsur; NSA, HCC (C456), F2109, Cynthia Reid.
112 *Arena Three* 2:7–9 (July – September 1965).
113 *Arena Three* 2:9 (September 1965), p. 12.
114 *Arena Three* 2:8 (August 1965), p. 11.
115 *Arena Three* 2:11 (November 1965), p. 17.
116 *Arena Three* 2:9 (September 1965), p. 12.
117 *Arena Three* 2:10 (October 1965), p. 11.
118 *Arena Three* 2:10 (October 1965), p. 13.
119 *Arena Three* 1:9 (September 1964), p. 7.

120 LSE, Hall Carpenter Archive / Albany Trust / 14/80, Letter from Esme Langley to Antony Grey, 10 May 1963.
121 NSA, HCC (C456), F2088, Diana Chapman. Contact with the American organisation, Daughters of Bilitis, and its magazine, *The Ladder*, can only have exacerbated such fears. See Faderman, *Odd Girls and Twilight Lovers*, p. 149 on the harassment members faced from the police and the FBI.
122 *Arena Three* 3:7 (August 1966), p. 5; *Arena Three* 5:9 (September 1968).
123 *Arena Three* 2:6 (June 1965), p. 11.
124 *Arena Three* 5:7 (July 1968), p. 14.
125 The notion of 'coming out' was, of course, a central tenet of GLF ideology. See Duberman, *Stonewall*.
126 *Arena Three* 7:11/12 (November/December 1970), p. 6.
127 *Arena Three* 8:4 (April 1971), pp. 6–7; *Arena Three* 8:6 (June 1971), p. 8.
128 *Arena Three* 3:6 (July 1966), p. 19.
130 *Arena Three* 2:9 (September 1965), p. 2.
131 NSA, HCC (C456), F2109, Cynthia Reid.
132 *Arena Three* 4:3 (March 1967), p. 1.
133 Oram, 'Little by little'.

Conclusion

In her interview with the Hall Carpenter Oral History Group, Diana Chapman claimed: 'The 1950s were a terrible decade for women.'[1] In doing so, she drew on a classic feminist representation of the immediate post-war decades as years of conservative femininity; arguments which have been reinforced by the conventional wisdom that the post-war years constituted an era of cultural austerity. However, lesbian accounts, including Chapman's own, offer a new perspective on post-war Britain, questioning the dominant representation of the 1940s and 50s. This evidence suggests that many women were challenging the cultural emphasis on domesticity as women's defining concern and presenting radically alternative modes of femininity, decades before the organised women's movement.

The ambiguities and contradictions in post-war notions of femininity afforded women a surprising degree of flexibility in the expression of alternative gender and sexual identities. Concepts such as 'tomboy', 'bachelor girl' and 'career woman' enabled women to forge social identities as single, economically independent and active women and to deploy these identities to express same-sex desire. Histories of sexuality in Britain have tended to present a monolithic, albeit historically contingent view of sexual identity, focusing, for example, on the figure of Radclyffe Hall and her fictional heroine, Stephen Gordon, as the archetypal lesbian identity model of the 1920s, or on the political lesbian as the dominant 1970s version of lesbianism. However, *Tomboys and Bachelor Girls* suggests a much more fluid and multiplicitous understanding of sexual identity, demonstrating the diverse range of sexual identity models current in post-war Britain. Lesbian accounts indicate the active role played by individual women in performing these identities in ways which were both situational and contingent.

Crucial to their deployment were a range of new spaces and communities which emerged out of expanding opportunities for women in the post-war decades. The development of unconventional occupational choices for women, such as the police and women's services, offered women greater opportunities to express alternative gender and sexual identities through work. An emerging lesbian consumer culture, in the context of wider social changes in accepted women's behaviour, played an important role in defining new models of lesbian identity based on butch/femme roles. However, while accounts of the role of consumerism in current lesbian and gay culture have presented consumer culture as a uniquely inclusive environment for lesbians and gay men, accounts of the post-war lesbian bar scene suggest that bar communities also operated to exclude certain identities in the past.

On an individual and collective level, lesbians sought to challenge and redefine accepted discourses on sexuality in the post-war decades. The picture of lesbianism and medico-scientific research, which emerges from lesbian accounts, points to a complex interplay between the medical profession and lesbianism generally, as well as between individual psychiatrists and lesbians. Personal accounts suggest that medical discourses continued to be highly influential in shaping women's understanding of lesbianism in the post-war decades. The published medical literature on homosexuality constituted an important point of reference for lesbians, while medical accounts and case histories offered an enduring model for narratives of identity formation. However, the histories of the lesbian magazine, *Arena Three*, and the social organisation, Kenric, indicate that this was not a unidirectional process. Members of these lesbian communities actively participated in scientific and medical research in the 1960s in an attempt to discredit established hostile accounts and foster greater understanding of lesbianism. Their stringent evaluation of research proposals and increasingly critical responses to research conclusions ensured that they were not located as passive objects of the medical gaze. Moreover, accounts of personal encounters between individual women and psychiatrists or counsellors provide unexpected evidence of collaboration. Not only did women actively seek psychiatric help in making sense of their sexuality, but psychiatrists also frequently engaged with their clients on a highly practical level, facilitating introductions between individual lesbians and disseminating information on the nature and location of existing lesbian communities.

Writing lesbian experience into post-war histories also has further implications for narratives of post-war Britain. Accounts of the development of a specific lesbian subculture, emerging in the 1950s, and the educational objectives of the first lesbian magazine in the 1960s, under-cut the notion of the 1960s as a decisive moment of radicalisation. Instead, they suggest a more gradual emergence of marginal cultures, predicated on diverse understandings of lesbian identity. More fundamentally, narratives of lesbian practices and collective action in the post-war decades as introspective and predicated on a political claim to 'normality', undermine assumptions of lesbian participation in an emerging 'counter-culture'.

Representations of the bar subculture and lesbian organisations such as the Minorities Research Group and Kenric, in particular challenge the accepted narrative of pre-Gay Liberation Movement politics. The conventional account of post-war sexuality, in particular, is either one of triumphant gays overcoming prejudice or a paradoxical deflation of the radical potential of pre-1970s sexual cultures. However, oral accounts of the British lesbian communities of this period point to a different interpretation, indicating that they incorporated a distinct political ideology which focused its claim to citizenship on the right to privacy or freedom of personal expression in the private sphere. In a similar argument to that made by Peter Wildeblood in his 1955 account of homosexuality, and by the Wolfenden Report's proposed legal reforms, these communities represented lesbians as 'ordinary' people with a right to express their emotional orientation in private.[2] However, this political message resists interpretation as a precursor to Gay Liberation movement politics. Evidence of encounters between members of the earlier lesbian communities, such as the Gateways night-club, and Gay Liberation Front activists, in 1971, indicate that the two political cultures were profoundly antithetical. Nevertheless, this evidence reconfigures our understanding of post-war sexual cultures as apolitical, demonstrating that issues of sexual deviance were hotly debated by lesbians and homosexual men in the post-war decades, against the backdrop of a vibrant social scene. These debates were not simply the beginning of a movement toward sexual liberation, culminating in the Gay Liberation movement, but offered significant alternative perspectives which engaged with contemporary social and cultural concerns.

Notes

1 NSA, HCC (C456), F2088, Diana Chapman.
2 Peter Wildeblood, *Against the Law* (London: Weidenfeld and Nicolson, 1955).

Epilogue

Our account of lesbianism in post-war Britain ends in 1971. However, the subsequent history of the women we have encountered could in many ways be said to bring us back to where we started in the archives. This story would therefore not be complete if we failed to consider the history of the Hall Carpenter Oral History Archive itself, and its role in shaping the ways in which post-war lesbian history can be imagined.

In the decade after 1971, new social and political conceptualisations of lesbianism proliferated. Following the demise of *Arena Three*, a group of women, including Angela Chilton and Jackie Forster, established a new lesbian organisation and magazine, *Sappho*. The magazine grew out of the monthly *Arena Three* Media Campaign meetings and was so named 'because [Sappho] was a wife, a widow, a mother and she started this college on Lesbos where women learned, loved and lived together and we felt that covered the lesbian scene as we knew it then'.[1] A highly active and visible lesbian group in the 1970s, Sappho held regular discussion groups and meetings, addressed by guest speakers on topics such as women and alcohol and lesbian motherhood. The Gay Liberation Front and the recently renamed Campaign for Homosexual Equality offered new opportunities for lesbians to campaign alongside gay men for lesbian and gay rights in this period, although many lesbians felt sidelined as women in this movement. The first British conference of the Women's Liberation Movement was held in Oxford in 1971 and many lesbians, including Roberta Henderson, Rosanna Hibbert, Sandy Martin, Sharley McLean and Jackie Forster were actively involved. Sappho was strongly influenced by current feminist ideas: Angela Chilton described the discussion meetings as being based around small 'consciousness-raising groups' and a Sappho group was active in campaigning for sexual orientation to be included as a category in the Sex Discrimination Act.

Jackie Forster's role as director of Sappho, and her background in the media, rendered her an obvious spokesperson for lesbian issues in the 1970s. She had come out publicly as a lesbian at Hyde Park's Speakers' Corner in 1969 and was a ubiquitous figure in media discussions of lesbianism in the subsequent decade. An obituary in 1998 described her as having been a 'veritable rent-a-dyke' in this period.[2] Heavily involved in lesbian activism in the 1970s and 1980s, Jackie Forster also became increasingly interested in lesbian history. In 1992 she joined the Management Committee of the Lesbian Archive and Information Centre, which had been established in London in 1984, and in 1995 she set up 'Daytime Dykes', a lesbian social group which visited historic lesbian sites in London. Her personal connections between lesbian socialising, activism and history from the 1960s to the 1990s are indicative of the broader links between lesbian campaigning and lesbian archives in this period.

The Hall Carpenter Oral History Archive, which represents the largest single archive of lesbian and gay personal narratives in the UK, exemplifies these connections between lesbian politics and history. Its history, and that of the larger archive of which it forms a part, is intimately connected with the development of lesbian and gay historical research in Britain and the place of oral history within it. In 1980, the political organisation, the Campaign for Homosexual Equality (CHE), established the Gay Monitoring and Archive Project (GMAP) to provide a media monitoring service which would support its campaigns against discrimination. In addition to its primary role of collating newspaper cuttings from the national press, GMAP received and housed the correspondence and files of earlier gay organisations. Subsequently becoming separated from CHE, the archive was operated from the flat of one of its founders, Julian Meldrum, and in 1982, was reborn as the limited company, Hall-Carpenter Memorial Archives Ltd.[3] Over the next two years, the archive added further material to its collection, including the extensive papers of the early homosexual campaigning organisation, the Albany Trust. It was in this period that the notion of a sound archive was first discussed. The archive had been offered a number of tapes of interviews, radio programmes and meetings relating to homosexuality and homosexual law reform, and, in August 1982, Julian Meldrum wrote to Jackie Forster, in her capacity as director of the lesbian magazine, Sappho, saying 'we are tentatively of the view that the best way we as a group can increase our usefulness to the lesbian community is through taking an interest in oral herstory, applying for (public) funds to develop this aspect of the archives, and to do so by employing one or

more (women) workers'.[4] The comment suggests a concern that the
recent donations of papers from predominantly male organisations were
weighting the archive toward a focus on male homosexuality. His belief
that oral herstory might provide a solution to redress the balance reflected
a growing faith in the value of oral history as a means of reclaiming
minority experience. From the 1960s onward, a growing body of
community publishing houses, oral-history groups and women's
consciousness-raising groups demonstrated a belief that marginal groups
could articulate and record their own experience and use this as the basis
for political action.

In 1984, the archive received a grant of £32 000 from the Greater
London Council (GLC), as part of a major strategy of funding minority
groups. This policy must be understood against the background of considerable tension between Labour local government and Conservative central
government in the 1980s. Sarah Green, in her analysis of lesbian feminist
groups in London in this period, has observed that:

> Two things particularly concerned [GLC leader, Ken] Livingstone: counter-
> ing discrimination against minority and disadvantaged groups, and
> bringing down the Thatcher government. That Livingstone and his
> colleagues saw the wooing of 'disadvantaged groups' as advantageous in
> Labour's struggle against Thatcherism at both local and national levels is
> clear ... The limited powers of the GLC enabled it at least to fund local
> groups for some kind of self-help service. The result was a grant-aid 'explo-
> sion' in London, where a large variety of groups, either never funded before
> or minimally funded, suddenly became the recipients of money, facilities,
> buildings and publicity.[5]

The Hall Carpenter Archive was one of these groups, enabling it to move
to the newly opened London Lesbian and Gay Centre in Cowcross Street,
Farringdon, and to establish both a Media Project and an Oral History
Project. The post of Oral History Project Co-ordinator was offered to
Margot Farnham, a schoolteacher in Waltham Forest, who began work in
February 1985. The appointment of a woman to the post was clearly
intended to represent the archive's commitment to the oral history project
as a means of increasing lesbians' presence within the archive, but the
project nevertheless set out to collect life-history interviews from both
lesbians and gay men. Assisted by a group of twelve volunteers, Margot
Farnham collected a total of sixty-four interviews, of which twenty-six
were with women. All were located within the London area.

A Hall Carpenter Oral History Group flyer requesting volunteers to
assist either in conducting interviews or in being interviewed, identified
the group's aims as follows:

> We want to address the limitations, distortions and omissions of conven-
> tionally produced history. We aim to record as many different experiences
> as possible and invite the contributions of all lesbians and gay men.[6]

This statement suggests that the organisers understood the project largely
as an attempt to add empirical evidence to the historical record through
the recording of lesbian and gay experiences. An insight into their specific
interests is provided by a list of projects on which they were working,
which included 'The Military', 'The Peace Movement', 'Religion and Spir-
ituality', 'Older Working-Class Women', 'Changes in Sexual Identity' and
'Irish Women'. The flyer added:

> We especially welcome working-class women, older people, people with
> disabilities and black or third world people who may like to use the equip-
> ment and resources to work on projects of their own choice. We want a
> collection and eventually publications and exhibitions that acknowledge
> our diversity and differences as well as strengthening the communities by
> making sure our achievements and histories are properly recorded.

This concern with 'difference' demonstrates the extent to which feminist
critiques of white, middle-class centred research techniques and theories
had influenced such projects by the mid-1980s. However, it is also
undoubtedly a reflection of GLC ideology, which understood the different
forms of discrimination experienced by minority groups as all deriving
from inequality in the capitalist system, and attempted to encourage
collaboration between them. Sarah Green has observed that this equal
opportunities policy was implemented by making its application a condition of all GLC grants and requiring grant-aided groups to include images
of minority groups in their publicity. 'In short', she argues, 'the GLC
explicitly intended to influence the activities, behaviour and ideology of
the white able-bodied majority towards minorities, especially by encouraging them to give away their power, or at the very least, to share it.'[7] That
the Hall Carpenter Oral History Group embraced this policy is evident
from the suggestion that people from other minority groups borrow the
equipment for their own projects. The extent to which they were successful in their own terms is difficult to assess, although a newsletter dated
'Winter 1985–6' gives some indication. In a further request for volunteers
to be interviewed, the newsletter asked, 'We particularly want to hear from
older people, people who have experienced World War 2 and people from
black, Asian and other minority groups'.[8] The absence of working-class
men and women from this list suggests that the Oral History Group
believed that it had been successful in locating lesbians and gay men from
different class backgrounds, but less so in representing age and ethnic
differences.

In the Spring of 1986, the demise of the GLC resulted in a loss of most of the Hall Carpenter Archive's funding. A fundraising working party was able to raise £3000, and the Oral History Group obtained funding from the London Borough Grants Scheme for another year. However, in March 1987, no further funding was available, and the Oral History Group ceased its work. The demise of the GLC and the subsequent loss of funding was ultimately the culmination of a long-term power struggle between a Conservative central government and Labour local authority. However, 1988 legislation prohibiting the 'promotion' of homosexuality as a 'pretended family relationship', enshrined in Section 28 of the Local Government Act 1988, is testament to the role played by anti-homosexual ideas in this debate. Anna Marie Smith has argued that the climate of fear developed by the AIDS epidemic in the late 1980s, and its link in the popular imagination with homosexuality, provided a pool of anti-homo-sexual feeling on which central government could draw in its power struggle with the GLC.[9] However, there is little evidence of the impact of this growth in anti-homosexual feeling on the Hall Carpenter interviews themselves. In response to the loss of GLC funding, the archive decided to find a 'safe' home for the collection, and deposited copies of the tapes with the British Library Sound Recording Department who commissioned a further sixty-four recordings, with the assistance of Margot Farnham, in 1990–91.

In total, the collection comprises sixty interviews with women, born between 1905 and 1965. While the larger collection is representative of a range of class, ethnic and age backgrounds, these differences are less apparent in the women born before 1950. Although there are a number of interviewees from working-class backgrounds, the group is dominated by middle- and upper-class educated professional women. Most had clearly played a significant role in the feminist and lesbian political communities of the 1970s or the earlier social groups of the 1960s. In addition to the interview with Jackie Forster, the group on which this research was based included three of the four founder members of *Arena Three*, Cynthia Reid, Julie Switsur and Diana Chapman; Angela Chilton, a founder member of the lesbian magazine, *Sappho*; several active members of the Women's Liberation Movement, including Roberta Henderson, Rosanna Hibbert, Sandy Martin and Sharley McLean; a number of influen-tial activists in the peace movement, including Pat Arrowsmith and Myrtle Soloman; and a founding member of the lesbian and gay Christian church, the Metropolitan Community Church. The participation of these women and others in this activist culture undoubtedly prompted their contribution to the Hall Carpenter Collection. Not only would they have been visible and accessible figures whom the interviewing team could approach, but their political commitments and experiences tied them to a culture which valued and enabled the articulation and sharing of personal testimonies. Their selection as interviewees reflects the emphasis in the construction of lesbian history, on politicised, community-based lesbian experience.

However, theirs is not the only lesbian history of post-war Britain. We began our discussion of post-war narratives with a quote from Nina Jenkins, in which she claimed:

> Do you know I can't – it's terrible, I mean I should be much more conscious of these sort of social things – but I don't ever recall words being used, in fact I'm not sure they were. I don't think they were because gay hadn't been invented; homosexual was a thing in books; lesbian was like a derogatory term that you hardly ever heard; and other people used things like poofs and queers. I loathed those words, they made my skin crawl, they still do. So I don't think any words were ever used. I think there was just an expectation that there were people like us and there were other people.[10]

This experience of lesbianism in post-war Britain as a silence, an absence from discourse was a common one, shared by many women. The ambiguities in concepts such as 'tomboy' and 'bachelor girl', which enabled them to be deployed as indicators of sexual dissidence, also afforded a protection from the explicit naming of a deviant sexual identity. For the majority of women who did not participate in the lesbian social communities of the 1960s or the political campaigns of the 1970s, this culture of ambiguity and silence would have continued to dominate the ways in which they conceptualised their lesbian identity. The stories of these women, and of their attempts to negotiate the experience of same-sex desire in the absence of an explicit discourse, represent a further untold history of post-war lesbianism.

Notes

1 NSA, HCC (C456), F1607–F1612, Jackie Forster.
2 Carole Woddis, 'Jackie Forster', *Independent* (31 October 1998).
3 Oliver Merrington, 'A Short History of the Hall-Carpenter Archives', http://hall-carpenter.tripod.com/hca/history.html.
4 LSE, Hall Carpenter Archive 2/4, correspondence between Julian Meldrum of the Hall Carpenter Archives and Jackie Forster of *Sappho* (5 August 1982). The term 'herstory' was widely used in the 1970s and 80s to indicate an attempt to add women's experience to the historical record.
5 Green, *Urban Amazons*, p. 136.

6 LSE, Hall Carpenter Archive 7/3, Hall Carpenter Oral History Group flyer, undated.

7 Green, *Urban Amazons*, p. 141.

8 LSE, Hall Carpenter Archive 7/3, Hall Carpenter News (Winter 1985-6).

9 Anna Marie Smith, *New Right Discourse on Race and Sexuality: Britain 1968–1990* (Cambridge: Cambridge University Press, 1994).

10 NSA, HCC (C456), F2499–F2501, Nina Jenkins.

Bibliography

Oral sources

Hall Carpenter Collection

NSA, HCC (C456), F1918–F1924, Olive (Ceri) Ager.
NSA, HCC (C456), F1326–F1327, Pat Arrowsmith.
NSA, HCC (C456), F2091–F2092, Elsa Beckett.
NSA, HCC (C456), F2088, Diana Chapman.
NSA, HCC (C456), F1622–F1624, Angela Chilton.
NSA, HCC (C456), F1359–F1360, Margaret Cranch.
NSA, HCC (C456), F1607–F1612, Jackie Forster.
NSA, HCC (C456), F2590, Jackie Forster.
NSA, HCC (C456), F1336–F1338, Antony Grey.
NSA, HCC (C456), F2561–F2565, Roberta Henderson.
NSA, HCC (C456), F2095–F2096, Rosanna Hibbert.
NSA, HCC (C456), F2087, Mabel Hills.
NSA, HCC (C456), F2499–F2501, Nina Jenkins.
NSA, HCC (C456), F2066–F2067, Helen Lilly.
NSA, HCC (C456) F2483–F2487, Sandy Martin.
NSA, HCC (C456), F2158–F2163, Sharley McLean.
NSA, HCC (C456), F1331–F1332, Nettie Pollard.
NSA, HCC (C456), F2109, Cynthia Reid.
NSA, HCC (C456), F2120–F2122, Gilli Salvat.
NSA, HCC (C456) F1328–F1330, Rene Sawyer.
NSA, HCC (C456), F2082–F2083, Myrtle Soloman.
NSA, HCC (C456), F2108, Julie Switsur.
NSA, HCC (C456), F2086, Jean White.
NSA, HCC (C456), F1325, Mary Wilkins.

Brighton Ourstory Project (eds), *Daring Hearts: Lesbian and Gay Lives of 50s and 60s Brighton* (Brighton: QueenSpark Books, 1992).

Hall Carpenter Lesbian Oral History Group (eds), *Inventing Ourselves: Lesbian Life Stories* (London: Routledge, 1989).
Neild, Suzanne and Rosalind Pearson (eds), *Women Like Us* (London: The Women's Press, 1992).

Archival sources

The National Archive (formerly the Public Record Office)

TNA, ADM 1/ 21067, WRNS accommodation.
TNA, AIR 2/12636, WRAF: Publicity.
TNA, AIR 20/10864, WRAF: Moral welfare 1960–1968.
TNA, CRIM 1/903, Rex v. Billie Joyce and others: Keeping a disorderly house/ Conspiring to corrupt public morals.
TNA, DPP 2/4338, 'The International Times', Lovebooks Ltd (publisher), Tom McGrath (editor): various editions considered for publication under the Obscene Publications Act, 1959. 1966–1969.
TNA, ED 136/467, Education Act 1944: Suggested amendments by various Members of Parliament 1944.
TNA, ED 136/480, Education Act 1944: Committee stage. Notes on amendments. Clauses 15–26. 1944.
TNA, HO 45/21917, Women Police: Increased establishment and expansion of duties in London area. 1945–1948.
TNA, MEPO 2/3169, Women Police: Recruiting booklet.
TNA, MEPO 2/4485, Running Horse Public House: Permitting Drunkenness/ disorderly conduct of undesirables: 1936.
TNA, MEPO 2/6158, Section House accommodation for women police.
TNA, MEPO 2/6159, Recruiting for women police: press advertisements 1934–1961.
TNA, MEPO 2/7680, Commissioner's Annual Report on drunkenness, licensed premises, clubs, betting, gaming etc. 1945–1965.
TNA, MEPO 2/8231, Memorandum from Superintendent Gargrave A4 Branch to D.I., 29 August 1962.
TNA, MEPO 3/758, The Caravan Club, 81 Endell Street WC1: Disorderly House: Evidence of Clarence Campion. Div. Det. Inspector. E; Minutes to Bow St Station 10 August 1934; Letter 11 August 1934.
TNA, MEPO 5/518, Pembridge Hall Section House for Women Police.
TNA, WO 32/10662, ATS Discharge Policy 1943–44.
TNA, WO 208/5137, ATS Policy Problems 1939–1948.
TNA, WO 277/6, Auxiliary Territorial Service 1939–1945.

Hall Carpenter Archive, London School of Economics

LSE, Hall Carpenter Archive 2/4, Correspondence between Julian Meldrum of the Hall Carpenter Archives and Jackie Forster of *Sappho*, 5 August 1982.
LSE, Hall Carpenter Archive 7/3, *Hall Carpenter News* (Winter 1985–6); Hall Carpenter Oral History Group flyer, undated.
LSE: Hall Carpenter Archive/Albany Trust /14/80, Letter from Esme Langley to Antony Grey, 'The Secretary, Homosexual Law Reform Society', 10 May 1963.

London Metropolitan Archive

LMA, PC / ENT / 2/12, List of applications for licences from 1 January 1936: London County Council Entertainments Committee.

Westminster City Archive

WCA, WBA: 804/56, Register of Licence Transfers, 9 May 1961–19 December 1972.

Newspapers and periodicals

Arena Three
Evening Echo (Hemel Hempstead)
Evening Post (Bristol)
Guardian
Medical News
Morning Telegraph (Sheffield)
News Letter: Belfast
News of the World
New Statesman
Out
She
Sunday Times
The Times
Titbits
Twentieth Century

Published primary sources

Allan, Mabel Esther, *Here We Go Round: A Career Story for Girls* (London: Heinemann, 1954).
Allen, Mary Sophia, *Lady in Blue* (London: Stanley Paul and Co., 1936).
Banks, Francis Richard, *The Penguin Guide to London* (London: Penguin, 1958).
Bannon, Ann, *Odd Girl Out* (San Francisco: Cleis Press, 2001 [1957]).
Bannon, Ann, *Beebo Brinker* (San Francisco: Cleis Press, 2001 [1962]).
Barnes, William, *A Century of Camden Housing* (London: London Borough of Camden, Housing Dept., 1972).
Baxter, Elizabeth Valerie, *Young Policewoman* (London: Bodley Head, 1955).
Bene, Eva, 'On the genesis of female homosexuality', *British Journal of Psychiatry* (1965), pp. 815–21.
Bibby, Cyril, *Sex Education* (London: Macmillan, 1945).
Bloom, Ursula, *Me – After the War: A Book for Girls Considering the Future* (London: John Gifford, 1944).
Board of Education, *Report of Consultative Committee on Differentiation of the Curriculum for Boys and Girls Respectively in Secondary Schools* (London: HMSO, 1923)
Board of Education, *Curriculum and Examinations in Secondary Schools: Report of the Committee of the Secondary School Examinations Council Appointed by the President of the Board of Education* (London: HMSO, 1943) [The Norwood Report].

Bolton, Mary, *Modern Careers for Girls* (London: W. Foulsham and Co. Ltd, 1957).

Bott, Elizabeth, *Family and Social Network* (London: Tavistock, 1957).

Bowlby, John, *Forty-four Juvenile Thieves: Their Characters and Home-Life* (London: Bailliere, Tindall and Cox, 1946).

Bowlby, John, *Maternal Care and Mental Health: A Report Prepared on Behalf of the World Health Organisation* (Geneva: World Health Organisation, 1952).

Bowlby, John, *Child Care and the Growth of Love* (Harmondsworth: Penguin, 1953).

Bowlby, John, 'The nature of the child's tie to his mother', *International Journal of Psycho-Analysis* 38–9 (1958).

Bremer, J., *Asexualisation: A Follow-up Study of 244 Cases* (Oslo: Oslo University Press, 1958).

Brew, J. Macalister, 'How the mind works', *Club News* (January 1945), p. 2.

Browne, Stella, 'Studies in feminine inversion', *Journal of Sexology and Psychanalysis* (1923).

Burns, Vincent G., *Female Convict* (Pyramid, 1959).

Cappon, Daniel, *Toward an Understanding of Homosexuality* (New Jersey: Prentice-Hall, 1965).

Caprio, Frank, *Female Homosexuality: A Psychodynamic Study of Lesbianism* (London: Peter Owen, 1957).

Carpenter, Edward, *The Intermediate Sex: A Study of Some Transitional Types of Men and Women* (London: Allen and Unwin, 1916 [1896]).

Central Housing Advisory Committee, *Dudley Report: Design of Dwellings* (London: HMSO, 1944).

Central Office of Information, *Britain: An Official Handbook* (London: HMSO, 1964).

Chesser, Eustace, *Sexual Behaviour: Normal and Abnormal* (London: Medical Publications, 1949).

Chesser, Eustace, *Live and Let Live: The Moral of the Wolfenden Report* (London: Heinemann, 1958).

Chesser, Eustace, *Women: A Popular Edition of the Chesser Report* (London: Jarrolds Publishers, 1958).

Chesser, Eustace, *Odd Man Out: Homosexuality in Men and Women* (London: Victor Gollancz, 1959).

Chesser, Eustace, *The Human Aspects of Sexual Deviation* (London: Jarrolds Publishers, 1971).

Comer, Lee, *Wedlocked Women* (Leeds: Feminist Books, 1974).

Compton-Burnett, Ivy, *More Women than Men* (London: Heinemann, 1933).

Condor, Stella, *Woman on the Beat: The True Story of a Policewoman* (London: Robert Hale, 1960).

Dallas, Dorothy M., *Sex Education in School and Society* (London: National Foundation for Education Research in England and Wales, 1972).

Dane, Clemence, *The Regiment of Women* (London: Heinemann, 1917).

Davies, Hunter (ed.), *The New 'London Spy'* (London: Corgi, 1966).

Davis, Katherine Bement, *Factors in the Sex Life of Twenty-Two Hundred Women* (London: Harper and Brothers, 1929).

Dickinson, Robert Latou and Lura Beam, *The Single Woman* (London: Williams and Norgate Ltd., 1934).

Doncaster, L. Hugh, *The Single Woman in Society* (London: Friends Home Service Committee, 1951).

Ellis, Havelock, *Studies in the Psychology of Sex, Complete in Two Volumes* (New York: Random, 1942 [1902]).

Epps, Phyllis, *British Journal of Delinquency* (January 1951), p. 187.

Fabian, Robert, *London After Dark* (London: The Naldrett Press, 1954).

Faithfull, L. M., *You and I, Saturday Talks at Cheltenham* (Chatto & Windus, 1927).

Forel, August, *The Sexual Question: A Scientific, Psychological, Hygienic and Sociological Study for the Cultured Classes* (London: Heinemann, 1906).

Freud, Sigmund, *The Standard Edition of the Complete Psychological Works of Sigmund Freud*, 24 vols., trans. James Strachey et al. (London: Hogarth Press, 1961), vol XIX.

Friedan, Betty, *The Feminine Mystique* (London: Gollancz, 1963).

Fry, Margery, *The Single Woman* (London: Delisle, 1953).

Gavron, Hannah, *The Captive Wife: Conflicts of Housebound Mothers* (London: Routledge & Kegan Paul, 1966).

I Want to be ... A 'Girl' Book of Careers (Watford: Hulton Press, 1957).

Gissing, George, *The Odd Woman* (London: T. Nelson and Sons, 1907).

Glass, S. J. and R. W. Johnson, 'Limitations and complications of organotherapy in male homosexuality', *Journal of Clinical Endocrinology* 4 (1944), pp. 540–4.

Goldring, Douglas, *The 1920s: A General Survey and Some Personal Memories* (London: Nicholson and Watson, 1945).

Hall, Radclyffe, *The Well of Loneliness* (London: Jonathan Cape, 1928; London: Virago, 1982).

Hall, Radclyffe, *The Unlit Lamp* (London: Cassell and Co., 1924).

Harvey, James, *Degraded Women* (Midwood, 1962).

Heller, C. G., and W. O. Maddock, 'The clinical uses of testosterone in the male', *Vitam. Horm.* 5 (1947), pp. 393–432.

Henry, Dr George W., *Sex Variants: A Study of Homosexual Patterns* (London: Cassell, 1950 [1941]).

Henry, Joan, *Women in Prison* (Perma, 1953).

Hewitt, Cecil Rolph, *A Licensing Handbook* (London: The Police Review Publishing Co., 1947).

Heyneman, Julie H., *Mary Sophia Allen, The Pioneer Policewoman* (London: Chatto and Windus, 1925).

Hilton, Jennifer, *The Gentle Arm of the Law: Life as a Policewoman* (Reading: Educational Explorers, 1967).

Hopkins, June, 'The lesbian personality', *British Journal of Psychiatry* 115 (1969), pp. 1433–6.

Hutton, Laura, *The Single Woman and her Emotional Problems* (London: Bailliere, Tindall and Cox, 1937).

Hutton, Laura, *The Single Woman: Her Adjustment to Life and Love* (London: Barrie and Rockliff, 1960).

Hyde, H. Montgomery, *The Other Love: A Historical and Contemporary Survey of Homosexuality in Britain* (London: Heinemann, 1970).

Jackson, Stanley, *An Indiscreet Guide to Soho* (London: Muse Arts, 1969).

Jephcott, Pearl, *Rising Twenty: Notes on Some Ordinary Girls* (London: Faber and Faber, 1948).

Kaye, Harvey, et al, 'Homosexuality in women', *Archives of General Psychiatry* 17 (Nov. 1967).

Kenyon, F. E., 'Studies in female homosexuality', *British Journal of Psychiatry* 114 (1968), pp. 1337–50.

Kinsey, Alfred, W. B. Pomeroy, C. E. Martin and P. H. Gebhard, *Sexual Behaviour in the Human Female* (Philadelphia: W. B. Saunders, 1953).

Krafft-Ebing, Richard von, *Psychopathia Sexualis* (London: Staples Press, 1965 [1886]).

Lamb, Felicia and Helen Pickthorn, *Locked-Up Daughters: A Parents' Look at Girls' Education and Schools* (London: Hodder and Stoughton, 1968).

Legge, Cecilia Mireio and Fred Frankiand Rigby, *Life and Growth* (London: Faber and Faber, 1950).

Loraine, J. A., et al, 'Endocrine function in male and female homosexuals', *British Medical Journal* 4 (1970), pp. 406–8.

Loraine, J. A., 'Patterns of hormone excretion in male and female homosexuals', *Nature* 234 (1971), 552–5.

Magee, Bryan, *One in Twenty: A Study of Homosexuality in Men and Women* (London: Secker and Warburg, 1966).

Mass Observation, *An Enquiry into People's Homes: A Report*, prepared by Mass Observation for the Advertising Service Guild (London: John Murray for the ASG, 1943).

Mass-Observation, *The Pub and the People: A Worktown Study* (London: Victor Gollancz, 1943).

Meyer-Bahlburg, Heino F. L., 'Sex hormones and male homosexuality in comparative perspective', *Archives of Sexual Behaviour* 6:4 (1977), pp. 297–325.

Milner, Marion, *The Human Problem in Schools: A Psychological Study Carried Out on Behalf of the Girls' Public Day School Trust* (London: Methuen and Co., 1938).

Ministry of Education, *Report of the Central Advisory Council for Education '15–18': The Crowther Report* (London: HMSO, 1959).

Mitchell, George and Terence Lupton, *The Liverpool Estate* (Liverpool: The University Press of Liverpool, 1954).

Moll, Albert, *Perversions of the Sex Instinct: A Study of Sexual Inversion* (Newark: Julian Press, 1931 [1891]).

Money, J., 'Use of an androgen-depleting hormone in the treatment of male sex offenders', *Journal of Sex Research* 6 (1970), pp. 165–72.

Myrdal, Alva and Viola Klein, *Women's Two Roles* (London: Routledge & Kegan Paul, 1956).

Neill, A. S., *Hearts Not Heads in the School* (Herbert Jenkins, 1945).

Newsom, John, *The Education of Girls* (London: Faber and Faber, 1948).

Philp, Albert Frederic and Noel Timms, *The Problem of the 'Problem Family': A Critical Review of the Literature Concerning the 'Problem Family' and its Treatment* (London: Family Service Units, 1957).

Progl, Zoe, *Woman of the Underworld* (London: Arthur Baker, 1964).

Rees, J. Tudor and Harvey V. Usill (eds), *They Stand Apart: A Critical Survey of the Problems of Homosexuality* (London: Heinemann, 1955).

Richardson, Helen, *Adolescent Girls in Approved Schools* (London: Routledge & Kegan Paul, 1969).

Rowntree, Benjamin Seebohm and George Russell Lavers, *English Life and Leisure: A Social Study* (London: Longmans, Green and Co., 1951).

Russell, George Lawrence, *Sex Problems in Wartime* (London: Student Christian Movement Press, 1940).

Smith, Marie Blanche, *The Single Woman of Today: Her Problems and Adjustment* (London: Watts and Co., 1951).

Spain, Nancy, *Why I'm Not a Millionaire: An Autobiography* (London: Hutchinson, 1956).

Spain, Nancy, *A Funny Thing Happened on the Way* (London: Hutchinson, 1964).

Storr, Anthony, *Sexual Deviation* (Harmondsworth: Penguin, 1964).

Swados, Felice, *House of Fury* (Berkley, 1959).

Tancred, Edith, *Women Police* (London: National Council of Women in Great Britain, 1951).

Tietjen, Arthur, *Soho: London's Vicious Circle* (London: Allan Wingate, 1956).

Tucker, Theodore F., *Parents' Problems and Sex Education* (London: The Bodley Head, 1948).

Ulrichs, Karl Heinrich, *The Riddle of 'Man-Manly' Love: The Pioneering Work on Male Homosexuality*, 2 vols., trans. Michael A. Lombardi-Nash (Buffalo, NY: Prometheus Books, 1994 [1864–80]).

Wildeblood, Peter, *Against the Law* (London: Weidenfeld and Nicolson, 1955).

Wilhelm, Gale, *Torchlight to Valhalla* (London: Random House, 1938).

Wilson, George B., *Alcohol and the Nation* (London: Nicholson and Watson, 1940).

Winner, Albertine, 'Homosexuality in women', *Medical Press and Circular* (September 3 1947), pp. 219–20.

Winicott, Donald W., *The Child and the Family: First Relationships* (London: Tavistock, 1962).

Winicott, Donald W., *The Family and Individual Development* (London: Tavistock, 1965).

Winsloe, Christa, *The Child Manuela* (London: Chapman and Hall, 1934).

Wober, Mallory, *English Girls' Boarding Schools* (London: Allen Lane, 1971).

Wolff, Charlotte, *Love Between Women* (London: Gerald Duckworth and Co., 1971).

Women's Employment Federation, *Careers: A Memorandum on Openings and Trainings for Girls and Women* (London: Women's Employment Federation, 1964).

Wyles, Lilian, *A Woman at Scotland Yard* (London: Faber and Faber, 1952).

Young, Brett, *White Ladies* (London: Heinemann, 1935).

Young, Michael and Peter Willmott, *Family and Kinship in East London* (Harmondsworth: Penguin, 1962).

YWCA Accommodation and Advisory Service and London Council for the Welfare of Women and Girls, *Staying in London: Hostels and Accommodation in London for Girls and Women* (1976/77).

Published secondary sources

Abbott, Sidney and Barbara Love, *Sappho Was a Right-On Woman* (New York: Stein and Day, 1972).

Abelove, Henry, 'The queering of lesbian/gay history', *Radical History Review* 62 (1995), pp. 44–57.

Abraham, Julie, *'Are Girls Necessary?' Lesbian Writing and Modern Histories* (London: Routledge, 1996).

Achilles, Nancy, 'The development of the homosexual bar as an institution', William Simon and John H. Gagnon, *Sexual Deviance* (New York: Harper and Row, 1967), pp. 228–44.

Ackroyd, Peter, *London: The Biography* (London: Vintage, 2001).

Addison, Paul, *Now the War is Over: A Social History of Britain 1945–51* (London: BBC and Jonathan Cape, 1985).

Adler, Sy and Johanna Brenner, 'Gender and space: lesbians and gay men in the city', *International Journal of Urban and Regional Research* 16:1 (1992), pp. 24–33.

Ainley, Rosa, *What Is She Like? Lesbian Identities from the 1950s to the 1990s* (London: Cassell, 1995).

Ardill, Susan and Sue O'Sullivan, 'Butch/femme obsessions', *Feminist Review* 34 (1990), pp. 79–85.

Attridge, Derek, Geoff Bennington and Robert Young (eds), *Post-Structuralism and the Question of History* (Cambridge: Cambridge University Press, 1987).

Auchmuty, Rosemary, '"You're a dyke, Angela!": Elsie J. Oxenham and the rise and fall of the schoolgirl story', in Lesbian History Group (ed.), *Not a Passing Phase: Reclaiming Lesbians in History 1840–1985* (London: The Women's Press, 1989), pp. 119–40.

Auchmuty, Rosemary, *The World of Girls* (London: The Women's Press, 1992).

Auchmuty, Rosemary, *The World of Women: Growing Up in the Girls' School Story* (London: The Women's Press, 1999).

Baker, Kathryn Hinojosa, 'Delinquent desire: Race, sex and ritual in reform schools for girls', *Discourse* 15:1 (1992), pp. 49–68.

Beddoe, Deirdre, *Discovering Women's History* (London: Pandora, 1993).

Beemyn, Brett and Mickey Eliason (eds), *Queer Studies: A Lesbian, Gay, Bisexual and Transgender Anthology* (New York: New York University Press, 1996).

Bell, Barbara, *Just Take Your Frock Off: A Lesbian Life* (Brighton: Ourstory Books, 1999).

Bell, David J., 'Insignificant others: Lesbian and gay geographies', *Area* 23:4 (1991), pp. 323–9.

Bell, David and Gill Valentine (eds), *Mapping Desires: Geographies of Sexualities* (London: Routledge, 1995).

Benstock, Shari, *Women of the Left Bank* (London: Virago, 1987).

Berg, Maxine, 'Women's work, mechanization and the early phases of industrialization in England', in Patrick Joyce (ed.), *The Historical Meanings of Work* (Cambridge: Cambridge University Press, 1987), pp. 64–98.

Berg, Maxine, 'What difference did women's work make to the Industrial Revolution?', *History Workshop Journal* 35 (1993), pp. 223–50.

Berger Gluck, Sherna and Daphne Patai (eds), *Women's Words: The Feminist Practice of Oral History* (London: Routledge, 1991).

Birmingham Feminist History Group, 'Feminism as femininity in the 1950s', *Feminist Review* 3 (1979), pp. 48–65.

Blackstone, Tessa, 'The education of girls today', in Juliet Mitchell and Ann Oakley (eds), *The Rights and Wrongs of Women* (Harmondsworth: Penguin, 1976), pp. 199–216.

Bland, Lucy, 'Trial by sexology? Maud Allen, Salome and the 'Cult of the Clitoris' case', in Lucy Bland and Laura Doan (eds), *Sexology in Culture: Labelling Bodies and Desires* (Cambridge: Polity Press, 1998), pp. 183–98.

Bland, Lucy and Laura Doan (eds), *Sexology in Culture: Labelling Bodies and Desires* (Cambridge: Polity Press, 1998).

Bland, Lucy and Laura Doan (eds), *Sexology Uncensored: The Documents of Sexual Science* (Chicago: University of Chicago Press, 1998).

Bocock, Robert, 'Choice and regulation: Sexual moralities', in Kenneth Thompson (ed.), *Media and Cultural Regulation* (London: Open University Press and Sage, 1994), pp. 70–104.

Boston, Sarah, *Women Workers and the Trade Union Movement* (London: Davis-Poynter, 1980).

Bourne, Stephen, *Brief Encounters: Lesbians and Gays in British Cinema 1930–1971* (London: Cassell, 1996).

Branca, Patricia, 'Image and reality: the myth of the idle Victorian woman', in Mary S. Hartman and Lois Banner (eds), *Clio's Consciousness Raised: New Perspectives on the History of Women* (London: Harper and Row, 1974), pp. 179–91.

Braybon, Gail and Penny Summerfield, *Out of the Cage: Women's Experiences in Two World Wars* (London: Pandora, 1987).

Breines, Wini, *Young, White and Miserable: Growing Up Female in the Fifties* (Boston: Beacon Press, 1992).

Bristow, Joseph, 'Being gay: Politics, identity, pleasure', *New Formations* 9 (1989), pp. 59–81.

Bristow, Joseph, *Sexuality* (London: Routledge, 1997).

Brivati, Brian, Julia Buxton and Anthony Seldon, *The Contemporary History Handbook* (Manchester: Manchester University Press, 1996).

Brown, Michael P., *Closet Space: Geographies of Metaphor from the Body to the Globe* (London: Routledge, 2000).

Bryant, Margaret, *The Unexpected Revolution: A Study in the History of the Education of Women and Girls in the Nineteenth Century* (London: London University Institute of Education, 1979).

Bullough, Vern and Bonnie Bullough, 'Lesbianism in the 1920s and 1930s: A newfound study', *Signs* 2:4 (1977), pp. 895–904.

Burchill, Graham, Colin Gordon and Peter Miller, *The Foucault Effect: Studies in Governmental Rationality* (London: Harvester Wheatsheaf, 1991).

Burnett, John, *A Social History of Housing, 1815–1970* (London: Methuen, 1986).

Burstyn, Joan, *Victorian Education and the Ideal of Womanhood* (London: Croom Helm, 1980).

Butler, Judith, *Gender Trouble: Feminism and the Subversion of Identity* (London: Routledge, 1990).

Butler, Judith, *Bodies That Matter: On the Discursive Limits of 'Sex'* (London: Routledge, 1993).

Campbell, Beatrix, 'A feminist sexual politics: Now you see it, now you don't', *Feminist Review* 5 (1980), pp. 1–18.

Cant, Bob and Susan Hemmings (eds), *Radical Records: Thirty Years of Lesbian and Gay History* (London: Routledge, 1988).

Card, Claudia, *Lesbian Choices* (New York: Columbia University Press, 1995).

Castells, Manuel, *The City and the Grassroots: A Cross-Cultural Theory of Urban Social Movements* (Berkeley: University of California Press, 1983).

Castle, Terry, *The Apparitional Lesbian: Female Homosexuality and Modern Culture* (New York: Columbia University, 1993).

Castle, Terry, *Noel Coward and Radclyffe Hall: Kindred Spirits* (New York: Columbia University Press, 1996).

Caunce, Stephen, *Oral History and the Local Historian* (Harlow: Longman, 1994).

Chakrabarty, Dipesh, 'Postcoloniality and the artifice of history: Who speaks for "Indian" pasts?', *Representations* 37 (1992), pp. 1–26.

Chamberlain, Mary, 'Reading narratives and cultural identity: Life stories from the Caribbean', unpublished paper given to the European Social Science History Conference, The Hague (27 February–2 March 2002).

Chauncey, George, *Gay New York: The Making of the Gay Male World, 1890–1940* (London: Flamingo, 1995).

Cohen, Derek and Richard Dyer, 'The politics of gay culture', in Gay Left Collective (eds), *Homosexuality: Power and Politics* (London: Allison and Busby, 1980), pp. 172–86.

Collis, Rose, *A Trouser-Wearing Character: The Life and Times of Nancy Spain* (London: Cassell, 1997).

Colomina, Beatriz (ed.), *Sexuality and Space* (New York: Princeton Architectural Press, 1992).

Conekin, Becky, Frank Mort and Chris Waters (eds), *Moments of Modernity: Reconstructing Britain 1945–1964* (London: Rivers Oram, 1999).

David, Hugh, *The Fitzrovians: A Portrait of Bohemian Society: 1900–55* (London: Michael Joseph, 1988).

Davidoff, Leonore, *Worlds Between: Historical Perspectives on Gender and Class* (Cambridge: Polity, 1995).

Davidoff, Leonore and Belinda Westover, *Our Work, Our Lives, Our Words: Women's History and Women's Work* (London: Macmillan, 1986).

Davidoff, Leonore and Catherine Hall, *Family Fortunes: Men and Women of the English Middle Class, 1780–1850* (Chicago: University of Chicago Press, 1987).

Davis, Madeline and Elizabeth Lapovsky Kennedy, 'Oral history and the study of sexuality in the lesbian community: Buffalo, New York, 1940–1960', *Feminist Studies* 12:1 (1986), pp. 7–28.

Davis, Madeline and Elizabeth Lapovsky Kennedy, *Boots of Leather, Slippers of Gold: A History of a Lesbian Community* (London: Routledge, 1993).

Dawson, Graham, *Soldier Heroes: British Adventure, Empire and the Imagining of Masculinities* (London: Routledge, 1994)

D'Emilio, John, *Sexual Politics, Sexual Communities: The Making of a Homosexual Minority in the United States, 1940–1970* (Chicago: University of Chicago Press, 1983).

Doan, Laura, *The Lesbian Postmodern* (New York: Columbia University Press, 1994).

Doan, Laura, '"Acts of female indecency": Sexology's intervention in legislating lesbianism', in Lucy Bland and Laura Doan (eds), *Sexology in Culture: Labelling Bodies and Desires* (Cambridge: Polity Press, 1998), pp. 199–213.

Doan, Laura, *Fashioning Sapphism: The Origins of a Modern English Lesbian Culture* (New York: Columbia University Press, 2001).

Doan, Laura and Sarah Waters, 'Making up lost time: contemporary lesbian writing and the invention of history', in David Alderson and Linda Anderson (eds),

Territories of Desire in Queer Culture (Manchester: Manchester University Press, 2000), pp. 12–28.

Dollimore, Jonathan, *Sexual Dissidence: Augustine to Wilde, Freud to Foucault* (Oxford: Clarendon Press, 1991).

Donoghue, Emma, *Passions between Women: British Lesbian Culture 1668–1801* (London: Scarlet Press, 1994).

Doty, Alexander, *Making Things Perfectly Queer: Interpreting Mass Culture* (Minneapolis: University of Minnesota Press, 1993).

Duberman, Martin, *Stonewall* (Harmondsworth: Penguin, 1993).

Duggan, Lisa, 'Making it perfectly queer', *Socialist Review* 22 (1992), pp. 11–31.

Dyhouse, Carol, 'Towards a "feminine" curriculum for English schoolgirls: The demands of ideology 1870–1963', *Women's Studies International Quarterly* 1 (1978), pp. 297–312.

Edge, Simon, *With Friends Like These: Marxism and Gay Politics* (London: Cassell, 1995).

Edwards, Elizabeth, 'Homoerotic friendship and college principals, 1880–1960', *Women's History Review* 4:2 (1995), pp, 149–63.

Emsley, Clive, *The English Police: A Political and Social History* (Hemel Hempstead: Harvester Wheatsheaf, 1991).

Evans, David, T., *Sexual Citizenship* (London: Routledge, 1993).

Evans, Mary, *A Good School: Life at a Girls' Grammar School in the 1950s* (London: Women's Press, 1991).

Faderman, Lillian, *Surpassing the Love of Men: Romantic Friendship and Love Between Women from the Renaissance to the Present* (London: The Women's Press, 1985).

Faderman, Lillian, *Odd Girls and Twilight Lovers: A History of Lesbian Life in Twentieth-Century America* (London: Penguin, 1992).

Faderman, Lillian, 'The return of butch and femme: A phenomenon in lesbian sexuality of the 1980s and 1990s', *Journal of the History of Sexuality* 2:4 (1992), pp. 578–96.

Faderman, Lillian (ed.), *Chloe Plus Olivia: An Anthology of Lesbian Literature from the Seventeenth Century to the Present* (London: Penguin, 1994).

Faraday, Annabel, 'Social definitions of lesbians in Britain 1914–1939' (PhD dissertation, University of Essex, 1986).

Faraday, Annabel, 'Lessoning lesbians: Girls' schools, coeducation and anti-lesbianism between the wars', in Carol Jones and Pat Mahoney (eds), *Learning Our Lines: Sexuality and Social Control in Education* (London: The Women's Press, 1989), pp. 23–45.

Farson, Daniel, *Soho in the Fifties* (London: Joseph, 1987).

Feinberg, Leslie, *Stone Butch Blues* (New York: Firebrand Books, 1993).

Felski, Rita, 'Introduction', in Lucy Bland and Laura Doan (eds), *Sexology in Culture: Labelling Bodies and Desires* (Cambridge: Polity Press, 1998), pp. 1–8.

Ferguson, Marjorie, *Forever Feminine: Women's Magazines and the Cult of Femininity* (London: Heinemann, 1983).

Ferris, Paul, *Sex and the British: A Twentieth Century History* (London: Mandarin, 1994).

Fischer, Erica, *Aimee and Jaguar: A Love Story, Berlin 1943* (New York: Harper Collins, 1996).

Forest, Benjamin, 'Hollywood as symbol: The significance of place in the construction of a gay identity', *Environment and Planning D: Society and Space* 13 (1995), pp. 133–57.

Foucault, Michel, *The History of Sexuality, vol.1: An Introduction* (Harmondsworth: Penguin, 1978).

Freedman, Estelle B., 'The prison lesbian: Race, class and the construction of the aggressive female homosexual 1915–1965', *Feminist Studies* 22:2 (1996), pp. 397–423.

Garber, Marjorie, *Vested Interests: Cross-dressing and Cultural Anxiety* (London: Routledge, 1992).

Gardiner, Jill, *From the Closet to the Screen: Women at the Gateways Club, 1945–85* (London: Pandora, 2003).

Gardiner, Juliet, *From the Bomb to the Beatles* (London: Collins and Brown, 1999).

Gilbert, Sandra M. and Susan Gubar, *No Man's Land: The Place of the Woman Writer in the Twentieth Century, Vol. II* (London: Yale University Press, 1993).

Giles, Judy, 'A home of one's own: women and domesticity in England 1918–1950', *Women's Studies International Forum* 16:3 (1993), pp. 239–53.

Gilmartin, Katie, 'We weren't bar people: Middle-class lesbian identities and cultural spaces', *GLQ* 3:1 (1996), pp. 1–51.

Gilmore, Leigh, 'Obscenity, modernity, identity: Legalizing "The Well of Loneliness" and "Nightwood"', *Journal of the History of Sexuality* 4:4 (1994), pp. 603–24.

Glick, Elisa, 'Sex positive: Feminism, queer theory, and politics of transgression', *Feminist Review* 64 (2000), pp. 19–45.

Gluck, Sherna Berger and Daphne Patai (eds), *Women's Words: The Feminist Practice of Oral History* (London: Routledge, 1991).

Gordon, Tuula, *Single Women: On the Margins?* (Basingstoke: Macmillan, 1994).

Gowing, Laura, 'History', in Andy Medhurst and Sally Munt (eds), *Lesbian and Gay Studies: A Critical Introduction* (London: Cassell, 1997), pp. 53–66.

Green, Sarah, *Urban Amazons: Lesbian Feminism and Beyond in the Gender, Sexuality and Identity Battles of London* (Basingstoke: Macmillan, 1997).

Griffin, Gabriele, *Heavenly Love? Lesbian Images in Twentieth-Century Women's Writing* (Manchester: Manchester University Press, 1994).

Groocock, Veronica, 'Chelsea girls', *Diva* (October 1996), pp. 42–3.

Groocock, Veronica, 'Gina Ware: Obituary', *Guardian* (1 September 2001), p. 23.

de Groot, Gerard J., '"I love the scent of cordite in your hair": Gender dynamics in mixed anti-aircraft batteries during the Second World War', *History* 8:265 (1997), pp. 73–92.

de Groot, Gerard, 'Lipstick on her nipples, cordite in her hair: Sex and romance among British servicewomen during the Second World War', in Gerard de Groot and Corinna Peniston-Bird (eds), *A Soldier and a Woman: Sexual Integration in the Military* (Harlow: Pearson Education, 2000), pp. 100–18.

Grosz, Elizabeth, *Space, Time and Perversion: Essays on the Politics of Bodies* (London: Routledge, 1995).

Hall, Catherine, 'The early formation of Victorian domestic ideology', in Sandra Burman (ed.), *Fit Work for Women* (London: Croom Helm, 1992), pp. 15–32.

Hall, Lesley, '"Disinterested enthusiasm for sexual misconduct": The British Society for the Study of Sex Psychology, 1913–47', Journal of Contemporary History 30 (1995).

Hall, Lesley, Sex, Gender and Social Change in Britain since 1880 (Basingstoke: Macmillan, 2000).

Hall, Marny, 'Private experiences in the public domain: Lesbians in organisations', in Jeff Hearn (ed.), The Sexuality of Organisations (London: Sage, 1989), pp. 125–38.

Hall, Stuart and Tony Jefferson, Resistance through Rituals: Youth Subcultures in Post-war Britain (London: Hutchinson, 1975).

Halperin, David M., 'Is there a history of sexuality?', in Henry Abelove (ed.), The Lesbian and Gay Studies Reader (London: Routledge, 1993), pp. 416–31.

Hamer, Emily, Britannia's Glory: A History of Twentieth-Century Lesbians (London: Cassell, 1996).

Hamnett, Chris and Bill Randolph, Cities, Housing and Profits: Flat Break Up and the Decline of Private Renting (London: Hutchinson, 1988).

Hart, Lynda, Fatal Women: Lesbian Sexuality and the Mark of Aggression (London: Routledge, 1994).

Harvey, David, Consciousness and the Urban Experience (Oxford: Blackwell, 1985).

Harvey, David, The Condition of Postmodernity (Oxford: Blackwell, 1989).

Hebdige, Dick, Subculture: The Meaning of Style (London: Routledge, 1979).

Heidensohn, Frances, Women in Control? The Role of Women in Law Enforcement (Oxford: Clarendon Press, 1992).

Hennessy, Peter, Never Again: Britain 1945–51 (London: Jonathan Cape, 1992).

Heron, Liz (ed.), Truth, Dare or Promise: Girls Growing Up in the 50s (London: Virago, 1985).

Heron, Liz (ed.), Streets of Desire: Women's Fictions of the Twentieth-Century City (London: Virago, 1993).

Hey, Valerie, Patriarchy and Pub Culture (London: Tavistock Publications, 1986).

Hickson, Alisdare, The Poisoned Bowl: Sex Repression in the Public School System (London: Constable, 1995).

Higgs, David (ed.), Queer Sites: Gay Urban Histories Since 1600 (London: Routledge, 1999).

Hindle, Paul, 'Gay communities and gay space in the city', in Stephen Whittle (ed.), The Margins of the City: Gay Men's Urban Lives (Aldershot: Arena, 1994), pp. 7–25.

Hodge, Andrew, Alan Turing: The Enigma (London: Vintage, 1992).

Holdsworth, Angela, Out of the Dolls House: The Story of Women in the Twentieth Century (London: BBC Books, 1988).

Houlbrook, Matt, 'Toward a historical geography of sexuality', Journal of Urban History 27:4 (2001), pp. 497–504.

Houlbrook, Matt, '"A Sun Among Cities": Space, identities and queer male practices, London 1918–57' (PhD dissertation, University of Essex, 2002).

Matt Houlbrook, Queer London: Perils and Pleasures in the Sexual Metropolis, 1918–1957 (Chicago: University of Chicago Press, 2005).

Howes, Keith, Broadcasting It: An Encyclopaedia of Homosexuality in Film, Radio and TV in the UK, 1923–1993 (London: Cassell, 1993).

Humphries, Steve, *A Secret World of Sex: Forbidden Fruit: The British Experience 1900–1950* (London: Sidgewick and Jackson, 1991).

Humphries, Steve and Pamela Gordon, *Forbidden Britain: Our Secret Past, 1900–1960* (London: BBC Books, 1994).

Hunt, Felicity (ed.), *Lessons for Life: The Schooling of Girls and Women 1850–1950* (Oxford: Oxford University Press, 1987).

Ingram, Gordon Brent, Anna-Marie Bouthillette and Yolanda Retter (eds), *Queers in Space: Communities; Public Places; Sites of Resistance* (Washington: Bay Press, 1997).

Inness, Sherrie, *The Lesbian Menace: Ideology, Identity and the Representation of Lesbian Life* (Amherst: University of Massachusetts Press, 1997).

Inness, Sherrie and Lloyd, Michele. E., 'G. I. Joes in Barbie Land: Recontextualizing butch in twentieth-century lesbian culture', in Brett Beemyn and Mickey Eliason (eds), *Queer Studies: A Lesbian, Gay, Bisexual and Transgender Anthology* (London: New York University Press, 1996), pp. 9–34.

Inwood, Stephen, 'Policing London's morals: the Metropolitan Police and popular culture', *London Journal* (1990), pp. 123–42.

Jagose, Annamarie, 'Way out: The category "lesbian" and the fantasy of the utopic space', *Journal of the History of Sexuality* 4:2 (1993), pp. 264–87.

Jeffrey-Poulter, Stephen, *Peers, Queers and Commons: The Struggle for Gay Law Reform from 1950 to the Present* (New York: Routledge, 1991).

Jeffreys, Sheila, *The Spinster and Her Enemies: Feminism and Sexuality, 1880–1930* (London: Pandora, 1985).

Jeffreys, Sheila, 'Butch and femme: Now and then', in Lesbian History Group (ed.), *Not a Passing Phase: Reclaiming Lesbians in History 1840–1985* (London: The Women's Press, 1989), pp. 158–87.

Jeffreys, Sheila, *Anticlimax* (London: The Women's Press, 1990).

Jeffreys, Sheila, *The Lesbian Heresy: A Feminist Perspective on the Lesbian Sexual Revolution* (London: Woman's Press, 1994).

Jeffreys, Sheila, 'The queer disappearance of lesbian sexuality in the academy', *Women's Studies International Forum* 17:5 (1994), pp. 459–72.

Jenkins, Alan, *The Twenties* (London: Book Club Associates, 1974).

Jenkins, Keith (ed.), *The Postmodern History Reader* (London: Routledge, 1996).

Jenson, Jane, 'Both friend and foe: Women and state welfare', in Renate Bridenthal, Claudia Koonz and Susan Stuard (eds), *Becoming Visible: Women in European History* (Boston: Houghton Mifflin, 1987), pp. 535–55.

Jerman, Betty, *The Lively-minded Women: The First Twenty Years of the National Housewives Register* (London: Heinemann, 1981).

Jivani, Alkarim, *It's Not Unusual: A History of Lesbian and Gay Britain in the Twentieth Century* (London: Michael O'Mara Books, 1997).

Kahn, Janet and Patricia A. Gozemba, 'In and around the Lighthouse: Working-class lesbian bar culture in the 1950s and 1960s', in Dorothy O. Helly and Susan M. Reverby (eds), *Gendered Domains: Rethinking Public and Private in Women's History* (London: Cornell University Press, 1992), pp. 90–106.

Keith, Michael and Steve Pile (eds), *Place and the Politics of Identity* (London: Routledge, 1993).

Kennedy, Elizabeth Lapovsky, 'Telling tales: Oral history and the construction of pre-Stonewall lesbian history', *Radical History Review* 62 (1995), pp. 58–79.

Koven, Seth and Sonya Michel, 'Gender and the origins of the Welfare State', *Radical History Review* 43 (1989), pp. 112–19.

de Lauretis, Teresa, 'Queer theory: Lesbian and gay sexualities: An introduction', *differences: A Journal of Feminist Cultural Studies* 3:2 (1991), pp. iii–xviii.

de Lauretis, Teresa, 'Sexual indifference and lesbian representation', in Henry Abelove, Michele Aina Barale and David M. Halperin (eds), *The Lesbian and Gay Studies Reader* (London: Routledge, 1993), pp. 141–58.

Lesbian History Group (ed.), *Not a Passing Phase: Reclaiming Lesbians in History 1840–1985* (London: The Women's Press, 1989).

Levine, Philippa, '"Walking the streets in a way no decent woman should": Women Police in World War I', *Journal of Modern History* 66 (1994), pp. 34–78.

Lewis, Jane, *Women in England: Sexual Divisions and Social Change, 1870–1950* (London: Wheatsheaf, 1984).

Lewis, Jane, 'Separate spheres: Threat or promise?', *Journal of British Studies* 30:1 (1991).

Lewis, Jane, *Women in Britain since 1945* (Oxford: Blackwell, 1992).

Lewis, John Parry, *Freedom to Drink: A Critical Review of the Development of the Licensing Laws and Proposals for Reform* (London: Institute of Economic Affairs, 1985).

Liddington, Jill, (ed.), *Female Fortune: Land, Gender and Authority* (London: Rivers Oram Press, 1999).

Light, Alison, *Forever England: Femininity, Literature and Conservatism between the Wars* (London: Routledge, 1991).

Lock, Joan, *The British Policewoman: Her Story* (London: Robert Hale, 1979).

McCormack, Ian, *Secret Sexualities* (London: Routledge, 1997).

McCrindle, Jean and Sheila Rowbotham (eds), *Dutiful Daughters: Women Talk About Their Lives* (Harmondsworth: Penguin Books, 1979).

McDermid, Jane, 'Women and education', in June Purvis (ed.), *Women's History: Britain, 1850–1945* (London: Routledge, 1995), pp. 107–30.

McDowell, Linda, 'Towards an understanding of the gender division of urban space', *Environment and Planning D: Society and Space* 1 (1983), pp. 59–72.

McDowell, Linda and Joanne P. Sharp, (eds), *Space, Gender, Knowledge: Feminist Readings* (London: Arnold, 1997).

McKibbin, Ross, *Classes and Cultures: England 1918–1951* (Oxford: Oxford University Press, 1998).

McLeish, Kenneth and Valerie, *Long to Reign Over Us: Memories of Coronation Day and Life in the 1950s* (London: Bloomsbury, 1992).

Marks, Pauline, 'Femininity in the classroom: An account of changing attitudes', in Juliet Mitchell and Ann Oakley (eds), *The Rights and Wrongs of Women* (Harmondsworth: Penguin, 1976), pp. 176–98.

Martin, Biddy, 'Lesbian identity and autobiographical difference[s]', in Bella Brodzki and Celeste Schenck (eds), *Life/Lines: Theorizing Women's Autobiography* (London: Cornell University Press, 1988), pp. 77–103.

Massey, Doreen, *Space, Place and Gender* (Cambridge: Polity Press, 1994).

Maynard, Steven, '"Respect your elders, know your past": History and the queer theorists', *Radical History Review* 75 (1999), pp. 56–78.

Meese, Elizabeth, 'When Virginia looked at Vita, what did she see; Or lesbian: femi-
     nist: woman – what's the differ(e/a)nce?', *Feminist Studies* 18:1 (1992), pp.
     99–117.

Merrington, Oliver, 'A Short History of the Hall-Carpenter Archives', http://hall-
     carpenter.tripod.com/hca/history.html.

Meyer, Leisa D., *Creating GI Jane: Sexuality and Power in the Women's Army Corps During World
     War II* (New York: Columbia University Press, 1996).

Mikulas, Teich and Roy Porter (eds), *Sexual Knowledge, Sexual Science: A History of Attitudes
     to Sexuality* (Cambridge: Cambridge University Press, 1994).

Miller, Neil, *Out of the Past* (London: Vintage, 1995).

Mort, Frank, *Cultures of Consumption: Masculinities and Social Space in Late Twentieth-Century
     Britain* (London: Routledge, 1996).

Mort, Frank, 'Mapping sexual London: The Wolfenden Committee on Homosexual
     Offences and Prostitution 1954–57', *New Formations* 37 (1999), pp. 92–112.

Moss, William W., *Oral History Program Manual* (London: Praeger Publishers, 1974).

Mouton, Michelle and Helena Pohlandt-McCormick, 'Boundary crossings: Oral
     history of Nazi Germany and Apartheid South Africa – a comparative perspec-
     tive', *History Workshop Journal* 48 (1999), pp. 41–63.

Munt, Sally, 'The Lesbian Flaneur', in David Bell and Gill Valentine (eds), *Mapping
     Desire* (London: Routledge, 1995), pp. 114–25.

Munt, Sally R., *Butch-Femme: Theorizing Lesbian Genders* (London: Cassell, 1997).

Munt, Sally R., *Heroic Desire: Lesbian Identity and Cultural Space* (London: Cassell, 1998).

Munt, Sally, 'The Lesbian Outlaw', *New Formations* 32 (1997), pp. 135–42.

Murray, Jenni, *The Woman's Hour: Fifty Years of Women in Britain* (London: BBC Books,
     1996).

Nestle, Joan (ed.), *The Persistent Desire: A Femme-Butch Reader* (Boston: Alyson Publica-
     tions, 1992).

Nestle, Joan, *A Restricted Country: Documents of Desire and Resistance* (London: Pandora,
     1996).

Newton, Esther, 'The mythic mannish lesbian: Radclyffe Hall and the New
     Woman', in M. Duberman, M. Vicinus and G. Chauncey (eds), *Hidden from
     History: Reclaiming the Gay and Lesbian Past* (New York: Penguin, 1989).

Norton, Rictor, *Mother Clap's Molly House: The Gay Subculture in England 1700–1830*
     (London: Gay Men's Press, 1992)

Norton, Rictor, *The Myth of the Modern Homosexual* (London: Cassell, 1997).

O'Brien, Lucy, *Dusty: A Biography of Dusty Springfield* (London: Sidgwick and Jackson,
     1999).

O'Connor, Justin and Derek Wynne (eds), *From the Margins to the Centre: Cultural Produc-
     tion and Consumption in the Post-industrial City* (Aldershot: Arena, 1996).

Ogborn, Miles, *Spaces of Modernity: London's Geographies 1680–1780* (London: The Guil-
     ford Press, 1998).

Oldfield, Sybil (ed.), *This Working-Day World: Women's Lives and Culture(s) in Britain
     1914–1945* (London: Taylor and Francis, 1994).

Oosterhuis, Harry, 'Richard von Krafft-Ebing's "Step-Children of Nature". Psychi-
     atry and the making of homosexual identity', in Vernon A. Rosario (ed.),
     Science and Homosexualities (London: Routledge, 1997), pp. 67–88.

Oram, Alison, '"Embittered, sexless or homosexual": Attacks on spinster teachers 1918–1939', in Lesbian History Group (ed.), *Not a Passing Phase: Reclaiming Lesbians in History 1840–1985* (London: The Women's Press, 1989), pp. 99–118.

Oram, Alison, *Women Teachers and Feminist Politics, 1900–1939* (Manchester: Manchester University Press, 1996).

Oram, Alison, '"Sex is an accident": Feminism, science and the radical sexual theory of Urania, 1915–1940', in Lucy Bland and Laura Doan (eds), *Sexology in Culture: Labelling Bodies and Desires* (Cambridge: Polity Press, 1998), pp. 214–30.

Oram, Alison and Annmarie Turnbull, *The Lesbian History Sourcebook* (London: Routledge, 2001).

Oram, Alison, 'Little by little? *Arena Three* and lesbian politics in the 1960s', in Marcus Collins (ed.), *The Permissive Society and its Enemies: Sixties British Culture* (London: Rivers Oram Press, forthcoming)

Partington, Angela, 'The days of the New Look: Consumer culture and working-class affluence', in Jim Fyrth (ed.), *Labour's Promised Land? Culture and Society in Labour Britain 1945–51* (London: Lawrence and Wishart, 1995), pp. 247–63.

Pedersen, Susan, 'The failure of feminism in the making of the British Welfare State', *Radical History Review* 45 (1989), pp. 86–110.

Pedersen, Susan, *Family, Dependence, and the Origins of the Welfare State: Britain and France 1914–1945* (Cambridge: Cambridge University Press, 1993).

Penn, Donna, 'Queer: Theorising politics and history', *Radical History Review* 62 (1995), pp. 24–42.

Perks, Robert and Alistair Thomson, *The Oral History Reader* (London: Routledge, 1998).

Pinney, Susanna, (ed.), *I'll Stand by You: The Letters of Sylvia Townsend Warner and Valentine Ackland* (London: Pimlico, 1998)

Plummer, Ken, *Telling Sexual Stories: Power, Change and Social Worlds* (London: Routledge, 1995).

Ponse, Barbara, 'Secrecy in the lesbian world', *Urban Life* 5 (1976), pp. 313–18.

Poovey, Mary, *Making a Social Body: British Cultural Formation, 1830–1864* (Chicago: University of Chicago Press, 1995).

Porter, Kevin and Jeffrey Weeks (eds), *Between the Acts: Lives of Homosexual Men 1885–1967* (London: Routledge, 1980).

Porter, Roy and Lesley Hall, *The Facts of Life: The Creation of Sexual Knowledge in Britain, 1650–1950* (New Haven: Yale University Press, 1995).

Power, Lisa, *No Bath But Plenty of Bubbles: An Oral History of the Gay Liberation Front* (London: Cassell, 1995).

Pugh, Martin, *Women and the Women's Movement in Britain 1914–1959* (Basingstoke: Macmillan, 1992).

Pugh, Martin, 'Domesticity and the decline of feminism, 1930–1950', in Harold L. Smith (ed.), *British Feminism in the Twentieth Century* (Aldershot: Edward Elgar, 1990), pp. 144–64.

Purvis, June, *A History of Women's Education in England* (Milton Keynes: Open University Press, 1991).

Purvis, June (ed.), *Women's History: Britain, 1850–1945* (London: UCL Press, 1995).

Quilley, Stephen, 'Constructing Manchester's "New urban village": Gay space in the entrepreneurial city', in Gordon Brent Ingram, Anna-Marie Bouthillette and Yolanda Retter (eds), *Queers in Space: Communities; Public Places; Sites of Resistance* (Washington: Bay Press, 1997), pp. 275–92.

Rabinow, Paul (ed.), *The Foucault Reader* (Penguin: Harmondsworth, 1994).

Ravetz, Alison, 'Housing the people', in Jim Fyrth (ed.), *Labour's Promised Land? Culture and Society in Labour Britain 1945–51* (London: Lawrence and Wishart, 1995), pp. 146–62.

Ravetz, Alison, *The Place of the Home: English Domestic Environments, 1914–2000* (London: E. and F. N. Spon, 1995).

Rich, Adrienne, *Compulsory Heterosexuality and Lesbian Existence* (London: Onlywomen Press, 1981)

Riley, Denise, *War in the Nursery: Theories of the Child and Mother* (London: Virago, 1983).

Roberts, Elizabeth, *Women and Families: An Oral History, 1940–1970* (Oxford: Blackwell, 1995).

Rosario, Vernon A. (ed.), *Science and Homosexualities* (London: Routledge, 1997).

Rose, Nikolas, *Governing the Soul: The Shaping of the Private Self* (London: Routledge, 1990).

Rose, Sonya O., *Limited Livelihoods: Gender and Class in Nineteenth Century England* (London: Routledge, 1992).

Rothenberg, Tamar, '"And she told two friends ...", Lesbians creating urban space', in David Bell and Gill Valentine (eds), *Mapping Desires: Geographies of Sexualities* (London: Routledge, 1995), pp. 165–81.

Rowbotham, Sheila, *A Century of Women: The History of Women in Britain and the United States* (London: Penguin, 1997).

Ruehl, Sonja, 'Inverts and experts: Radclyffe Hall and the lesbian identity', in Rosalind Brunt and Caroline Rowan (eds), *Feminism, Culture and Politics* (London: Lawrence Wishart, 1982), pp. 15–36.

Rule, Jane, *Lesbian Images* (London: Peter Davies, 1976).

Rupp, Leila J., *A Desired Past: A Short History of Same-sex Love in America* (Chicago: University of Chicago Press, 1999).

Rupp, Leila J., '"Imagine my surprise": Women's relationships in mid 20th century America', in Martin Duberman, Martha Vicinus and George Chauncey (eds), *Hidden from History: Reclaiming the Gay and Lesbian Past* (London: Penguin, 1991), pp. 395–410.

Ryan, Jenny and Hilary Fitzpatrick, 'The space that difference makes: Negotiation and urban identities through consumption practices', in Justin O'Connor and Derek Wynne (eds), *From the Margins to the Centre* (Aldershot: Arena, 1996), pp. 169–201.

Scott, Joan, 'The evidence of experience', *Critical Inquiry* 17 (1991), pp. 773–97.

Sedgwick, Eve Kosofsky, *Epistemology of the Closet* (London: Harvester Wheatsheaf, 1991).

Segal, Lynne, 'A feminist looks at the family', in John Muncie, Margaret Wetherell, Rudi Dallos and Allan Cochrane (eds), *Understanding the Family* (London: Sage, 1995), pp. 295–316.

Segal, Lynne, 'Look back in anger: men in the fifties', in Rowena Chapman and Jonathan Rutherford (eds), *Male Order: Unwrapping Masculinity* (London: Lawrence and Wishart, 1988).

Seidman, Steven (ed.), *Queer Theory / Sociology* (Oxford: Blackwell, 1996).

Serlin, David Harley, 'Christine Jorgensen and the Cold War closet', *Radical History Review* 62 (1995), pp. 137–65.

Shands, Kerstin, *Embracing Space: Spatial Metaphors in Feminist Discourse* (London: Greenwood Press, 1999).

Sheridan, Dorothy (ed.), *Wartime Women* (London: Mandarin, 1991).

Sheridan, Dorothy, 'ATS women: Challenge and containment in women's lives in the military during the Second World War' (MLitt dissertation, University of Sussex, 1988).

Shields, Rob, *Places on the Margin: Alternative Geographies of Modernity* (London: Routledge, 1991).

Simpson, Mark, *Anti-Gay* (London: Cassell, 1996).

Sinfield, Alan, *Out on Stage: Lesbian and Gay Theatre in the Twentieth Century* (London: Yale University Press, 1999).

Sinfield, Alan, *The Wilde Century: Effeminacy, Oscar Wilde and the Queer Moment* (London: Cassell, 1994).

Sissons, Michael and Philip French, *Age of Austerity, 1945–1951* (Oxford: Blackwell, 1986).

Smith, Anna Marie, *New Right Discourse on Race and Sexuality: Britain 1968–1990* (Cambridge: Cambridge University Press, 1994).

Smith, Harold L., 'The womanpower problem in Britain during the Second World War', *The Historical Journal* 27:4 (1984), pp. 925–45.

Smith, Harold L., 'British feminism and the equal pay issue in the 1930s', *Women's History Review* 5:1 (1996), pp. 97–110.

Smith, Patricia Juliana, *Lesbian Panic: Homoeroticism in Modern British Women's Fiction* (New York: Columbia University Press, 1997).

Smith, Patricia Juliana (ed.), *The Queer Sixties* (London: Routledge, 1999).

Soja, Edward W., *Postmodern Geographies* (London: Verso, 1989).

Spain, Daphne, *Gendered Spaces* (Chapel Hill: University of North Carolina Press, 1992).

Spender, Dale (ed.), *The Education Papers: Women's Quest for Equality in Britain 1850–1912* (London: Routledge & Kegan Paul, 1987).

Spivak, Gayatri Chakravorty, 'Subaltern studies: Deconstructing historiography' in her *In Other Worlds: Essays in Cultural Politics* (London: Methuen, 1987), pp. 197–221.

Stanley, Liz, 'Romantic friendship? Some issues in researching lesbian history and biography', *Women's History Review* 1:2 (1992), pp. 193–216.

Stanley, Liz, *Sex Surveyed 1949–1994: From Mass Observation's 'Little Kinsey' to the National Survey and the Hite Report* (London: Taylor and Francis, 1995).

Steedman, Carolyn, *Landscape for a Good Woman* (London: Virago, 1986).

Steedman, Carolyn, 'State–sponsored autobiography', in Becky Conekin, Frank Mort and Chris Waters, *Moments of Modernity: Reconstructing Britain 1945–1964* (London: Rivers Oram, 1999), pp. 45–54.

Stein, Arlene, 'Sisters and queers: The decentring of lesbian feminism', *Socialist Review* 22:1 (1992), pp. 33–55.

Stein, Arlene, 'All dressed up but no place to go? Style wars and the new lesbianism', in Corey K. Creekmur and Alexander Doty (eds), *Out In Culture: Gay, Lesbian and Queer Essays on Popular Culture* (London: Cassell, 1995), pp. 476–83.

Stewart-Pack, Angela, and Jules Cassidy, *We're Here: Conversations with Lesbian Women* (London: Quartet, 1977).

Stone, Tessa, 'The integration of women into a military service: The WAAF in the Second World War' (PhD dissertation, University of Cambridge, 1998).

Stone, Tessa, 'Creating a (gendered?) military identity: The Women's Auxiliary Air Force in Great Britain in the Second World War', *Women's History Review* 84 (1999), pp. 605–24.

Summerfield, Penny, *Women Workers in the Second World War: Production and Patriarchy in Conflict* (London: Croom Helm, 1989).

Summerfield, Penny, 'Approaches to women and social change in the Second World War', in Brian Brivati and Harriet Jones (eds), *What Difference Did the War Make?* (Leicester: Leicester University Press, 1993), pp. 63–79.

Summerfield, Penny, *Reconstructing Women's Wartime Lives: Discourse and Subjectivity in Oral Histories of the Second World War* (Manchester: Manchester University Press, 1998).

Summerfield, Penny and N. Crockett, 'You weren't taught that with the welding: lessons in sexuality in the Second World War', *Women's History Review* 1 (1992).

Sutherland, Douglas, *Portraits of a Decade: London Life 1945–1955* (London: Harrap, 1988).

Taylor, Eric, *Women Who Went to War 1938–46* (London: Robert Hale, 1988).

Terry, Jennifer, 'Theorizing deviant historiography', *differences* 3 (1991), pp. 55–74.

Thane, Pat, 'Women since 1945', in Paul Johnson (ed.), *Twentieth Century Britain: Economic, Social and Cultural Change* (London: Longman, 1994).

Thorpe, Rochella, 'A house where queers go: African-American lesbian nightlife in Detroit, 1940–1975', in Ellen Lewin (ed.), *Inventing Lesbian Cultures in America* (Boston: Beacon Press, 1996), pp. 40–61.

Tinkler, Penny, *Constructing Girlhood: Popular Magazines for Girls Growing Up in England 1920–1950* (London: Taylor and Francis, 1995).

Tosh, John, *The Pursuit of History: Aims, Methods and New Directions in the Study of Modern History* (London: Longman, 1991).

Traub, Valerie, 'The rewards of lesbian history', *Feminist Studies* 25: 2 (1999), pp. 363–94.

Valentine, Gill, 'Negotiating and managing multiple sexual identities: Lesbian time-space strategies', *Transactions of the Institute of British Geographers* 18 (1992), 237–48.

Valentine, Gill, 'Desperately seeking Susan: A geography of lesbian friendships', *Area* 25 (1993), pp. 109–16.

Valentine, Gill, '(Hetero)sexing space: Lesbian perceptions and experiences of everyday spaces', *Environment and Planning D: Society and Space* 11 (1993), pp. 395–413.

Valentine, Gill, 'Out and about: Geographies of lesbian landscapes', *International Journal of Urban and Regional Research* 19 (1995), pp. 96–111.

Valentine, Gill (ed.), *From Nowhere to Everywhere: Lesbian Geographies* (New York: Harrington Park Press, 2000).

Vernon, James, '"For some queer reason": The trials and tribulations of Colonel Barker's masquerade in interwar Britain', *Signs* 26:1 (2000), pp. 37–62.

Vernon, James, 'Telling the Subaltern to speak: Mass Observation and the formation of social history in post-war Britain', Proceedings of the International Congress, 'History Under Debate', Santiago de Compostela, July 1999.

Vickery, Amanda, 'Golden age to separate spheres? A review of the categories and chronology of English women's history', The Historical Journal 36:2 (1993), pp. 383–414.

Vicinus, Martha (ed.), Suffer and be Still: Women in the Victorian Age (Bloomington: Indiana University Press, 1972).

Vicinus, Martha, 'Sexuality and power: A review of current work in the history of sexuality', Feminist Studies 8:1 (1982), pp. 133–56.

Vicinus, Martha, 'Distance and desire: English boarding school friendships, 1870–1920', Signs 9:4 (1984), pp. 618–19.

Vicinus, Martha, Independent Women: Work and Community for Single Women: 1850–1920 (London: Virago, 1985).

Vicinus, Martha, '"They wonder to which sex I belong": Women's relationships in mid twentieth century America', Feminist Studies 18:3 (1992), pp. 467–97.

Vicinus, Martha, 'Lesbian history: All theory and no facts or all facts and no theory?', Radical History Review 60 (1994), pp. 57–75.

Vidler, Anthony, 'Bodies in space/ Subjects in the city: Psychopathologies of modern urbanism', differences 5:3 (1993), pp. 29–51.

Walkowitz, Judith, City of Dreadful Delight: Narratives of Sexual Danger in Late-Victorian London (London: Virago, 1992).

Waller, Jane and Michael Vaughan–Rees, Women in Wartime: The Role of Women's Magazines 1939–1945 (London: Macdonald Optima, 1987).

Walter, Aubrey (ed.), Come Together (London: Gay Men's Press, 1980).

Warner, Michael (ed.), Fear of a Queer Planet: Queer Politics and Social Theory (Minneapolis: University of Minnesota Press, 1993).

Waters, Chris, 'Havelock Ellis, Sigmund Freud and the state: Discourses of homosexual identity in interwar England', in Lucy Bland and Laura Doan (eds), Sexology in Culture (Cambridge: Polity Press, 1998), pp. 165–80.

Webster, Wendy, Imagining Home: Gender, Race and National Identity 1945–64 (London: UCL Press, 1998).

Weeks, Jeffrey, Coming Out: Homosexual Politics in Britain from the Nineteenth Century to the Present (London: Quartet Books, 1977).

Weeks, Jeffrey, Sex, Politics and Society: The Regulation of Sexuality Since 1800 (London: Longman, 1981).

Weeks, Jeffrey, Sexuality and Its Discontents (London: Routledge & Kegan Paul, 1985).

Weeks, Jeffrey, Making Sexual History (Cambridge: Polity, 2000).

Weeks, Jeffrey (ed.), The Lesser Evil and The Greater Good: The Theory and Politics of Social Diversity (London: Rivers Oram, 1994).

Weightman, Barbara A., 'Gay bars as private places', Landscape 24 (1980), pp. 9–16.

Weightman, Barbara A., 'Commentary: Towards a geography of the gay community', Journal of Cultural Geography 1 (1981), pp. 106–12.

Weightman, Gavin and Steve Humphries, The Making of Modern London 1914–1939 (London: Sidgwick and Jackson, 1984).

Wheelwright, Julie, Amazons and Military Maids (London: Pandora, 1989).

White, Hayden, *The Content of the Form: Narrative Discourse and Historical Representation* (London: John Hopkins University Press, 1987).

Whittle, Stephen, 'Consuming differences: The collaboration of the gay body with the cultural state', in Stephen Whittle (ed.), *The Margins of the City: Gay Men's Urban Lives* (Aldershot: Arena, 1994), pp. 27–42.

Wiesen Cook, Blanche, 'The historical denial of lesbianism', *Radical History Review* 20 (1979), 60–5.

Wiesen Cook, Blanche, '"Women alone stir my imagination": Lesbianism and the cultural tradition', *Signs* 4:4 (1979), pp. 718–39.

Williams, Gwylmor Prys and George Thompson Blake, *Drink in Great Britain 1900 to 1979* (London: Edsall, 1980).

Wilson, Elizabeth, *Women and the Welfare State* (London: Tavistock, 1977).

Wilson, Elizabeth, *Only Halfway to Paradise: Women in Post-war Britain 1945–1968* (London: Tavistock, 1980).

Wilson, Elizabeth, 'Forbidden love', *Feminist Studies* 10:2 (1984), pp. 213–26.

Wilson, Elizabeth, 'Memoirs of an anti-heroine', in Bob Cant and Susan Hemmings (eds), *Radical Records: Thirty Years of Lesbian and Gay History* (London: Routledge, 1988), pp. 42–50.

Wilton, Tamsin, *Lesbian Studies: Setting an Agenda* (London: Routledge, 1995).

Winchester, H. P. M. and P E. White, 'The location of marginal groups in the inner city', *Environment and Planning D: Society and Space* 6:1 (1988), pp. 37–54.

Wittig, Monique, 'One is not born a woman', in Henry Abelove, Michele Aina Barale and David M. Halperin (eds), *The Lesbian and Gay Studies Reader* (London: Routledge, 1993), pp. 103–9.

Wolfe, Maxine, 'Invisible women in invisible places: Lesbians, lesbian bars, and the social production of people/environment relationships', *Architecture and Behaviour* 8:2 (1992), pp. 137–58.

Young, Ken and John Kramer, *Strategy and Conflict in Metropolitan Housing: Suburbia versus the GLC 1965–1975* (London: Heinemann, 1978).

Yow, Valerie Raleigh, *Recording Oral History: A Practical Guide for Social Scientists* (London: Sage, 1994).

Zimet, Jaye, *Strange Sisters: The Art of Lesbian Pulp Fiction 1949–69* (London: Penguin, 1999).

Zimmerman, Bonnie, 'What has never been: An overview of lesbian feminist literary criticism', *Feminist Studies* 7:3 (1981), pp. 451–75.

Zimmerman, Bonnie, 'The politics of transliteration: Lesbian personal narratives', *Signs* 9:4 (1984), pp. 663–82.

Zita, Jacquelyn N., 'Gay and lesbian studies: Yet another unhappy marriage?', in Linda Garber (ed.), *Tilting the Tower* (New York: Routledge, 1994), pp. 258–76.

Index